BEGINNING TEACHING:

BEGINNING LEARNING

SECOND EDITION

BEGINNING TEACHING:

BEGINNING LEARNING

in primary education

SECOND EDITION

Edited by
Janet Moyles and Gillian Robinson

Open University Press
Buckingham · Philadelphia

Open University Press
Celtic Court
22 Ballmoor
Buckingham
MK18 1XW

email: enquiries@openup.co.uk
world wide web: www.openup.co.uk

and
325 Chestnut Street
Philadelphia, PA 19106, USA

First Published 1995
Reprinted 1996 (twice), 1997, 1998, 1999, 2000

First published in this second edition 2002

A catalogue record of this book is available from the British Library

ISBN   0 335 21129 1 (pb)

Library of Congress Cataloging-in-Publication Data
Beginning teaching, beginning learning in primary education/edited by Janet Moyles and Gillian Robinson. – 2nd ed.
      p. cm.
   Includes bibliographical references and index.
   ISBN 0-335-21129-1 (pbk.)
      1. First year teachers–Great Britain.   2. Student teachers–Great Britain.
   3. Elementary school teachers–Great Britain.   I. Moyles, Janet R.
   II. Robinson, Gillian.

LB2844.1.N4 B44 2002
372.11–dc21   2001045820

Typeset by Graphicraft Limited, Hong Kong
Printed in Great Britain by Biddles Limited, Guildford and King's Lynn

Contents

Notes on the editors and contributors   vii
Foreword by Professor Colin Richards   xi
Acknowledgements   xiii
Abbreviations   xiv

Introduction   1
    Janet Moyles and Gillian Robinson

Part 1 Learning to teach   13

1 Begin at the beginning: working in the Foundation Stage   15
   Nansi Ellis
2 A place for everything . . . ? The teaching and learning
   environment   30
   Janet Moyles
3 Seeing clearly: observation in the primary classroom   48
   Linda Hargreaves
4 Identifying the positive within yourself: action planning
   for competence   73
   Neil Kitson
5 Inside the learning mind: primary children and their
   learning potential   90
   Roger Merry

Part 2   Teaching to learn   105

6   What shall we do today? Planning for learning – children
    and teachers!   107
    Janet Moyles
7   Fruit salads and wild gardens! Developing investigative
    thinking and skills in children   127
    Tina Jarvis and Lee Woods
8   Mummy's face is green! Developing thinking and skills
    in art   143
    Gillian Robinson
9   Telling the whole story: developing children's oral skills
    and imagination within the literacy hour   157
    Jane Hislam
10 Getting it write! Supporting and responding to children's
    writing   173
    Marilyn Foreman and Nikki Gamble
11 All the children want to do is get on with it! ICT in
    primary education   191
    Nick Easingwood
12 Keeping track: assessing, monitoring and recording
    children's progress and achievement   209
    Morag Hunter-Carsch

Part 3   Responsibilities, roles and relationships   233

13 Putting the bananas to bed! Becoming a reflective primary
    teacher   235
    Siân Adams
14 Dialogue with difference: teaching for equality in primary
    schools   249
    Alison Shilela
15 All children are special: but some are more special than
    others! Special educational needs in the primary school   267
    Jenny Lansdell
16 It takes two to tango: working with experienced teachers   284
    Wendy Suschitzky and Barbara Garner
17 I don't want to worry you, but . . . ! Teachers and the law   297
    Christopher Curran

Concluding remarks
The road to Damascus: learning from continuing experiences   313
    Janet Moyles, beginner teachers and tutors

Index   318

Notes on the editors

and contributors

Siân Adams is currently a researcher at Anglia Polytechnic University working on a project related to effective pedagogy in the early years. She recently completed a PhD on teachers' reflective practices and was a main contributor to the writing of *StEPs: A Framework for Playful Teaching*. She has also published a number of articles on early years practices. Prior to working as a researcher she was an advisory teacher in a local authority and a class teacher in early years settings.

Christopher Curran is a senior lecturer in educational studies at Anglia Polytechnic University. He teaches students across a range of courses for undergraduates and postgraduates, as well as on in-service degree courses for serving teachers. He has a particular expertise in the work of para-professional staff, also a main area of research interest. He is also tutor-in-charge of developing the Foundation Degree in Learning Support at APU and is currently undertaking his own doctorate.

Nick Easingwood is a senior lecturer in ICT coordinator in education at Anglia Polytechnic University. He teaches ICT in the curriculum to students on undergraduate and postgraduate ITE courses, as well as on in-service degree courses for serving teachers. Co-editor of *ICT and Literacy, Information and Communications Technology, Media, Reading and Writing*, he is committed to the use of ICT as a means of enhancing teaching and learning across all areas of the curriculum. He is currently working on a range of other publications in the area of ICT.

Nansi Ellis is the primary education adviser for Association of Teachers and Lecturers (ATL), where she works with teachers and support staff to develop policy and advice on primary and early years education. Formerly a primary teacher in both Wales and England, she subsequently joined QCA, managing the early years team throughout the development of the Foundation Stage curriculum guidance. She has a degree in philosophy and a particular interest in gender issues.

Marilyn Foreman is a senior lecturer and subject leader in English at Anglia Polytechnic University. She teaches on undergraduate and postgraduate ITT courses, early childhood studies courses and classroom learning assistant (CLA) diploma courses. Formerly a primary teacher, her research interests are in the areas of children's language and the discourse of classrooms.

Nikki Gamble is now a literacy consultant and was formerly a member of staff at the School of Education, Anglia Polytechnic University where she taught on a number of primary undergraduate and postgraduate programmes. Nikki's main teaching and academic interests are in children's literature, reading development and new literacies. She serves on a number of national and international committees with a focus on children's literacy and books.

Barbara Garner is a part-time lecturer in primary education and also a classroom teacher. Having been an advisory teacher and a counsellor, she considers herself to be a generalist, though she has expertise in early years education and in primary mathematics. She has a wide range of interests and has published several practical papers on different aspects of primary education.

Linda Hargreaves is Senior Lecturer in primary education at Homerton College where she works in early years and primary music education. She has used observational methods extensively, first at the University of Leicester as an ORACLE observer in 1978–9, and subsequently in studies of small rural schools. More recent observational research includes the ORACLE 1990s' replication studies of primary–secondary transfer published in *Inside the Primary Classroom – 20 Years on*, and the ESRC-funded SPRINT Interactive Teaching project with Janet Moyles and other contributors to this book.

Jane Hislam lectures in primary English at the University of Leicester, having previously worked for the advisory service and as a classroom teacher. Research and teaching interests include children's literature and oral storytelling and she has lectured and given workshops widely in this field. She has also worked with other contributors on the ESRC-funded SPRINT project looking at interactive teaching in the literacy hour. Her publications include articles about oral story and children's literature. She has also written a monograph for the Society for Storytelling.

Morag Hunter-Carsch lectures in primary education at the University of Leicester, having previously worked as a researcher. Her research and teaching interests are mainly in the area of reading and evaluating learning with particular reference to children with special educational needs. She has written and edited several books and articles on various aspects of literacy and its assessment and been part of an ESRC-funded project on literacy hour teaching.

Tina Jarvis is Senior Lecturer in primary science and technology at the University of Leicester and Director of the Primary PGCE programme. She is also Co-Director of the SciCentre and has published very widely in the area of her expertise. Her research includes investigating English and Australian children's perceptions of technology and science and the development of children's expertise in planning.

Neil Kitson lectures in primary education at the University of Leicester. He has worked for several years both as a teacher and as an advisory teacher for drama. He has published and broadcast widely on a variety of issues and is currently involved in developing materials in relation to competences for teachers. He has also been part of a funded project investigating interactive teaching in the literacy hour.

Jenny Lansdell is Deputy Dean of Education at Anglia Polytechnic University and a chartered educational psychologist. She has taught children of all ages, including those with severe learning difficulties in special schools and those experiencing specific difficulties with literacy in mainstream schools. Her research interests include the language of mathematics, working with parents to support struggling readers, special needs in the early years and quality in teacher education and she has published in these and other areas.

Roger Merry is Senior Lecturer in primary education at the University of Leicester with research interests in cognitive psychology, special needs education and English teaching. He is author of *Successful Children: Successful Teaching* and his previous publications range from book chapters and journal articles in these areas, to children's stories and activity books with characters like Sid Genius and Gertie Grimble. He has been co-director of a funded project investigating literacy hour teaching.

Janet Moyles is Professor of Education and Research at Anglia Polytechnic University and an early childhood education specialist, particularly in the areas of play, teaching and learning. Her books include *Just Playing?*, *Organizing for Learning in the Primary Classroom, The Excellence of Play* (ed.) and, more recently, *StEPs: A Framework for Playful Teaching*, which has arisen from a recent research project. She has directed a number of funded research projects related to effective pedagogy and has also written a variety of articles on different aspects of early years and primary education.

Gillian Robinson is Reader in Education, Director of Research Degrees and Lecturer in Art and Design at Anglia Polytechnic University. She received her MA and PhD from the University of London. Her book *Sketch-books: Explore and Store* was published in 1995 and by Heinemann USA in 1996. A co-authored book *Developing Art Experience* was published in 1997. Her continuing research interests are focused around the value of sketch-books and journals as a cross-curricular tool for developing creativity and thinking skills. She is also a practising painter working mostly in mixed media.

Alison Shilela is Head of Primary Initial Teacher Training at Anglia Polytechnic University. She has taught children and adults in Britain and worked as a Manager for Cambridgeshire Multicultural Education Service before joining APU. Alison spent four years teaching Namibian refugees in Zambia and one year teaching at the Universite de Dakar. Her research interests currently include the recruitment and retention of male primary teachers, the issue of faith schools, mentoring and school development, and the issues of equality and social justice in programme design for initial teacher education.

Wendy Suschitzky is a tutor working within initial teacher education and Deputy Director of the Primary PGCE programme at the University of Leicester. Formerly an early years teacher, who has also worked in community education, her main teaching and research interests are in the areas of teacher education, mentoring, equal opportunities in children's learning.

Lee Woods is currently Head of Primary Maths and Science at Anglia Polytechnic University School of Education. Prior to her move into higher education, she worked in a variety of schools spanning a 20-year teaching career. Although she started in the secondary sector she moved into the primary phase just as the National Curriculum was being introduced. Her current main research interests include the effective teaching and learning of mathematics in primary schools.

Foreword

Professor Colin Richards

The first edition of this book was published in 1995. A great deal has happened to both primary education and primary teacher education since then. Many things have changed but some have remained the same. You, as would-ber primary teachers, need to be knowledgeable about both.

What has happened during the past six years? The National Curriculum has been reviewed and a revised version put in place. The book's chapters on aspects of the foundation curriculum and the primary curriculum deal with this. National testing has become ever more important. The book gives you important ideas about assessment and testing.

In particular the government has introduced two major 'special measures' – the National Literacy and Numeracy Strategies – to, in its own words, 'lever up standards in the basics'. The book introduces you to these but does not believe that they are THE answer to all the primary school's problems. Information and communication technology is increasingly important and it receives its due place within the book.

Very significantly the government has introduced major changes in the way would-be teachers are prepared for their first jobs. The government wants you to be *trained*; the authors of this book believe you need to be *educated* about primary education as well as being *trained*. That's why the book addresses you as *student* teachers, not as *trainees*.

However much some things have changed, the kind of qualities you need as a primary teacher are the same as they have always been. To be a *professional* teacher, you need to be reflective; aware of how children learn; able to provide an appropriate learning environment; able to work with other adults; able to observe, assess and plan; and, very importantly, need to enjoy your work and the satisfaction that comes from working with young children. The book helps you meet these needs – as you will seek to meet the learning and other needs of the children you teach.

Becoming a primary school teacher is a demanding, difficult, exhausting and at times can be a fazing experience but it is also immensely rewarding, incredibly fascinating, never-for-a-moment boring (unless you make it so!) and often so very humorous. This book captures what it's like – enjoy and learn from it.

Acknowledgements

Many thanks and much appreciation should go to the students and tutors associated with Anglia Polytechnic University and the University of Leicester who have contributed in various ways to the production of the second edition, not least those tutors from both institutions (and beyond, in the case of Linda Hargreaves and Nansi Ellis) who have contributed chapters. Photographs are courtesy of teachers and children in schools around the country including St Thomas of Canterbury (C. of E.) Infant School, brentwood, and Gillian Robinson, Cherry Fulloway and Janet Moyles.

It's also worth adding the editors' thanks to all those of you in institutions who have made a second edition of this book worthwhile. We hope this edition continues to support your work and develop all our students and newly qualified teachers' knowledge, skills and professional development.

Further acknowledgements are given in individual chapters.

Abbreviations

We have tried to keep educational jargon to a minimum in the book but, inevitably, there are certain acronyms or phrases given specific meaning in education. The following represents a list of terminology which it would be useful for students and NQTs to understand.

APU	assessment of performance unit
ATL	Association of Teachers and Lecturers
ATs	attainment targets and tests within NC subjects
BEd/BA(Ed)	Bachelor of Education/Bachelor of Arts (Education)
CA	classroom assistant
citizenship	part of the NC related to children developing social and political awareness
CLA	classroom learning assistant
DES	Department of Education and Science, later to become the DfE
DfE	Department for Education, the previous name for DfEE
DfEE	Department for Education and Employment, the government body in charge of education
DLOs	desirable learning outcomes
E2L	English as a second language or EAL (English as an additional language) or EFL (English as a foreign language)
early years or early childhood education	applied usually to the education of 3- to 7/8-year-olds but increasingly focused on 3–5-year-olds in the Foundation Stage

ELGs	early learning goals
ERA	Education Reform Act
FS	Foundation Stage, guidance on curriculum for children aged 3–5 years in all settings, e.g. nurseries, playgroups, reception classes
HEI	higher education institution, e.g. university, college
HMI	Her Majesty's Inspectorate, now Ofsted, see below
IAP	individual action planning
ICT	information communications technology
in loco parentis	adopting the role and responsibilities of a 'good parent'
ITE	initial teacher education (preferred by most academics to ITT)
ITT	initial teacher training
KS1 and KS2	the NC gives four age-related stages of education, with Key Stages 1 and 2 relating to primary children aged from 5–7 and 7–11 respectively.
LEA	Local Education Authority
NC	National Curriculum
NCC	National Curriculum Council, subsumed within SCAA and later QCA
NLS	National Literacy Strategy
NNS	National Numeracy Strategy
NQT	newly qualified teacher
Ofsted	Office for Standards in Education, the body which governs school and ITT course inspections
parents	Anyone who has the legal guardianship of a child
PE	physical education
pedagogy	the study of teaching and learning
PGCE	Postgraduate Certificate in Education
PoS	Programmes of Study in the NC
PSHE	personal/social/health education
pupils	children in the context of school/ing
QCA	Qualifications and Curriculum Authority, which subsumed SCAA
QTS	Qualified Teacher Status
RE	religious education
RoA	record(s) of achievement
SATs	standard attainment tasks
SCAA	schools Curriculum and Assessment Authority
SCITT	school-centred initial teacher training
SEN	special educational need(s)
SENCO	special educational needs co-ordinator
SMSC	social, moral, spiritual and cultural education

TAs	teacher assessments
TE	teaching experience, or TP (teaching practice or placement)
TTA	Teacher Training Agency, which has charge of all ITT/ITE courses
Year groups	those years which now constitute the years of schooling for primary childen from ages 5 to 11, e.g. Year 1 = 5- to 6-year-olds, Year 2 = 6- to 7-year-olds, through to Year 6 = 10- to 11-year-olds. There is a designated Year R for reception children (those who are rising 5) now within the FS guidance.

Introduction

Janet Moyles and Gillian Robinson

Cameo 1

A student teacher going into a junior school for his first placement was asked, 'Why on earth do you want to teach?' He confidently replied 'Well, I really like being with children and helping them learn.' He was somewhat surprised at the teacher's response: 'Oh, if only that was what it is all about!'

Cameo 2

(From a student teacher's journal about work with a Year 4 class)
'The best moment this half-term was when all the children together performed a dance/drama about the water-cycle from beginning to end – five weeks' work – and said they really enjoyed it! I felt a great sense of achievement because, in the first week's dance session, they didn't have a clue – and neither did I!'

Cameo 3

The student has spent nearly a week with a class of 5-year-olds on her first teaching experience. In planning the final day, the teacher has suggested that Julia might take the class for the Friday morning and 'try out' being a class teacher. Plans have been made and Julia goes through in her mind just how everything will go. The morning is spent on various activities and runs quite smoothly, if rather noisily. The teacher, who has just entered the classroom, reminds the student that the children will need some time to pack away the equipment. Julia uses what she believes to be the teacher's method of getting the children to put everything away, saying clearly 'Listen

everybody . . . it's time to stop now. Put your things away and go and
sit on the carpet.' Pandemonium reigns. The children appear to have
gone berserk, rushing around the room, colliding with each other and
dropping things on the floor. Even worse, the classroom looks like a
herd of animals has passed through – and the teacher's standing
there watching!

In the beginning . . .

Beginning teachers, whether students or those entering their first teaching posts, rightly have high ideals about the kind of teachers they want
to be and the kind of classroom ethos they want to foster. Nearly always,
as in the second cameo, they share a delight in actually being with
children and participating in the fun and enjoyment of new learning.
These are, however, only a very few aspects of the role of teacher, albeit
arguably the best bits! As the teacher in the first cameo indicates, the
requirements of the professional role extend well beyond 'just teaching'
a class of children. There are many skills and attributes needed, as will be
evidenced through the chapters of this book. Many of these will be
acquired through the processes of initial teacher education courses but
since the advent of the multiplicity of standards for students and newly
qualified teachers, the time on courses for thinking more widely around
the professional aspects of teaching as well as curriculum content have
become somewhat limited.

The third cameo serves to emphasize that children and teaching can
seemingly be extremely unpredictable and that the balance of primary
classroom life is sometimes poised on a ruler edge (if not quite a knife
edge). The student did everything 'right' yet the outcome was disastrous
for her confidence, at least in the short term. What this situation highlights is that it is not sufficient merely to emulate the actions and behaviours of another in order to learn to teach. How simple it would be if, as
some in authority would occasionally lead us to believe, one could walk
into a classroom armed with subject knowledge, the desire to teach and
a belief that what one taught is what the children learn. The real world
is far less predictable but infinitely more varied, exciting and challenging, as we shall discover.

Whereas we all might wish that someone could wave a magic wand
and save us from Julia's encounter in the third cameo, these experiences
are all part of learning to be a teacher. From the outset you need to be
clear of one thing: *no one can teach you how to teach* anymore than
anyone can teach you how to learn. Both happen in tandem – or at least
they should do – hence the title of this book *Beginning Teaching: Beginning Learning*. Learning to teach is all about what *we as teachers* bring

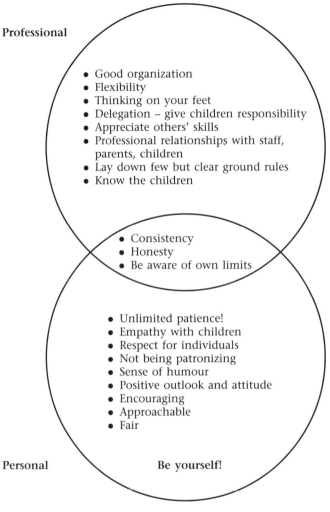

Professional

- Good organization
- Flexibility
- Thinking on your feet
- Delegation – give children responsibility
- Appreciate others' skills
- Professional relationships with staff, parents, children
- Lay down few but clear ground rules
- Know the children

- Consistency
- Honesty
- Be aware of own limits

- Unlimited patience!
- Empathy with children
- Respect for individuals
- Not being patronizing
- Sense of humour
- Positive outlook and attitude
- Encouraging
- Approachable
- Fair

Personal

Be yourself!

Figure 0.1 What makes a good teacher?

that develops our professional personalities in harmony with our own personalities.

Every teacher is a mix of the personal and the professional and, whereas the professional may take a few knocks in the beginning stages like Julia, keeping the personal esteem intact is vital; I may be an awful teacher but that does not mean I am inevitably an awful person! One common activity which teaching students often undertake is to identify what makes a 'good teacher' and to try to separate out those professional skills which may need to be developed and the personal skills already existing. Inevitably, this is not necessarily as clear cut as Figure 0.1 suggests but does show how one group of students began to celebrate some of their many desirable competences, which ensured that they did not get overwhelmed or de-skilled from the perpetual onslaught of new learning.

In any profession, the learning curve between a state of being a 'novice' and that of being an 'expert' (Berliner 1994; Casbergue and Allen 1997) is inevitably steep because there are always so many new issues to deal with simultaneously. Even when a certain level of expertise has been gained, new initiatives often challenge existing securities – as many teachers have discovered over the past few years. Whatever apparently rigorous and difficult roles people have had in previous experiences, entrants to the teaching profession (as well as those with significant experience) may suddenly find themselves confronted with an overload of challenges. Because early years and primary education concerns 3- to 11-year-old children – and often fairly large numbers of them at once – these challenges are nearly always immediate and unrelenting: the children just do not go away while we get our acts together! What needs to be acknowledged is that, with support and encouragement from others, the vast majority of people succeed as effective teachers and thoroughly enjoy their vocation. Any teacher education course, of whatever duration or type, is only the *start* of a professional career; the beginning of learning about teaching.

Intentions of this book

This book, like its predecessor, addresses all those just entering teaching either as students or as newly qualified teachers. It will also be of interest to those whose job it is to help these individuals learn about pedagogy. The original book grew out of increasing concern on the part of course tutors that the emphasis in teacher education is now so focused on *subject* curriculum that many of the underlying issues that make the 3–11 years of education and schooling special are given insufficient prominence. At the time of this second edition, the concerns among many academics, students and teachers are over the level of *prescription* that is currently received from the many government agencies – for example, Qualifications and Curriculum Authority (QCA), Teacher Training Agency (TTA), Office for Standards in Education (Ofsted), The Task Forces on Literacy/Numeracy and numerous government papers – which have increasingly reduced the autonomy of such professionals and determined much of what must be included in teacher training at initial and continuing professional development levels.

At the same time, and in many ways conversely, much has been written recently about creative teaching, children's perceptions on teachers and reflective teaching strategies (see, for example, Woods 1995; Woods and Jeffrey 1996; Ghaye and Ghaye 1998; Day 1999; Pollard and Filer 1999), which has led some academics and teachers to challenge whether prescribing curriculum and teaching strategies will result in children achieving to their highest potential.

By undertaking this second edition and incorporating some of this new thinking, we hope to redress some of the necessary balance to ensure not just a *trained* teaching workforce but *educated* and reflective teachers.

Like its predecessor, this book does not aim to do everything or be all things to all people. We have used the expertise of individual tutors to support students' learning and teaching in those aspects where we feel that prescription is not sufficient to give students the wherewithal to question and to extend their own thinking and practices. Clearly there is more about which we could have written; this is why we give further reading at the ends of chapters so that readers have access to other sources should they require further support.

First, a brief background to the current context of primary and early years education is given together with an introduction to some of the concepts you will meet in reading the book as a whole. (See pp. xiv–xvi for a note of the abbreviations and special terminology used.) Second, the structure of the book is explained and information given regarding the chapters.

The context of early years and primary education

In England, as in many other countries in the world, a deep economic recession in the 1980s led to relatively high levels of unemployment. On the understandable basis of attempting to give their children more than they themselves had experienced, being 'in work' became the ultimate goal of many parents for their children and, parallel to this, came the pressures of being 'well educated' in order ostensibly to achieve such employment. Rightly or wrongly, education – or more properly *schooling* – became viewed, by politicians and the general public alike, as the panacea for many of society's problems. Huge pressures of accountability were put on teachers – appraisal of teacher performance became a paramount issue at this time (see Moyles 1988) – and it was inevitable that what was taught in the name of education also came under national scrutiny (Department of Education and Science 1988).

It was within this framework that the National Curriculum (NC) for England and Wales became a legislated requirement in 1989, standards for new teachers were imposed in 1998 and performance-related pay for qualified teachers appeared in 2000 – to name but a few! This focus on teaching, learning and curriculum is set to continue for many years.

Some things have changed for the good; in the earlier book, the issue of early years education featured way down any list of educational and political priorities. However, growing knowledge from research, in particular, about children's development and the early formulation of dispositions to learning in our youngest citizens, as well as downward pressures from Key Stage 1 (KS1) of the NC, have put early years firmly on the political and public agenda, culminating in 2001 with a Select Committee Report to the government on the early years and the many issues that it embraces (House of Commons Education and Employment Committee 2001). Since the year 2000, the Foundation Stage has offered guidance on curriculum experiences for 3- to 5-year-olds across all early education settings and set early learning goals (ELGs) for all young children at the point of transfer into mainstream school.

The NC curriculum for primary aged children has, since 1989, undergone a number of both reductions and extensions, resulting in the current documentation used in schools, the subject of which is the focus of all initial teacher training (ITT) courses. All ITT providers are also visited by government inspectors and judged on the basis of their ability to deliver all components of the curriculum but, increasingly, the focus has been on English and mathematics. In fact, in the latter two areas many academics and teachers rue the fact that these subjects are now conceived quite narrowly in terms of literacy and numeracy, with specific inspection of these aspects a regular feature of academic life, affecting both tutors and students. Inspection reports on ITT provision (as they are for individual schools) are available for public scrutiny through the Ofsted website (www.ofsted.gov.uk). The full NC – including religious education – has to be taught *by law* to all children aged 5–11 years in state primary schools, with maths and English (from 1995) being formally assessed in KS1 at age 7 years and KS2 at age 11 years. The DfEE's website includes very full information on all aspects of curriculum including support with teaching activities and can be found at www.dfes.gov.uk.

As well as curriculum subjects, the NC aims to reflect the entitlement of all children to have access to a broad, balanced and relevant curriculum, which accounts for differentiation, progression and continuity, in order that every child should achieve his or her full potential (Department of Education and Science 1989). In practice, this means that the subject curriculum has to be extended to incorporate all the broader curriculum aspects such as citizenship and personal and social education. Clearly, just in content terms, there will be much that new teachers will need to learn and address in order to show their capabilities and competence across such a broad curriculum sweep.

It needs to be remembered that a subject-dominated curriculum takes *knowledge*, and the handing *down* of that knowledge, as its basis. However, it is widely acknowledged that, for primary age children, the *processes* of their learning are far more important (see Merry 1998). To teach primary aged children effectively, one must first recognize what they already bring to the learning situation, just as teacher education courses try to use the existing strengths of students as the basis of professional development.

The subject dominance has impacted heavily on teacher education: Circular 4/98 (Department for Education and Employment 1998) clearly spells out what ITT courses are expected to accomplish by way of students meeting a range of standards (see Jacques and Hyland 2000). So while a major part of course time is to be spent on subject curriculum with a specific focus on literacy and numeracy, students are also assessed – and self-assess – on a significant number of standards, all of which must be met for Qualified Teacher Status (QTS) to be awarded. Further standards are incorporated into the induction year processes for NQTs (see Teacher Training Agency (TTA) 1999 or the website at www.teach-tta.gov.uk). In addition, there are specific periods of time (dependent on the overall length of the course) that students must spend in schools in direct contact with practising teachers and children. (Since around 1993, the relationships between institutions and the people within them have been known as 'ITT partnerships'.) Both tutors and teachers, during Ofsted inspections, award students specific grades for aspects of their teaching and, in order to be successful, partnerships must demonstrate high degrees of congruence between these gradings and those of the inspectors. As with other aspects, there are changes being made to the requirements which means that tutors and students, as well as the partnership teachers, need continually to change and adapt practices to meet the current situation. There are specific standards for early years teachers which must be met in addition to the general primary standards. For all teachers, in addition to curriculum knowledge, the areas of focus currently include:

- planning, teaching and class management;
- monitoring, assessment, recording, reporting and accountability;
- other professional requirements, including knowledge of aspects of the law related to sex and race discrimination, health and safety, child protection, pupil welfare, discipline and teachers' common law duty, professional development.

It goes without saying that the combination of these demands is overwhelming to students, course providers and schools. Therefore, it is no surprise to find that many of these issues are now insufficiently covered on many teacher education courses despite continuing goodwill all round. Hence the need for a book of this type, which explores some of these vitally important but potentially neglected areas and a selection of related issues that we feel are important for beginning teaching and learning about teaching.

The structure and content of the book

The book has three parts: the first addresses the issue of learning to teach, the second explores a variety of strategies needed by beginner teachers in teaching to learn, while the third part deals with responsibilities, roles and relationships which are now so vital to the partnership within the teacher education enterprise. Within sections there are several chapters, each of which carries its own questions, references and suggested further reading. Each chapter is written in a straightforward style and begins with a one or more cameos of life in primary classrooms as it is experienced by beginner teachers so as to offer an immediate point of reference with everyday encounters. This feature has been particularly welcomed by readers of the first edition.

In the first of the five chapters constituting Part 1, we begin at the beginning with a new chapter by Nansi Ellis on the Foundation Stage in which she examines the background to this relatively new aspect of English education and outlines its main features. Nansi argues that early years teachers are often the most passionate about their work and find this the most exciting and rewarding period in which to engage in children's learning. She argues that this stage is vital to all the children's futures both as school pupils and as people and welcomes the current focus on early years education and the closer working relationships formed with parents at this stage. ALL students should read this chapter because it sets the framework for thinking about how children learn and how we can best teach when we work from the starting point in children's current capabilities.

This chapter is followed by Janet Moyles's up-dated chapter exploring aspects of the classroom as a learning context. Rather than dealing with the pragmatics of the classroom, the emphasis is on delving into teachers' beliefs and values, behavioural and home/school issues, children's independence and the processes of teaching and learning, to understand how structures and routines affect potential learning opportunities.

Part of any teacher's repertoire must include observing what is happening in the classroom context. In Chapter 3, Linda Hargreaves offers further examples of effective observational techniques, which she has grounded firmly in a clear rationale for practice as she did in the first edition. She continues to challenge us to think about the differences between looking and observing and emphasizes the importance of observation as part of teacher-based, formative assessment to help in the identification of a child's, and teacher's, needs.

Teacher education must start from the basis of acknowledging what beginner teachers bring to their own learning. Neil Kitson, in his up-dated chapter, examines the background to the notion of teacher competences and explains what these mean in the context of initial teacher education (ITE) and the TTA standards. He argues that while the standards will remain the same, students' response to them will alter as they develop professionally and extend their own learning about teaching. The example given is of one Postgraduate Certificate in Education (PGCE) course's documentation through which students identify their strengths and needs and make individual action plans for future development. In Chapter 5, as in the previous edition, Roger Merry concentrates on how we can begin to understand children through identifying aspects of our own learning and reflecting on how we approach tasks. He covers such aspects as perception, memory and learning strategies, reviews some general trends in how children develop and considers the curriculum in relation to purpose, relevance and attention to differentiation. His chapter now includes reference to the current research into cognitive development and brain studies, a growing feature of cognitive theory.

In Part 2, Teaching to Learn, the seven chapters focus on different aspects of curriculum including an extended chapter on developing investigative thinking in science and maths and three new chapters dealing with arts-based education, reading and writing and ICT. This section constitutes a kind of 'sandwich' in which we start with planning for teaching and learning and conclude with how we keep track, monitor and record achievement – in the middle, we explore the different curriculum bases as the context for teaching and learning. Having emphasized how we all learn through our own experiences, Janet Moyles in Chapter 6 begins to explore how we can plan for children's learning within the context of their own interests and motivations while still complying with subject curriculum requirements.

Developing investigative skills, creativity and problem solving strategies must have high priority for primary age children (as well as their teachers) for these provide the tools with which to approach the formal task of school learning. The next five chapters highlight these skills and processes. First, in Chapter 7, using science, technology and maths situations, Tina Jarvis and Lee Woods illustrate some of the many concepts which provide a sound basis for learning and emphasizes the need to ensure that children are given sufficient opportunity to explore a variety of questions and solutions in a logical and systematic way. Gillian Robinson, in Chapter 8, accentuates similar points but does so in the context of exploring children's approaches to arts-based education and introduces the notion of sketchbooks as a form of on-going thinking and learning for children and adults. As a practising artist herself, Gill highlights the importance of a broad and balanced curriculum in which the arts are given their rightful place and treated with the importance they deserve as contexts for creating adaptable and flexible thinkers. Her concern at the marginalization of art through the need to meet the demands of the heavily prescriptive and assessed aspects of the curriculum, is shared by many teachers who feel that the benefits to be derived from allowing children's creative expression to emerge and develop is well rewarded through better powers of concentration and imagination.

Using a wide variety of examples, Jane Hislam's chapter develops the theme of creativity in another direction, exploring ways of creating an effective classroom context for the development of children's imaginative powers through the structured framework of storytelling and oracy-based activities across the curriculum. Communication and co-operation are vital ingredients in primary education for teachers and children. This theme is further developed in a new chapter by Marilyn Foreman and Nikki Gamble in Chapter 10, when they examine the many ways in which reading and writing can contribute to children's enjoyment of the spoken and written word and provide some excellent learning activities in the process. In his truly cross-curricular Chapter 11, Nick Easingwood encourages readers to think about computers as tools for teaching and learning, which are good at handling large amounts of data, and do so in motivating and stimulating ways. He shows how the wealth of standards to be achieved in information communications technology (ICT) by beginning teachers, can be handled effectively and enjoyably through a range of activities and also offers clear practical advice about the location of computers and about safety aspects which often concern those new to the teaching.

Part 2 ends with Morag Hunter-Carsch's chapter on record keeping, monitoring and assessment of children's achievements, in which she outlines some of the theory and practices of recording, evaluating and assessing not only children's learning but monitoring the planning and implementation of the curriculum by the teacher.

The third and final section has five chapters. The first of these focuses on the big issue of reflective practice in teaching. Siân Adams makes it clear that the continuing professional development of teachers is enhanced and extended significantly by engaging in the process of reflection on what we do, why we do it and how we make second-by-second decisions in our response to the continuing demands of children and other adults in the classroom. Using evidence from a research study and her own PhD work, Siân helps readers to realize that reflecting on what one does is the key to both understanding ourselves as teachers and making provision for effective learning and teaching.

In the new Chapter 14, Alison Shilela explains why working for equality in education is fundamental to a successful learning environment for children and teachers. She expresses her strong belief that our role as teachers is not simply in offering all learners the same chances, but to breathe life into those opportunities. In a lively and passionate chapter, Alison explains both some of the fundamental understandings about equality and also some of the chief misunderstandings. She emphasizes the need to work within equal opportunities guidelines and the necessity for teachers who understand and respect the range of values and differences in our modern society. This is followed by another new chapter on special educational needs (SEN) by Jenny Lansdell. Since the first edition of this book, the incidence of special needs in primary schools has grown considerably. Jenny both explains the context of SEN and also the different forms this may take, as well as ensuring that readers increase their knowledge of the legislation in this area. She emphasizes the importance of teachers in developing a caring and supportive ethos within the classroom and exhorts us to realize that the key to effective practice with all children is our ability to establish what a child's specific needs are and then find ways of creating opportunities for enabling that child to succeed.

In their revised chapter, Wendy Suschitzky and Barbara Garner explore the many issues involved in the role of the mentor teacher and the establishment of mutual respect and partnerships between beginner teachers and those who will support their professional development in the school context.

Chris Curran's final chapter explains the law as it applies to teachers in schools and in the context of (1) the duty of care, (2) physical contact with pupils, (3) punishment and (4) the teacher as an employee. He emphasizes the need for primary teachers, as caring professionals, to adopt the roles and responsibilities of 'good parents'. Chris gives guidance on coping with a vast array of professional responsibilities and how these are expressed in practice. While some of the issues may appear somewhat severe, he emphasizes that most teachers go through the whole of their professional lives without untoward incidents occurring. Knowing the framework of the law and what to do in preventing as well as handling difficult circumstances, is half-way to ensuring that potential incidents are minimized and we rest easy in our beds!

The very brief conclusion to the book ensures that the voices of beginning teachers are heard as they explain to readers their experiences in the early days of teaching and learning.

As will be obvious by now, the scope of the book is very broadly based but by keeping the focus on the learning partnership between the beginner teacher and the children, we have hoped to make it manageable and useful. Primary teachers do need to have a good grasp of subject knowledge and how it can be translated into classroom practices to ensure children's learning: this is now covered in detail in all ITE courses. But this is only part of a broader primary curriculum, which subsumes many other factors as we have seen. Whatever the intensity and rigours of the primary curriculum, the children and their teachers both need to gain enjoyment and satisfaction from the educational process and a real desire to continue learning: school and learning should be fun for everyone. Beginner teachers are usually welcomed by the children because they bring new ideas and different ways of doing things. As one 8-year-old child wrote in a letter to a student – the spelling faithfully reproduced: 'We are very greatful that you came to help us in your spare time and we're sorry that your liveing'!!

Here's the hope that you will always be able to see the humorous side of school.

References and further reading

Barnes, R. (1999) *Positive teaching, positive learning*. London: Routledge.

Berliner, D. (1994) Teacher expertise, in A. Pollard and J. Bourne (eds) *Teaching and Learning in the Primary School*. London: Routledge/Open University.

Casbergue, R. and Allen, R. (1997) Evolution of novice through expert teachers' recall: implications for effective reflection on practice, *Teaching and Teacher Education*, 13(7): 741–55.

Cooper, P. and McIntyre, D. (1996) *Effective Teaching and Learning. Teachers' and Students' Perspectives*. Buckingham: Open University Press.

Day, C. (1999) *Developing Teachers: The Challenges of Lifelong Learning*: London: Falmer Press.

Department of Education and Science (1988) *The Education Reform Act*. London: HMSO.

Department of Education and Science (1989) *The Implementation of the National Curriculum in Primary Schools*. London: HMSO.

Department for Education and Employment (1998) Circular 4/98 *Teaching: High Status, High Standards*. London: HMSO.

Ghaye, A. and Ghaye, K. (1998) *Teaching and Learning Through Critical Reflective Practice*. London: David Fulton.

House of Commons Education and Employment Committee (2001) *Early Years: First Report Volumes I and II*. London: HMSO.

Jacques, K. and Hyland, R. (2000) *Achieving QTS. Professional Studies: Primary Phase*. Cleveland: Learning Matters.

Merry, R. (1998) *Successful Children: Successful Teaching*. Buckingham: Open University Press.

Moyles, J. (1988) *Self-Evaluation: A Primary Teacher's Guide*. Windsor: NFER/Nelson.

Pollard, A. and Filer, A. (1999) *Social World of Pupil Career: Strategic Biographies through Primary School*. London: Cassell.

Woods, P. (1995) *Creative Teachers in Primary Schools*. Buckingham: Open University Press.

Woods, P. and Jeffrey, B. (1996) *Teachable Moments: The Art of Teaching in Primary Schools*. Buckingham: Open University Press.

Part 1

Learning to teach

1

Begin at the beginning:

working in the Foundation Stage

Nansi Ellis

Cameo 1

The assignment given to final year BEd students is to design their ideal nursery. One group decides to consider the aims and values of their nursery, and how that will affect its design and function. They visit nurseries, early years units and Early Excellence Centres, to see how others have answered these questions.

Cameo 2

As the reception children arrive, they immediately go to a table where the teacher has written their names on pieces of card. With their parents' help, they find the correct card and take it to the classroom assistant who marks the register. Ravinder turns her card over and says, 'Look, this side is me in English, and this is me in Gujurati!'

Cameo 3

The home corner in the reception class has been set up as a restaurant with menus and posters made by the children. Earlier, the class discussed places where they have eaten and the teacher made a list of questions that might be asked at a restaurant. These are now stuck on the wall where the children can see them and the adults use them as prompts in the role-play. A parent is helping one group of children to make matzos, while another group washes and sets out fruit to be eaten at the restaurant. The teacher takes photographs of Joseph writing Zoë's order on his pad and of Rachel counting out change.

Introduction

This chapter explores the new England-wide curriculum guidance related to our youngest children, those aged between 3 and nearly 6 years of age. Through the students in cameo 1, we will consider the aims and values that underpin the Foundation Stage (FS), as this stage is known, and how our practice can be based on those values. The FS teacher works with a dilemma, however: children and their learning are at the heart of education, but they, and we, must work towards prescribed outcomes. The new guidance does not provide all the answers, and in exploring relationships with children and their parents, in our assessments, planning and teaching methods, we need to find ways of dealing with this tension.

Early years professionals are often passionate about their work and will argue that early years teaching is the most exciting and rewarding there is. We work with children, and with their families and communities, in a more immediate way than at any other stage in education. The children we teach are enthusiastic, they are eager to find out about the world and they want to do it 'now'. We see children develop, becoming more secure in their skills and abilities, more confident to explore and to learn. We see them learning: Ravinder, in the second cameo, recognizes her name; later, she will recognize the letters of her name in other words; perhaps she will want to write her name on her paintings and then to write the names of her friends. Children are changing daily, and we face the challenge of supporting their learning and harnessing their eagerness. We have to be creative in order to maintain the children's enthusiasm, and flexible in order to meet the immediate need; and we must know enough about our children's development to provide the right opportunities at the right time. As early years professionals, we also know that this stage is vital for children's future: we help children to develop the skills and the attitudes on which all future learning depends.

The vital importance of early years education is finally being recognized in legislation. The Conservative government in 1995, set up a mechanism for funding nursery education. However, the 'nursery vouchers' that parents could 'spend' in different forms of provision quickly became unpopular. The desirable learning outcomes (DLOs), developed to provide some accountability, led to misunderstandings, and pressure on early years professionals to introduce overly formal teaching with tangible outcomes (also jokingly known as 'death by worksheet'). Following its election in 1997, the Labour government made a commitment to reviewing the DLOs and ensuring properly funded, high quality, early years places for children whose parents wanted early education in a range of settings outside the home.

The Foundation Stage

The response to the review of the DLOs, carried out by the Qualifications and Curriculum Authority (QCA), demonstrated an overwhelming desire for a distinct and coherent 'Foundation Stage', based on clearly articulated values and accompanied by detailed guidance. There was also a groundswell of opinion that formal teaching, worksheets and tests were against all the principles of good early years practice.

We also know that high quality in early years is not just about children learning to read, write and count; that it is very difficult to define and even harder to measure (see Lindsay and Desforges 1998). This is partly because, in the early years, we focus on the *processes* of learning and not on the outcomes. Early education is about enjoyment and enthusiasm for learning, independence and social skills: attitudes and dispositions that are difficult to quantify. The learning process is better served by play and exploration, which are hard to measure, than by teaching children to reach particular goals. In addition, it is difficult to measure our impact as teachers, while also acknowledging the large part that parents and carers play in their children's learning (Henry 1996).

The Foundation Stage is about more than school provision. It is about ensuring high-quality education in a wide range of settings, including pre-schools, playgroups, childminder networks, nursery schools, and nursery and reception classes in state maintained and independent schools. Close relationships with families and communities, which the early years professional has always valued, are strengthened through links with the national childcare strategy, and further reinforced in Early Excellence Centres and Beacon Nurseries, established to develop and promote good practice in integrating early education, day care, family learning, home support, training and other provider support. Following the success of initiatives such as 'Headstart' and High/Scope, good quality early education, linked with the Sure Start programme which aims to raise achievement in the most socially and economically deprived areas, is acknowledged as the foundation of lifelong learning, benefiting both children and society.

The new curriculum guidance (Qualifications and Curriculum Authority 2000) provides the starting point for all funded settings, including schools, as they develop a high quality curriculum. It is also intended to inform those who 'receive' children into Year 1 classes, where they begin the national curriculum, when some children will be just 5 and others will be nearly 6 years of age. It is organized as six areas of learning, which represent both subjects and broader 'themes' (as discussed in Chapter 6):

1 personal, social and emotional development;
2 communication, language and literacy;

Early years teaching is the most exciting and rewarding there is

3 mathematical development;
4 knowledge and understanding of the world;
5 physical development; and
6 creative development.

It does not resolve the tension between processes and outcomes. However, it does embed the outcomes (the early learning goals (ELG), which most children are expected to achieve by the end of their FS experience) within good, principled practice, with effective teaching based firmly on children's learning processes. New research being carried out for the DfEE/QCA will provide guidance to practitioners on effective pedagogy within the FS (Moyles *et al.* 2001; Sylva and Siraj-Blatchford 2001).

FS teachers can sometimes feel part of both school and the foundation stage: sometimes we don't quite belong in either. Early years student teachers may work and train with pre-school providers with little formal training, but whose knowledge is based on many years' experience. In a particular school as a reception class teacher, you may be the only one with early years experience, and teachers' professional development opportunities may revolve around national curriculum test data, or bear little relation to early years classroom practices. The tensions can affect

We need to know our children, know what they can do, what they enjoy and what they find challenging

the two worlds differently: professionals outside school may be struggling to reconcile new outcomes and accountability with firmly held views of good early years practice. We as teachers, on the other hand, are well versed in measuring and comparing; many of us need to rediscover the values and the vision that brought us into teaching in the first place. Is it possible for us to hold on to the ideals and vision of the FS in today's real world of teaching?

Aims and values

In the first cameo, the BEd students quickly decided that in order to provide good quality education, their nursery must have clearly defined aims and values. They agree that the nursery curriculum 'should start with children, taking into account everything we know about their learning, their motivation, and their impressive intellectual and emotional powers' (Drummond 1998: 108). We would do well to start here as we consider the Foundation Stage.

The FS starts with children. For a small child, being 3 is very different from being 2 or being 4. The FS is about us as teachers celebrating what it means to be 3 (or 4 or 5) years of age and not constantly striving to make children 'be' something else. This means that we need to know our children, know what they can do, what they enjoy and what they find challenging. We must help them to feel secure and valued.

The more we know about children's learning, the better we can encourage them to see themselves as learners, as Roger Merry indicates in
Chapter 5. Children want to learn, they want to make sense of the world
around them and they want to be able to tell people, especially their
teachers, about it. They are not seen as passive vessels, waiting to be
filled with knowledge and moulded into well-behaved citizens: instead
they are enthusiastic and active learners, needing to be nurtured and
supported in their quest for knowledge and their attempts to form relationships (see, for example, Bruce 1987: 17; Webber 1999: 140ff). As we
find out more about the way our brains develop, so we can help children
to explore the learning process and to make meaningful links in their
learning (see Kotulak 1996).

We can then match our teaching methods with children's learning
processes. The FS is about encouraging children's enjoyment of learning,
and their view of learning as a natural part of their lives. Teaching is
about us harnessing that desire and enthusiasm, so that these young
children gain a zest and enthusiasm for learning. It is here that we have
to consider the outcomes: the curriculum must be rigorously planned,
based on where the children are and what they can do, but we will also
have long-term aims for children's learning (see Chapters 6 and 12).

Getting to know the children

The children we teach come with very different experiences. The majority may never have attended this kind of setting before: some may never
have been away from home without their parents or familiar adults; this
may be their first experience of school with its strange rules and big,
noisy children. They may speak little or no English, they may be fluent
readers, they may be unable to tie their own shoelaces. Children may
join at different times of the year, perhaps beginning part-time. The
school may put classes together initially and split them later on. Children may come from many different settings or directly from the home;
or they may come from a nursery within the school. They may come
with very sketchy previous records, or none at all, or the school may
have good links with feeder settings and a policy on transferring records.
We need to get to know these children, to decide what it is we need to
know in order to give them the best opportunities: this information may
also be needed as a 'baseline' from which to measure the progress they
make.

How will we get to know these children? Initially, their parents and
carers will be a vital source of information, as they are the people who
know their children best. According to induction standards, the new
teacher must liaise effectively with parents and carers, by providing reports,

discussing targets and encouraging parents to support their children. In the FS we are encouraged to think more broadly: parents are children's first, and enduring, educators (Qualifications and Curriculum Authority 2000: 9) and we can discover a great deal about children's preferences, abilities, needs and background in discussion with their parents.

Links with parents

The good FS teacher also knows that if parents and carers feel welcome and valued, their children are more likely to feel the same. In cameo 2, children and parents are involved in a ritual at the beginning of each day. The teacher has learnt that Ravinder's family speak Gujurati, and has asked her mother to write Ravinder's name on her card. Taking the register becomes relatively painless, and the ritual provides security for the child and involves parents. It shows the children that their backgrounds and home languages are important and valued (a point taken up later by Alison Shilela in Chapter 14). We must remember that parents too come with different experiences, and by making space for them to come into the nursery with their children, and providing displays explaining what the children might be doing and why, we can involve parents in their children's learning. This could influence the ways in which they will support their children later in their school lives.

Parents may also be ambivalent about learning and outcomes: they want their child to be happy, to enjoy school and to make friends. They also want their child to 'do well'. For some, this will mean 'doing better' than other children: learning to read and write quicker, scoring higher marks in tests, getting more sums right. This may mean that they want to see evidence of what their children have done; or that they will want to coach them to 'pass' any assessments we carry out. We need to explain what 'doing well' might look like, and be clear about how the curriculum, assessment and teaching methods we use will enable children to progress.

In creating links with parents, as teachers we may want to consider:

- Welcoming parents: how can we start and end the day/session so that there is time to talk to parents?
- Providing information: what is the school policy? Is there a brochure? Does it explain the FS? Are there opportunities for using photographs or video to explain what the children are learning?
- Staying in touch: some schools make a point of phoning parents with good reports as well as telling them of problems. Is information translated into community languages? Is there anyone who can help translate displays, or provide support for parents who are not confident with English?

- Involving parents: are parents encouraged to help in the classroom? Are they encouraged to stay with their children for a while at the beginning of the day?

Assessment practices

Part of the excitement and the challenge of the FS is that children are changing every day: this means we need to observe and assess on a regular basis (more guidance in Chapters 3 and 12). As we get to know these children, so it becomes important to value what we find. Although it would be so much easier if all the children were the same, particularly if they were all equally mature and ready to learn, assessment allows us to find and value the *positive* in every child, and to celebrate their current stage and achievements.

Tensions arise when we need to use assessment to measure against prescribed outcomes. We can celebrate a child's achievement of the ELGs – and we see this in cameo 3, where the teacher records Rachel using number names in order in a familiar context. By building a collection of records, the teacher celebrates Rachel's achievement of this particular goal for mathematical development. Induction standards require the new teacher to recognize the level that a pupil is achieving and make accurate assessments against attainment targets and performance levels, and when we are required to provide a snapshot of all children's attainment in a formal 'assessment', we may be encouraged to make comparisons that reflect unfavourably on particular children.

In thinking about assessment, we need be clear how far it helps us to know our children, and to show individual progress. As professionals, we need to agree what records of achievement and progress will be useful to share as children move up the school, so that we build up a more complete picture of the children we teach. We may want to consider:

- Planning: identifying opportunities for observation and assessment and using different sorts of assessment for different purposes.
- Recording: different methods for different purposes – photographs, video, tape recording, taking notes and collecting children's written work?
- Other people: can support staff observe particular children, activities or equipment? How can parents be involved?
- Using the assessments: how useful is the information we collect – for celebrating children's progress; for measuring against outcomes; for self-evaluation?

All of these feature in following chapters.

Children as learners

Assessing children shows not only what they know and can do but also how they learn, as Roger Merry explains so clearly in Chapter 5. We can also learn a great deal from ongoing research into learning.

Recent research into brain function (eloquently explained by Greenfield 1998) has shown that there is a huge growth in the number of synapses (connections between the brain cells) after birth, followed by a time of 'pruning', when the least used connections are eliminated. The young child's brain, up to the age of about 10 years, has more synapses than at any other time of life. The brain is highly 'plastic', and new learning creates new pathways and networks, which improve brain function. Children need physical activity, concrete and relevant experiences to aid this learning.

Studies in cognitive psychology, particularly in recent years by Meltzoff (1999) show children trying to make sense of the world in a very methodical and collaborative way. They have theories about the way the world works; they make predictions and test them out, using ideas from other children and adults to refine their theories. They start to play 'pretend' games, showing that they understand that some things are real and others are not. At around 4 or 5 years, they begin to realize that people can have different beliefs from their own: Chantal knows her dad hid the presents in the cupboard, but she knows that her brother still believes they are under the bed where he last saw them.

For children to be successful as learners, they need to develop 'super skills' of learning. According to Sir Christopher Ball, 'motivation, socialisation and confidence are the most important [of these]' (Royal Society of Arts 1994: 11). Pascal and Bertram (undated), divide these 'super-skills' into dispositions to learn, respect for self and others and emotional well-being, and suggest that dispositions include resilience, organizational skills, curiosity, concentration, inventiveness, self-management and openness (see, too, Park: 1998).

Children's own play is arguably the best way of developing these 'super skills', and it is well worth reflecting on our own practices. Play enables children to take charge of their own learning: to test things out and reinforce their learning; to act out feelings and take on board new ideas; and to bring all of these things together to make sense of the world (Bruce 1991; Moyles 1994). It is important that we can at least explain to parents how children's playing enables them to learn, and that we consider what kind of evidence we can provide for our assertions. Cameo 3 shows a particular kind of play, planned by the teacher, but children will also initiate their own play. It may be worth while carrying out an audit of the classroom or playground, to see what kind of provision is available for children to play, to learn through movement and their senses, to make choices and decisions about their learning, and to carry out in-depth and long-term exploration. Of course, children who manage their own learning, who explore issues that arouse their curiosity, may not reach the outcomes we had in mind for them: we must try to balance their aims with our own.

Curriculum planning

The Qualifications and Curriculum Authority's curriculum guidance does allow some flexibility: it defines the curriculum as 'everything children do, see, hear or feel in their setting, both planned and unplanned' (Qualifications and Curriculum Authority 2000: 1). It is not a national curriculum. There are no 'core' subjects: each area of learning is equally important. 'Stepping Stones' towards the goals are not attainment targets (ATs), but suggestions of stages that children may move through on their way to the goals. The curriculum should be about what we want children to learn (see for example Hanson 1998; Whitaker 1998).

Importantly, many of the goals reflect the 'super-skills'. The goals for personal, social and emotional development are divided into dispositions and attitudes; self-confidence and self-esteem; making relationships; behaviour and self-control; self-care; and a sense of community. Creative development covers imagination, responding to experiences, and expressing and communicating ideas; and physical development includes moving with confidence and imagination, showing awareness of space, themselves, and others. The guidance shows many of the goals being achieved by children who are playing.

Both outcomes and process are important in planning for continuity and progression too. The children will ultimately transfer to Year 1 and move into the National Curriculum and that needs to be a smooth transition. Children who watch, question and investigate, who design and build using tools and information communications technology (ICT) (all goals for knowledge and understanding of the world) are developing skills needed to access the National Curriculum, and contexts for these can be planned to fit with the whole school curriculum. Communication, language and literacy, and mathematical development were developed so that they fit with the literacy and numeracy strategies, but can be taught in a way appropriate to the Foundation Stage. Children who learn through playing in different contexts and with different people will have a head start in personal/social/health education (PSHE) and citizenship, with its four interrelated sections of developing confidence and responsibility and making the most of their abilities; preparing to play an active role as citizens; developing a healthy, safer lifestyle; developing good relationships and respecting the differences between people.

Observation of children's play and exploration will provide insights into the ways in which they can be challenged

The induction standards for newly qualified teachers also state that the newly qualified teacher (NQT) must plan effectively with regards to equality of opportunity and to meet the needs of children with special needs and this is woven through QCA's guidance. It is not enough to plan a wonderful curriculum if Reese spends the whole time cycling round and round the playground and Jasmin never gets a chance to use the computer. Observation of children's play and exploration will provide insights into the ways in which they can be challenged, the areas in which they are working on the boundaries of their capabilities and can be helped to move on, and the issues with which they need time to grapple and assimilate knowledge.

Continuous assessment takes on huge significance, giving 'insight into children's interests, achievements and possible difficulties in their learning from which next steps in learning and teaching can be planned. It also helps ensure early identification of special educational needs and particular abilities' (Qualifications and Curriculum Authority 2000: 24). From that knowledge comes the ability to plan a meaningful curriculum for each child. Curriculum planning must also show how children will move towards the goals for each area of learning and the stepping stones, and the learning and teaching sections of each area of learning give useful suggestions for planning purposes. Of course, children don't learn in straight lines, nor do they learn in neat blocks: Cameo 3 shows a single activity encompassing all of the areas, with children able to work at their own pace, but with planned ways of supporting and scaffolding their learning through class discussion and questions. Planning must also acknowledge that children need to consolidate their learning, use skills in different contexts, and experiment with what they know rather than just keep plodding on towards the next level: there must also be provision for depth and breadth of knowledge and experience.

Our understanding of the outcomes we wish for our children's learning, including the early learning goals, is also important, so that we can ensure that their learning has a purpose. If we can make the links between children's aims and our own, we will be providing a curriculum that at least begins to balance the outcomes of learning with the processes.

In planning the curriculum, we need to bear in mind:

- the areas of learning: are all six being covered over time?
- the children: can they *all* access the learning? How can their learning be extended?
- resources: is there a choice of resources, or contexts in which they can be used? Are there opportunities for learning outdoors?
- the early learning goals: how will the children progress towards the goals?
- other adults in the classroom: do they know what the children are learning? Do they know how they can support the learning, is it helpful to discuss appropriate vocabulary or skills, which they can use or teach?
- the school: how does FS planning fit within the school's frameworks?

Teaching methods

Knowledge of children's ways of learning should influence our teaching methods. Some children learn in very physical and active ways, others need time to think things through before coming back to try again. They also learn at different rates, and some may look like they are regressing for a while before leaping forwards in their thinking. We need to provide stimulating and varied input; a well-resourced environment; and a structure comprising both active times, when children can manipulate their environment and see how things work, and quiet times to consider the evidence and formulate theories. This brings us back to play: 'what children are involved in when they initiate the task . . . The skill of the adult educator is in entering the child's play, led by the initiative of the child, as a partner who shares the process' (Bruce 1991: 17).

This kind of teaching needs to encompass a wide range of teaching strategies. QCA's curriculum guidance suggests a number of strands which, along with rigorous planning and assessment, make up effective teaching.

These include modelling positive behaviour and using rich language; using questioning that asks children to think, rather than recall facts; direct teaching, when appropriate, of skills and knowledge, either adults or other children; and supporting, motivating and enabling children (Qualifications and Curriculum Authority 2000: 22–4). Some of this will be planned; some may be spontaneous, in responding to the particular needs of a child. Guidance for inspectors (Office for Standards in Education 2000) provides some useful questions about teaching strategies, which teachers can use for self-evaluation.

Knowledge of individual children is important too: when to intervene with useful questions or suggestions, and when to stay quiet are good teaching skills we all need to acquire. Finding the time to listen will give important messages, as well as providing models for the children's own behaviour. Having consistently high (but realistic) expectations of children's abilities and behaviour encourages children to meet them. Providing space and time for children to become engrossed in their own activities and to explore issues in depth, encourages them to see themselves as learners and explorers and to value what they find. Sensitively joining in with some of those activities shows children that we value their efforts and that we see their work as important.

Various studies have looked at different forms of early education. Lawrence *et al.* (1997) report on a longitudinal study in the USA of children who took part in different forms of pre-school. At the age of 23 years, those who had attended formal skills-based, direct-instruction settings still seemed to be at a distinct disadvantage compared with both the 'free play' settings and those which used the High/Scope 'plan, do, review' model, having experienced more arrests, discipline and educational problems. Sylva's (1998) research shows the importance of teaching that allows children to direct their learning and make their own decisions (quoted in David 1999: 11). The evidence suggests that this kind of teaching develops social and personal skills, giving long-term advantages both in terms of learning and social responsibility.

Conclusion

Is it possible to keep children at the heart of our teaching? Although QCA's guidance does not provide us with all the answers, it is evident that the emphasis is now shifting. The FS is a key stage based on principles. In this age of targets and accountability, it is easy to lose sight of values and look only to outcomes. Early years professionals have fought a hard battle to persuade government to recognize the principles and values that underpin early learning. *They are the same values that underpin later learning and teaching.*

Teachers are accountable for children's learning. In the FS this means more than accountability for children's attainments of particular levels. We are accountable also for children's motivation and enjoyment, their friendships and self-esteem. This is a fundamental part of the FS, not an addition to an already overcrowded National Curriculum.

We still have measurable outcomes, but the ways in which children reach them are equally important. Early years experts have always known the importance of play. QCA's curriculum guidance provides 'official' acknowledgement of the vital place of play in children's learning.

The nature of teaching in the FS arises from the nature of learning, and is firmly based around the children and not vice versa. We are expected to develop our professional knowledge and skills, and to evaluate them, in a way that is useful for us and our children, rather than to meet external targets. Equally importantly, we are encouraged to trust our expertise.

The FS will no doubt be subject to changes in time, but it currently goes some way towards enshrining the best of early years thinking and practice in government policy. Much of that thinking underpins teaching throughout the primary school, but government strategies do not often reflect it. If we, the early years key professionals, can translate the theory into practice, the balance may shift further towards principled education, based on children's needs and talents, with teachers held accountable for the things which really matter.

Some further issues to consider

1 What principles and beliefs underpin your teaching, and how are these reflected in your teaching, planning and record keeping? Consider asking your mentor about their beliefs, and observing them. You could ask your teacher-mentor to do the same for you.
2 How can you plan towards outcomes, while remaining focused on individual children, their needs, their talents, their ways of learning? Does the planning format you use enable you to do that? Talk to other teachers about their strategies.
3 What does 'being accountable' mean? How are you accountable to the government? To Ofsted? To your headteacher? To the parents? To the children? Think about what these groups need and want from you.

References and further reading

Ball, C. (1999) *The Learning Agenda: Reform or Revolution.* Derby: University of Derby.
Bennett, N., Wood, L. and Rogers, S. (1997) *Teaching Through Play: Teachers' Thinking and Classroom Practice.* Buckingham: Open University Press.

Bruce, T. (1987) *Early Childhood Education.* London: Hodder and Stoughton.

Bruce, T. (1991) *Time to play in Early Childhood Education.* London: Hodder and Stoughton.

David, T. (1999) Changing minds: teaching young children, in T. David (ed.) *Teaching Young Children.* London: Paul Chapman.

David, T. and Nurse, A. (1999) Inspections of under fives' education and constructions of early childhood, in T. David (ed.) *Teaching Young Children.* London: Paul Chapman.

Department for Education and Employment (2000) *The Induction Period for Newly Qualified Teachers.* London: HMSO.

Drummond, M. J. (1998) Starting with children: towards an early years curriculum, in ATL (ed.) *Take Care, Mr Blunkett: Powerful Voices in the New Curriculum Debate.* London: ATL.

Greenfield, S. (1998) *The Human Brain: A Guided Tour.* London: Phoenix.

Hanson, D. (1998) From good intentions, in ATL (ed.) *Take Care, Mr Blunkett: Powerful Voices in the New Curriculum Debate.* London: ATL.

Henry, M. (1996) *Young Children, Parents and Professionals: Enhancing the Links in Early Childhood.* London: Routledge.

Kotulak, R. (1996) *Inside the Brain: Revolutionary Discoveries of How the Mind Works.* Kansas City, MO: Andrews and McMeel.

Lawrence, J., Schweinhart, J. and Weikart, D. (1997) *Lasting Differences: The High/Scope Preschool Curriculum Study Through Age 23.* Ypsilanti, MI: High/Scope Press.

Lindsay, G. and Desforges, C. (1998) *Baseline Assessment: Practice, Problems and Possibilities.* London: David Fulton.

Meltzoff, A. (1999) *The Scientist in the Crib: Minds, Brains and How Children Learn.* London: Morrow Press.

Moyles, J. (1989) *Just Playing? The Role and Status of Play in Early Education.* Milton Keynes: Open University Press.

Moyles, J. (1991) *Play as a Learning Process in your Classroom.* London: Cassell.

Moyles, J. (1994) *The Excellence of Play.* Buckingham: Open University Press.

Moyles, J., Adams, S. and Musgrove, A. (2001) *Study of Effective Early Pedagogy.* Report for the DfES/QCA. Chelmsford/London.

Office for Standards in Education (2000) *Inspecting Subjects 3–11: Guidance for Inspectors and Schools.* London: HMSO.

Parliamentary Office of Science and Technology (2000) *Early Years Learning.* London: HMSO.

Park, J. (1998) Motivating young people to learn, in ATL (ed.) *Take Care, Mr Blunkett: Powerful Voices in the New Curriculum Debate.* London: ATL.

Pascal, C. and Bertram, A. (undated) Accounting Early for Lifelong Learning. University College, Worcester (an unpublished discussion paper).

Qualifications and Curriculum Authority (2000) *Curriculum Guidance for the Foundation Stage.* London: HMSO.

Royal Society of Arts (1994) *Start Right* (The Ball Report). London: R.S.A.

Sylva, K. and Siraj-Blatchford, I. (2001) Effective Pedagogy in the Early Years. Report for the DfES/QCA. London/Oxford.

Webber, B. (1999) Assessment and learning, in T. David (ed.) *Teaching Young Children.* London: Paul Chapman.

Whitaker, P. (1998) Education at the edge, in ATL (ed.) *Take Care, Mr Blunkett: Powerful Voices in the New Curriculum Debate.* London: ATL.

2

A place for everything . . . ? The teaching and learning environment

Janet Moyles

Cameo 1

Billy, aged 4 years, watches the new teacher closely in the nursery classroom, scrutinizing her face with a puzzled expression at every opportunity. He does this for several days, saying nothing, and the teacher bides her time feeling that Billy is simply getting used to her being with that class. Eventually, she asks Billy why he seems so puzzled. 'What you got that blue-stuff on your eyes for?' Billy asks gruffly (meaning the teacher's eye shadow). Instead of rushing in with an answer the teacher reflects for a moment and then asks of the boy 'Why do you think it's there?' Quick as a flash Billy retorts, 'Is it 'cos your 'tending to be a witch?'

Cameo 2

The beginner teacher takes great trouble to set up a new 'travel agents' stimulus area in the classroom. It has an appropriate sign, brochures, pens and paper, telephone, maps of the world, travel posters for Disneyworld, a computer, a cash register and a furniture arrangement which, as far as possible, reflects a real travel agency. Next morning, when the class of 8-year-olds arrive, there is great delight in the area and everyone wants to be the first to play. There is much jostling, pushing, arguing and, eventually, a few tears as the shop ends up in a demolished heap. The young teacher is devastated by the quick demise of her hard work and vows never to set up such an area again.

Cameo 3

It is customary at the end of the day, for the Year 1 children in Jackie's class sit on the carpet for quiet reflection and a story. The children mostly listen quietly and attentively to each other and to the teacher. However, there are always one or two children who constantly tug at the fraying edges of the carpet and set other children off pulling at the loose threads. Jackie asks them in a kindly but firm manner, several times, to 'Please stop making the carpet worse' but every day her story is interrupted, and eventually stopped, in order to remove the offending children.

Introduction

The cameos raise very different issues about the classroom as a con-text for teaching and learning. On the one hand, a primary teacher needs to be a very organized and aware person, with a clear rationale for managing such things as a broad curriculum, teaching and learning resources, mounds of paperwork while, on the other hand, being able to give maximum time and effort to managing children and their learn-ing. Young children, like Billy, are no less intelligent or less thinking than adults; they just operate at a different level of understanding and constantly strive to make meaning from the sometimes bewildering (and contradictory) world in which they find themselves (see Moyles 1997).

No doubt you are questioning why, in the second cameo, despite all this teacher's care and effort, she apparently did not succeed? What more did she need to understand about the children and the learning context in order to achieve her intentions? Similarly, in the third cameo, why does this experienced teacher fail to pay attention to something relatively small which continually undermines her authority during story time and, worse still, causes interference to children's concentration, enjoyment of the occasion and potential learning? The answer to these and other questions lies in understanding some crucial factors (some of which are explored in other chapters within this book), which inextricably interrelate in the primary classroom and significantly affect its organiza-tion and management, namely:

- teachers: their beliefs and values and how these underpin all other elements of classroom organization and management;
- children: their family backgrounds, age phases and individual learning and behavioural needs which must be addressed;
- the learning environment: the indoor and outdoor classroom and its resources (human and physical).

In this chapter, albeit briefly, we will examine these three issues and what they mean to the beginner teacher, using examples from classroom experiences and questions to focus attention on the issues.

Beliefs that matter

All of us bring to teaching memories of our own lives in school, perceptions about what it is to 'teach' and beliefs about how classroom systems should be. As part of coursework, some PGCE students explored the notion of what makes a 'good' teacher and their thoughts are shown in Figure 2.1.

The very first statement, 'Believe in what you do' is simple but profound. Within us all lurks the 'ghost of pupil past' that influences both

B elieve in what you do
ase what you do on children's interests and needs

A pproachable personality is vital
lways try to think positively and react thoughtfully

S ense of humour is essential – second sight is useful!
tructured approach to planning and management

I n touch with differing abilities and interests
ntegrates all children into class whatever race, sex or disability

C ontrol and respect must be *earned*: children treated equitably
ommunication skills must be excellent

T otally firm, fair and flexible
reats everyone with respect

E xplains things clearly and explicitly
xpects to be listened to and listens in return

A ware of everything and open to new ideas
nalytical and self-reflective

C onfident, calm, caring, collected and child-orientated
reative and imaginative

H appy classroom and happy, secure children
ome background is acknowledged and understood

I nfinitely patient and consistent
maginative and enthusiastic, inspiring and in touch

N egotiates learning intentions and outcomes
eed for planning, observation and evaluation recognized

G eneral knowledge and common sense is used in teaching
ET ORGANIZED!

Figure 2.1   What makes a good teacher

negatively and positively what we believe about children, teachers and education. You will, no doubt, have heard statements like:

'Children today are not as well behaved as they used to be.'
'Children just don't listen these days.'
'Literacy and Numeracy, the basics, are what really matter in primary school.'

or even

'No one forgets a good teacher!'

These beliefs about children, teachers and education may or may not reflect how *you* feel about these things but certainly echo others' perceptions. Holding such views would make a vast difference to the way each of these people might themselves teach children, organize the curriculum, or manage the classroom. Hence, we can begin to understand why there are so many different views about education prevailing in our society. An added difficulty within teaching is that while the schooling system operates for all, ostensibly on the basis of equality of opportunity, each individual within the system – child and teacher – is different and has a differing level of, expectation, capability, understanding and need.

Not only must you, as a beginner teacher, engage with other people's beliefs and views regarding educational issues but you must determine what YOU believe. Without this personal construct – of children, the teacher's role and the learning environment – it is an uphill struggle to establish yourself as a competent and confident class teacher. Reflecting on your own teaching is a vital part of your self-evaluation and professional development as Siân Adams explains in Chapter 13.

People aged 3–11 years

As we have seen in Nansi Ellis's chapter, when children enter the Foundation Stage of education, they already bring with them a wide range of experiences. Parents and other family members are their first 'educators' (see Hurst and Joseph 1998; Drury *et al.* 2000) and, as teachers, we must not ignore what children bring from their past (however brief that past!). From the time they enter early years settings, children are also developing greater and greater levels of independence in their actions and thinking – the very move from home to a nursery setting represents the main beginning of independence from the family. Having made that break, however, children may find themselves in a number of different settings before finally arriving in mainstream education sometime around their fifth birthday. Whatever the new environment, children react to being in a different sociocultural framework with a large number of (relatively unknown) other children and adults and this can affect significantly their behaviour and self-concept – as it would with all of us. If you don't believe me, just think how you feel entering the new school in which you will spend your teaching practice or induction year! It's no different emotionally for young children.

Family background

Whatever children bring with them, an effective teacher will ensure that early experiences are endorsed within the classroom structures. For example: children from different ethnic backgrounds will have their cultures represented within home corner materials, and 'the family' will reflect a range of types of structures to be found in modern society. The effective teacher will also want to *extend* children's experiences and offer them a range of broader options. One example might be the child who arrives with very stereotypical gender views (like the 3-year-old boy who told me it was women's work to pick up the jigsaw pieces from the floor!) or those who have not yet learned to cope with children different from themselves (Alison Shilela explores these issues in Chapter 14). Remember, we cannot change anything so fundamental as the child's background. What has to 'change' is the way adults respond to them on the basis of accepting the children's background as a starting point for managing learning and ensuring continuity and coherence.

Continued contact with parents is a specific feature of primary education and most parents want to work with us as teachers in achieving the best for their children (see Hughes *et al.* 1994) and in working with children with special needs (as Jenny Lansdell explains in Chapter 15). In primary classrooms, teachers are *in loco parentis* (as Chris Curran discusses in Chapter 17), replacing the parent in dealing as diligently as we can with the children's needs during our time with them.

Managing learning with different age groups

Many primary ITE courses now specialize in either advanced early years courses in which students learn to work with those aged 3–7 years or in specialist KS1/KS2 courses (5–11 years). Courses will normally make some differentiation between phases but will emphasize the notions of continuity and progression across primary education. Just because a child is a 7-year-old does not mean, for example, that he or she no longer needs access to practical aids for number work or should cease to have experiences with constructional toys. Throughout the primary years children are developing a wide range of skills and constructing knowledge and understanding through their interactions and, as they increasingly gain ability to work from more abstract concepts, their teaching and learning

Throughout the primary years children are developing a wide range of skills and constructing knowledge and understanding

needs and the organization of these will gradually change. For example, older children may be expected to work more collaboratively and undertake more complex problem solving tasks, which will require a very different classroom organization and teaching style.

For younger children, it is not a question of 'watering-down' the activities that would be given to junior children: far from it! Rather it is necessary to understand the distinct emphases required in focusing on young children, in developing their learning effectively and in examining the particular classroom strategies required by the teacher (see, for example, Edgington 1998: Moyles *et al.* 2001). (Figure 2.2 represents an attempt to explain to PGCE students the differing emphases between teaching 3- to 5-year-olds and older children.)

The main headings within the diagram in Figure 2.2 do not necessarily change for older children but the focus becomes increasingly dominated by the KS1 and KS2 National Curriculum requirements. The Foundation Stage has its own areas of learning and teachers of younger children still require a sound knowledge of the subject elements within these areas, for it is probably true to say that the younger the child, the securer our own knowledge of different curriculum aspects needs to be. Whereas one explanation may be sufficient for an older primary child, the same concept may need explaining in many diverse ways to find an explanation that 'fits' the younger child's (or special needs child's) different ways of

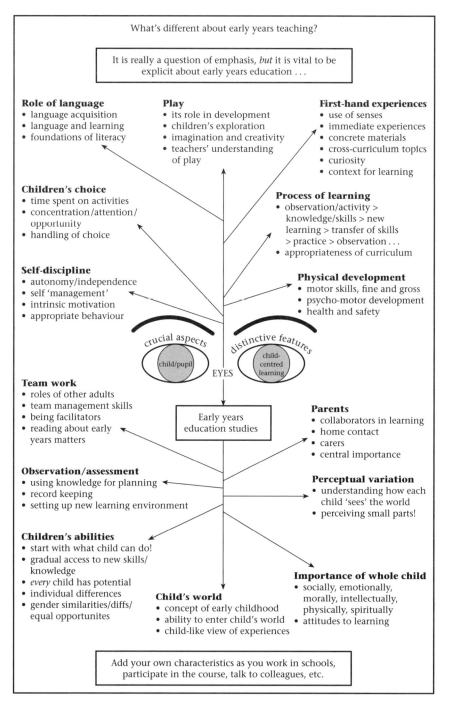

What's different about early years teaching?

It is really a question of emphasis, *but* it is vital to be explicit about early years education . . .

Role of language
- language acquisition
- language and learning
- foundations of literacy

Play
- its role in development
- children's exploration
- imagination and creativity
- teachers' understanding of play

First-hand experiences
- use of senses
- immediate experiences
- concrete materials
- cross-curriculum topics
- curiosity
- context for learning

Children's choice
- time spent on activities
- concentration/attention/ opportunity
- handling of choice

Process of learning
- observation/activity > knowledge/skills > new learning > transfer of skills > practice > observation . . .
- appropriateness of curriculum

Self-discipline
- autonomy/independence
- self 'management'
- intrinsic motivation
- appropriate behaviour

Physical development
- motor skills, fine and gross
- psycho-motor development
- health and safety

crucial aspects   distinctive features
child/pupil   child-centred learning
EYES

Team work
- roles of other adults
- team management skills
- being facilitators
- reading about early years matters

Early years education studies

Parents
- collaborators in learning
- home contact
- carers
- central importance

Observation/assessment
- using knowledge for planning
- record keeping
- setting up new learning environment

Perceptual variation
- understanding how each child 'sees' the world
- perceiving small parts!

Children's abilities
- start with what child can do!
- gradual access to new skills/ knowledge
- *every* child has potential
- individual differences
- gender similarities/diffs/ equal opportunites

Child's world
- concept of early childhood
- ability to enter child's world
- child-like view of experiences

Importance of whole child
- socially, emotionally, morally, intellectually, physically, spiritually
- attitudes to learning

Add your own characteristics as you work in schools, participate in the course, talk to colleagues, etc.

Figure 2.2

making meaning. Creating classroom structures that allow a sustained language and communications opportunities (see Whitehead 1999) and on-going observations and assessments leading to planning for provision of learning experiences, are key areas for FS teachers (Fisher 1996).

A sound understanding of child development and the process of learning is vital for all primary teachers if they are to organize and manage the classroom appropriately for different age groups (Merry 1998). Regrettably, this is one aspect which has received decreasing emphasis on primary ITE courses over the last few years. Beginner teachers must be prepared to ask appropriate searching questions related to children's development during curriculum sessions and to enhance their own understanding through reading and interpreting observations of children across the age phases.

Children's independence

Children across the primary school years are developing independence in a variety of ways, particularly in thinking, confidence, self-esteem and development.

Thinking

Like Billy in the first cameo, many children work out explanations for themselves about phenomena (Tina Jarvis and Lee Woods explain this more fully in Chapter 7). He is not being rude or cheeky, trying to be funny or being 'cute': he is simply making a guess based on prior experience (in this case, a face-painting session). This trial and error way of working is very typical of primary aged children and should be fostered for we all learn a great deal by our mistakes and our guesses. The management of learning situations must allow children to raise serious, sensible questions, which receive equally serious answers (see de Boo 1999). The type of 'What colour is it?', 'What shape is it?' questions, so frequently asked, are actually confusing to children who are well aware that the questioner knows the answers already and, therefore, see no point in responding. Children often think it must be some kind of 'catch' question, which can lead to a failure to respond through uncertainty or embarrassment that, in turn, may lead the teacher to believe that the child has poor language skills. The classroom structures need to allow opportunities for exploring open-ended questions, more appropriate in developing higher-order thinking skills to challenge understanding and ensure the teacher learns about the children's learning (see Costello 2000).

Confidence

The children in the second scenario were so keen and confident in the classroom that they temporarily 'forgot' the conventions of behaviour which they had been taught. They would need to be told that their *behaviour* was inappropriate on this occasion, rather than being 'blamed' for what had happened to the travel agency. Blame leads to children eventually deciding that they are 'no good' or making the 'I'm useless' type of comment, a form of 'labelling' so destructive of self-worth. The problem with labels is that people so often live up to the image the label suggests, so that being 'naughty' or 'good' or 'difficult' leads to exactly that kind of behaviour being exhibited. In turn, being 'difficult' gains some children the level of attention they demand (inevitably meaning that other children get less) and generates a self-fulfilling prophecy on the part of teacher and child with the child becoming more difficult and the teaching continually reaffirming the label. As a consequence, classroom management is made more problematic in that much time and energy is taken up in dealing with difficult children rather than ensuring teacher-time is more equitably distributed (see Barnes 1999 for some useful strategies).

Giving children responsibility for making decisions about classroom rules and routines, ensures that they take ownership and responsibility for their own actions as well as democratic decisions about other people's behaviour.

Development
Children of 3–8 years are gradually developing physical competence, which allows greater independence of movement and action. It is positively cruel to keep children in this age phase sitting still for long periods of time! (After 8 years, children tend to refine and hone existing skills through general maturity rather than making any great leaps in development (see Maude 1996, 2001)). Although the children in the third scenario appear to be 'naughty', children naturally manipulate things around them and explore increasing control over their fine motor skills. Ironically, it may well be that fraying the carpet edge was actually helping one child to concentrate! It could equally be that one of the 'frayers' is still socially quite immature and finds sitting within a confined space in close proximity to others quite distressing. Perhaps one or both of the children have not yet acquired age-appropriate levels of emotional stability, in which case fraying the carpet may be a symptom of underlying anxiety about, for example, whether the parent or carer will turn up at the end of the day. The message is clear: *understand the children as individual people* and organize and manage the classroom with this knowledge in mind. Think of them as people with all the emotions and needs that you yourself have – though at a different phase in life. Make one-to-one as well as collective relationships with them. Dealing with individual needs is not simply a matter of considering a child's learning needs but of understanding 'where they are' physically, socially and emotionally as well (as Jenny Lansdell explains in Chapter 15). For the children who cannot physically sit still for any extended period, it may

be more appropriate that they draw a picture during story time or are asked to make pictorial or written notes during periods of teacher exposition to the whole class. This kind of thinking is at the very heart of child-centred education, the provision of a differentiated curriculum and effective classroom management.

Organizing and managing the teaching and learning environment

The classroom represents 'home' for five or more hours of each weekday during term times for children and teachers alike. Its prime function is to 'house' the teacher and the learners in a kind of 'workshop' (or playshop!) context that supports crucial interactions between them. The teacher must translate knowledge of children and pedagogy into classroom organization and management structures to everyone's benefit, no mean feat given that few people will have been totally responsible for 30+ other people before! The vital elements that must be considered are:

- the physical environment both indoors and out;
- structures (including routines) and resource management;
- rights, responsibilities and rules;
- communication.

Each of these will be explored briefly and references given to useful further reading. While you read, try to think about classrooms within your recent experience so as to give meaning to the issues.

Physical environment

The classroom or class base is part of a larger school building, which was built in a particular time in history under the philosophies of education that existed at those times. Very early state elementary schools, for example, had large halls where vast numbers of children were taught *en masse* to read, write and do basic number skills. Schools built in the 1920s to 1930s show a growing emphasis on outdoor activities for children, being characterized by having open-air quadrangles (often containing gardens and outdoor play areas) around which long draughty corridors spawn individual classrooms, with up to 50 children in each! Designs of schools built in the 1960s and 1970s reflect a belief in the interactive and collaborative nature of children's learning and are often open-plan, where two or more classrooms are merged together and teachers are intended to function as a team. Whatever the building, teachers must operate current ideologies and practices making the most of whatever they have to promote effective teaching and learning experiences.

There is much to learn from the way in which teachers organize the seating arrangements

Take a moment to turn to the classroom plan in Figure 3.3 (in Linda Hargreaves's chapter). It reflects a very typical kind of layout for an infant classroom and contains direct 'clues' as to the activities of the children and, therefore, the practices of the teacher. Many areas of curriculum, including subjects, are represented within the layout, for example language and personal/social skills (the café), literacy (the library area), technology (constructional toys and 3-D models), art (painting), science (water play) and mathematics (sorting and puzzles). This layout immediately suggests a KS1 classroom, where children may be given some choice in their activities, albeit choosing from those learning experiences provided by the teacher in specific areas of the room, or be direction within specific sessions, e.g. the literacy hour. A teacher's ideology superimposes on any physical classroom space a way of working for that teacher and the children. Such aspects are worth noting on your next visit to a classroom. Does the classroom you visit have an arrangement of grouped tables, individual desks in rows facing the front, tables or desks arranged in 'work bays'? All of these arrangements will say something to the observer about the preferences of the teacher.

There is much to learn from the way in which teachers organize the seating arrangements. People whose ideology lies in a child-centred type of education can be quite horrified at the sight of rows of desks and chairs, which tend to signify whole-class teaching. Collaborative group work requires tables to be organized in such a way that co-operation and interaction between children can take place, for example, that they can all see each other's faces and share resources. Such arrangements, however, can positively hinder children attempting to undertake concentrated, individual work or hamper the teacher in trying to demonstrate to the whole class. The organization of the desks or tables needs to be contingent on the types of activities that are taking place – the 'fitness for purpose' notion (see Alexander *et al.* 1992).

Carpet areas are excellent for bringing a cosy 'togetherness' to shared events in the classroom, be it poetry or story (as in cameo 3), in plenary sessions, discussions or singing together. They may not be so useful for older children (physically large 11-year-olds can find sitting on a carpet cross-legged rather demeaning) or for a teacher's detailed exposition on a special topic. It may be far more useful if the carpet area is detailed as a stimulus area (see Moyles 1989) so that children can follow up such a teacher-directed session with a more first-hand, direct experience, as might be the case with the travel agency (once the ground-rules are established!).

When entering a classroom in which you are going to work for the first time, it is advisable to make a plan as this both helps to fix the area in your mind and also offers the opportunity of rechecking at home when you are thinking through future learning activities. It is also useful for observation purposes as suggested by Linda Hargreaves in Chapter 3.

It is as well to remember that the 'outdoor classroom' is as important as the indoor environment when it comes to teaching and learning, especially with younger children. There is growing evidence that children need more physical activity than they currently have in school (see Maude 2001) and government and media alike constantly raise the issue of children's physical fitness and inclinations to sporting activities. As Bilton (1998) explains, anything that can be done indoors can be done outside – and be done even bigger! Aspects of the science and geography curricular done outside with older children, for example studying naturally-occurring phenomena and identifying wild-life, have the advantage of being based on reality. With younger children, taking the 'Garden Centre' role play area outside, for example, means that mapping your journey to buy seeds and plants (using wheeled vehicles for gross motor development, too!) can bring in a wide range of aspects of Knowledge and Understanding of the World and offer opportunities for 'messy' water and soil activities, which would be less satisfactory indoors.

Structures and routines

By structures is meant the way the classroom operates so that children are clear what they are doing and do not need to expend time and energy in constantly finding out where things are and what they must do. Routines represent the order in which things happen and are usually related to the daily and weekly timetable for the class.

Timetables are usually determined by the school, at least in outline, with several sessions being 'fixed times', for example, hall periods or assemblies. Within the constraints of the required curriculum, teachers have the task of deciding on the best use of time within what is left either individually or in year groups. In reality, much time is now spent fitting in everything else around the Literacy and Numeracy hours. Making good use of teaching and learning time is vital as we must ensure that the 'whole child' is educated and not just schooled in literacy and numeracy. Citizenship is a burgeoning area of focus for politicians and public alike and demands its own curriculum time.

Making observations of our own classrooms can reveal that children are, for example, spending much of their time waiting for teacher attention; this may be because the daily structures and routines are inappropriate and need reconsidering. Perhaps children are too dependent on the teacher for resources or tasks, or are given insufficient guidance on what to do when they are 'stuck'. A class discussion generating a set of ideas of what to do when you need help, such as ask another child, look in a book, do another task until the teacher can see you, can quickly alleviate this problem even with young children.

Routines are helpful though we should guard against them becoming 'routinous' and, therefore, boring. A little deviation from routine helps to keep children and teacher alert and interested, for example, try taking the children outside for literacy hour activities using a 'treasure hunt' idea – find words, read, do tasks from their reading, communicate with others and happily feedback in the plenary on their different experiences.

Such routines as those involved in children entering and leaving the classroom or in tidying up need constant attention. Does it happen smoothly or do the children fidget and tussle with each other? Often, as in the carpet cameo above, children and teachers simply get overly familiar with a situation and what should be dealt with quickly, becomes a constant thorn in everyone's side! Routines are useful but familiarity can breed contempt! (The caretaker, a classroom assistant or a willing parent might be asked to repair that carpet.)

Demanding levels of responsibility from the children appropriate to their age by, for example, ensuring that they are responsible for the access/retrieval and upkeep/maintenance of resources (we need *all* the pieces in a word game or jigsaw!), ensures that they are not dependent on the teacher or other classroom adult for every item of equipment. This also means that materials should be located and labelled appropriately; older children can do this in negotiation with the teacher and even the youngest children can do the labelling though location may be the teacher's decision. Train and trust the children! Expect them to behave appropriately in all matters and most of them will. A quality classroom is likely to be one where there is a place for everything and everything is mainly in its place! You should not use precious time at the end of each day for sorting out the classroom when there is marking, preparation, display, records and a wealth of other tasks on which your time is more profitably spent.

Rights, responsibilities and rules

Children and teachers have the right to the best possible classroom experiences – and that also means behaving appropriately towards each other. Issues should be discussed, responsibilities of each party determined and ground-rules established. Both teachers and learners should feel able to raise issues that affect them working effectively in the classroom, for example both are likely to be affected by noise – constant shouting or nagging will usually make this situation worse, whereas discussion about alleviating the situation can result in a quiet, working atmosphere being maintained by the children. As a general rule, children should be given responsibility for going to the toilet without asking, though this may be dependent on the school layout. A sensible rule which children will readily accept is 'one at a time'. Whatever the rule, it should be established quickly, with firmness and consistency: this applies equally to any rules made. When asked about their 'best' teachers, a majority of junior age pupils chose fairness and consistency as the chief qualities (see Cullingford 1991; Pollard and Filer 1999). If, for any reason, changes to the rules are required, these should be communicated, renegotiated, written up and read out for all to see and hear, agreed and firmly put into effect as efficiently as possible.

Behaviour

It would be trite to suggest that if you get the classroom organization and management sorted out there will be no behaviour problems. We have, however, only to think about the number of times there is a fuss and disagreement over quite minor incidents – a child tripping over another, arguments over resources – to realize that many behavioural issues are at least related to classroom structures. Bored children also misbehave, so achieving work at an appropriate standard relieves some problems. Most primary children enjoy school, appreciate the relationship they have with teachers and want to be part of the stimulating activities. Many behavioural problems can be contained within acceptable boundaries once teacher and child have 'got the measure of each other' and a working relationship agreed. This happens when the teacher makes time to work with individuals, knows them individually and responds to their needs. Treating children as people and giving them appropriate respect means that many children will respond with appropriate levels of responsibility and care for others. (The teacher's role in ensuring safety is dealt with in Chapter 17).

Communication

Primary teachers usually excel at explaining to children what to do and how to do it. Communication, however, often breaks down because teachers fail to tell children *why* they are undertaking a certain activity and what they are expected to *know* and *do* as a result. So much is taken for granted in the primary classroom and yet, as many cameos in this book show, children often have a very different level of understanding to adults and need explicit guidance.

There will be many different levels at which we communicate with children requiring different *classroom groupings*. Talking to them as a whole class to establish the groundwork for something to which all children will contribute or demonstrating a new technique are examples. Grouping by ability for some activities, will mean that we can work to stretch the abler children or give closer attention to a group requiring additional help. Grouping by task will be helpful where resources are perhaps limited and only a few children at a time can have access to practical equipment. With younger children, groupings are commonly by friendship and there may also be occasion where sex groupings might be used, particularly where the teacher is attempting to encourage boys to use the home-corner provision or girls to become more adventurous with the constructional materials. A useful research-based text on grouping and its different forms and outcomes is given by Sukhnandan and Lee (1998).

Communication with other adults is also an important skill. As a student on a teacher education course, there will be many occasions on which you will work with others as part of learning about classroom practice. In fact, students sometimes feel like 'piggy-in-the-middle' when they receive regular, if sometimes conflicting advice, from a range of tutors, class teachers and support staff! Regular communication with a more experienced teacher such as a mentor, can ensure that adversity is kept in perspective and the classroom runs as smoothly as possible – time needs to be set aside for mentoring as Wendy Suschitzky and Barbara Garner stress in Chapter 16. These types of communication happen with less frequency as one becomes a teacher with full responsibility for the class – in fact it can be quite an isolated job in a typical closed classroom situation. You may well have help from nursery nurses (if you work within the early years) and, increasingly, classroom assistants (CAs) across both KS1 and KS2 classrooms (see Moyles and Suschitzky 1997a, 1997b). Parents, further and higher education students, sixth formers, and professionals whose advice is sought about particular children are also likely to number among your regular visitors. As teachers, we really must help them to help us and the children, which means being clear before they arrive what their role is and what support is needed. In the case of CAs, unless it is vital to the activity that they sit and listen to the story, for example, request their help in preparing the next batch of materials, repairing books, labelling materials or, better still, working to provide extended learning opportunities for individual children.

One level of communication which is often forgotten is that of communicating with yourself – reflecting on your experiences and needs. What did *you* do today? How did you feel about it? What skills have you used and what needs do you have for tomorrow or next week? Take time out to reflect on your beliefs about teaching and learning and talk to others about your successes and inevitable occasional disasters! (For more on reflective practice and its usefulness to teachers, see Chapter 13 and Ghaye and Ghaye 1998; Day 1999.)

Conclusion

When considering classroom organization and management issues it is inappropriate to focus wholly on the pragmatics of organizing indoor and outdoor physical space, for each environment carries its own unique constraints. It is far more vital to get at the roots of why different teachers' practices are as they are. The crucial aspect involved is what teachers believe – about themselves, the children, the purposes of education and schooling, curriculum processes and the ethos of the particular school. Alexander (2000: 540) explains the processes of teaching and learning in these terms:

> pedagogy is both act and discourse. Pedagogy encompasses the performance of teaching together with the theories, beliefs, policies and controversies that inform and shape it . . . Pedagogy connects the apparently self-contained act of teaching with culture, structure and mechanisms of social control.

Having a clear rationale for organizing and managing a classroom in a particular way needs to be explored by beginner teachers based on their own beliefs and developing ideology of effective pedagogy. Constant reflection on how it all works is crucial to continuing success and evolution of effective practice. The best primary classroom practitioners operate a wide range of skills; an excellent piece of research highlighting these can be found in Gipps *et al.* 2000.

To put all this in perspective, let us return to the second cameo. This teacher felt that her course had taught her that children would learn much about the work of travel agents (as well as some geographical knowledge, multi-cultural understanding and opportunity to use literacy and numeracy skills) from having this first-hand experience presented to them in the classroom. However, this element was still not within her understanding of children's responses to such experiences. She had been taught on her ITE course, but had not yet absorbed it into her own value systems, that most children need exploration of new materials and contexts before being expected to deal in any depth with the concepts presented. The student could have:

- given children the responsibility for setting up the travel agency in the classroom, so that at each stage they were exploring the materials and the context;
- asked the children to present rules for use of the travel agency and to decide what was and was not acceptable behaviour;
- made her own rules as to how the travel agency should be used and put up an appropriate sign;
- allowed children to use the travel agency only when she was available to supervise their activities.

If your instinct is towards the first and second options, it is likely that you are a 'child-centred' person who puts thoughts about the children's learning experiences first. If you chose the final two options these, on the whole, reflect a more 'teacher-centred' reaction. Which one would you have chosen? Why? How are these values and ideals likely to influence your classroom organization and management?

References and further reading

Alexander, R. (2000) *Culture and Pedagogy: International Comparisons in Primary Education.* Oxford: Blackwell.

Alexander, R., Rose, J. and Woodhead, C. (1992) *Curriculum Organisation and Classroom Practice in Primary Schools.* London: DES.

Barnes, R. (1999) *Positive Teaching: Positive Learning.* London: Routledge.

Bilton, H. (1998) *Outdoor Play in the Early Years: Management and Innovation.* London: David Fulton.

Costello, P. (2000) *Thinking Skills and Early Childhood Education.* London: David Fulton.

Cullingford, C. (1991) *The Inner World of the School: Children's Ideas about Schools.* London: Cassells.

Day, C. (1999) *Developing Teachers: The Challenges of Lifelong Learning.* London: Falmer Press.

De Boo, M. (1999) *Enquiring Children: Challenging Teaching.* Buckingham: Open University Press.

Drury, R., Miller, L. and Campbell, R. (2000) *Looking at Early Years Education and Care.* London: David Fulton.

Edgington, M. (1998) *The Nursery Teacher in Action: Teaching 3, 4 and 5 Year Olds,* 2nd edn. London: Paul Chapman.

Fisher, J. (1996) *Starting from the Child.* Buckingham: Open University Press.

Ghaye, A. and Ghaye, K. (1998) *Teaching and Learning through Critical Reflective Practice.* London: David Fulton.

Gipps, C., McCallum, B. and Hargreaves, E. (2000) *What Makes a Good Primary School Teacher? Expert Classroom Strategies.* London: Routledge/Falmer.

Hughes, M., Wikeley, F. and Nash, T. (1994) *Parents and Their Children's Schools.* Oxford: Blackwell.

Hurst, V. and Joseph, J. (1998) *Supporting Early Learning: The Way Forward.* Buckingham: Open University Press.

Kyriacou, C. (1998) (2nd edn) *Essential Teaching Skills.* Oxford: Blackwell.

Maude, P. (1996) 'How do I do better?' From movement development into early years physical education, in D. Whitebread (ed.) *Teaching and Learning in the Early Years.* London: Routledge.

Maude, T. (2001) *Physical Children: Active Teaching.* Buckingham: Open University Press.

Merry, R. (1998) *Successful Children: Successful Teaching.* Buckingham: Open University Press.

Moyles, J. (1989) *Just Playing? The Role and Status of Play in Early Education.* Milton Keynes: Open University Press.

Moyles, J. (1994) *The Excellence of Play.* Buckingham: Open University Press.

Moyles, J. (1997) 'Just for fun? The Child as Active Meaning Seeker,' in Kitson, N. and Merry, R. (eds) *Teaching in the Primary School: A Learning Relationship.* London: Routledge.

Moyles, J. and Adams, S. (with others) (2001) *StEPs: A Framework for Playful Teaching in the Early Years.* Buckingham: Open University Press.

Moyles, J. and Suschitzky, W. (1997a) *Jills of All Trades . . . ? Classroom Assistants in KS1 Classes.* London: ATL and University of Leicester.

Moyles, J. and Suschitzky, W. (1997b) *The Buck Stops Here . . . ! Nursery Teachers and Nursery Nurses Working Together.* Leicester: Esmée Fairbairn Charitable Trust/ University of Leicester.

Moyles, J. (1992) *Organizing for Learning in the Primary Classroom: A Balanced Approach to Classroom Management.* Buckingham: Open University Press.

Moyles, J. (1994) *Classroom Organisation.* Bright Ideas for Early Years Series. Leamington Spa: Scholastic Publications.

Pollard, A. and Filer, A. (1999) *Social World of Pupil Career: Strategic Biographies through Primary School.* London: Cassell.

Sukhnandan, L. and Lee, B. (1998) *Streaming, Setting and Grouping by Ability: A Review of the Literature.* Slough: NFER.

Whitehead, M. (1999) *Supporting Language and Literacy Development in the Early Years.* Buckingham: Open University Press.

3

Seeing clearly: observation in the primary classroom

Linda Hargreaves

Cameo 1

Behaviour is not always what it seems

Somehow Dan always seems to be on the far side of the room or to be walking in that direction. He 'messes about' with his friends during science or technology or other group or individual work sessions. His teacher, Mrs Bennett, decides to take a closer look at Dan's behaviour. Every 10 minutes or so, during the next science session, she notes Dan's whereabouts and what he is doing. She keeps the notes on a page of her spiral notebook. By doing this she can see what Dan is doing at times when he is not attracting her attention by causing a disturbance. She uses a simple code: I = in base; O = out of base, and M = moving (see Figure 3.1). The results surprise her for while there were many Ms and Os, as she follows his movements she realizes that:

1 his journeys are usually task-oriented rather than task-avoiding, for example finding a book, getting something for the investigation;
2 the 'messing about' seems to be initiated by other children as Dan passes them, but the disturbance results from Dan obviously trying to get back to his investigation.

In other words, he seems to be trying to be involved in his task most of the time. It dawns on her that she has been assuming that Dan causes the disturbances because he is out of base. To check her initial observation she uses a similar technique with Dan in the next couple of practical sessions, and sometimes makes a point of going over to his group at times when he is in his place. Strangely enough the number of 'O's and M's she records decreases and Dan seems to stay

Child: Dan Curriculum area science Weds 5th, Oct .
Task: Comparing supermarket washing up liquids for
suddiness:
work out how to do fair test and then carry it out.

Time	I = In O = Out M = Mobile	Activity	Interacting with ...
1105	I	Talking about soap suds task	-own group
11.12	M	Collecting yogurt pot from sink. Sam goes to sink - picks up 2 pots – holds one to each eye – 'binoculars' Dan laughs / back to place	Sam
11.20	I	Timing how long suds are lasting	No i/a
1130	M - O	Returning pots to sink. Sam is filling pots with hot water creating more suds. Dan turns away – S. grabs his sleeve and pulls him back – D. tugs himself free → back to table	Sam
1136	I	Writing / doing diagram	No i/a
11.45	M	Tidying up at Sam's group's table – gets cloth	Can't tell ??
11.55	I	(whole class – reporting back) listening intently	none

Figure 3.1 Tracking Dan

in his base much more often. If this is an 'observer effect', she is quite
pleased about it.

Cameo 2

Unexpected pains

Liz is a trainee teacher in a Year 1 class who is testing a hunch that
boys are more likely to answer questions in the numeracy hour,
whereas girls are more likely to answer (or, perhaps, to be asked)
more questions in the literacy hour. She decides to video the class,
and so that she can film the children's faces, which would help in
making out their answers, she stands just to one side of the teacher.
While watching the video afterwards and counting up the number
of questions answered by girls and boys, she notices a sequence of
events that she would not otherwise have seen. During the session,

Date ..20.9.......... ... Curriculum area(s) ..Sci/tech.....
Topic..forces...........Task..bridge task.............

Group 3	planning	measuring mass	measuring length	evaluation/reflection
Dawn	✓✓✓		✓ (talks)	
Julie	✓✓✓	✓?	✓✓✓	✓
Yvette	✓	*?check		

Examples/notes:

D: — now it'll need loads of these
    little ones

J : count them into 10s so it'll be
    100g in each pile

Y : Lets put the blue ones on first so
    it'll be more weights

D: Yeah . good idea (laughs)

Figure 3.2 Group work observation grid: observing science and technology activities

Jack had become quite upset because of a pain in his tummy, and yet he had been perfectly fine a few minutes earlier. The teacher had asked him a question, which he could not answer, and so she had used her usual technique of saying, 'Can anyone help, Jack?' When the other child answered correctly, she had accepted the answer and moved on to the next question but forgot to turn her attention back to Jack. When Liz watched the video she realized that Jack had changed his attitude from eagerly participating, to looking down at the floor and fiddling with his shoes. He did not put his hand up again. Then, about five minutes later, he complained of the pain. Liz realized how important it must have been to Jack, that the teacher completed her interaction with him.

Cameo 3
Observation uncovers misunderstanding
Figure 3.2 shows how a teacher who was observing Yvette, Dawn and Julie's technology skills, discovered the children's basic misunderstanding about mass. They were trying to build a paper bridge, which would span a 25 cm gap, and hold at least 1.5 Kg. They had used up all the bigger standard weights, passed the 1Kg mark and were now down to the 10 gram weights. Some of these were made of blue plastic, others were of brass. As shown in Figure 3.2, Yvette decided to use the blue plastic 10g weights first, because, she said, 'It'll be more weights'. Later, the teacher asked Yvette why they had used the blue weights first. She replied, 'They're lighter because they're plastic so you need more.'

Cameo 4
How do you paint talk?
One afternoon, 3-year-old Jamie chooses to paint, for the first time. His first two paintings consist of heavy thick zig-zag brush strokes that fill the paper. He tells Jan, a nursery nurse, that one is a picture of his mum and the other is his sister. Next he is going to paint his gran. Jan decides to watch him. He begins by drawing a fine 'tadpole' portrait of his gran, talking to himself as he does so. Then he says, 'And now some talking'; using a brush loaded with thick red paint, he starts at the mouth zig-zagging the brush all over his gran's portrait, and gradually covering the figure and filling all the space around it. Jamie, Jan realizes, still has to learn which human characteristics can be painted and which cannot.

Cameo 5
Observation reveals who goes where
The staff of a nursery unit routinely use observation of the children's choices of activity in their record-keeping system by plotting the child's movements on a plan of the nursery. Generally, this is done for each child once a term unless the plan shows that a child is choosing a very limited range of activities, or is flitting from one activity to another without really settling down. An example of a plan is shown in Figure 3.3. Sometimes they note the time the child arrives at an activity and the time he or she leaves it, but usually they just record the order of the activities and add a plus (+) sign for each ten minutes that the child stays at one activity. The child's choices, plotted on the plan, usually suffice as a graphic record. The staff use the tracks as a basis for discussion about the children's progress in the nursery and recently the tracks have shown that boys are rarely choosing the book area.

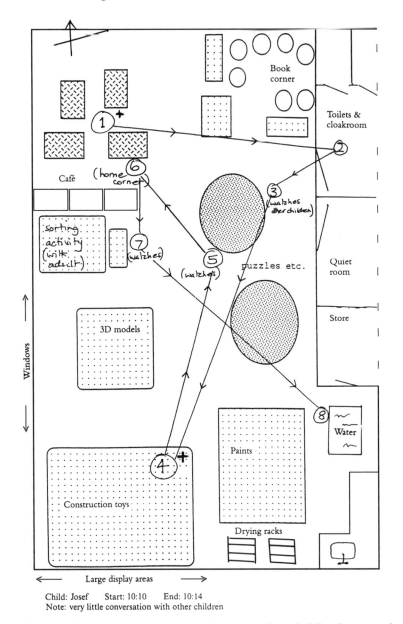

Child: Josef   Start: 10:10   End: 10:14
Note: very little conversation with other children

Figure 3.3 Using a classroom plan to track a child's choices of activity

Introduction

Observation is one of the most difficult things for a teacher to do in the classroom. Observing means learning to stay detached from the on-going action and letting it take its course. Good teaching, on the other hand, means supporting or 'scaffolding' a child's learning, asking questions, pre-empting mistakes, checking understanding and ensuring a measure of success. Yet observation must be part of this process. Good teaching also involves finding out what a child can do without help, in order to be able to provide, *or withdraw,* support at the critical points in the learning process (Wood 1988; Wood and Wood 1996). Yet observation-based research has shown that teachers do most of the talking in classrooms (Flanders 1964) and very little listening, watching, or indeed observing how children learn (Galton *et al.* 1980, 1999).

Growing awareness of the role of observation in teaching during the 1990s has meant that classroom observation is becoming an essential professional skill in the teacher's repertoire. It has been a vital element of the training of nursery nurses and pre-school practitioners for many years (Oates 1991), but its use as a mode of teacher-based assessment in the early 1990s, in primary science for example (see Cavendish *et al.* 1990), has introduced it into everyday practice. Used as a means of formative assessment, as in cameo 3, observation can be very revealing. The teacher in that episode discovered that these children did not understand that a 10g mass weighs 10g regardless of what material it is made of. If the teacher had relied simply on the written outcome of the children's task, or if she had intervened in the girls' discussion about what to do, she would not have identified this misconception. In other words, close observation, as a form of assessment is essential if a child's learning progress is to be based on firm foundations. Close observation of every classroom learning situation would be impossible, but some observation, built into the teacher's planning as described in Chapter 6, and using simple methods like that described in cameo 1, is both possible and very valuable.

Unfortunately, having recently gained a place in the teacher's repertoire, observation has become associated with the process of school inspection in which it is used simply to *judge* a teacher's performance, as it is by Ofsted. If used to *describe* children's and teachers' behaviour it has a much more informative role to play, and recent developments that encourage teachers to become more involved are likely to increase the professional importance of observation as a practitioner's research strategy (see Everton *et al.* 2000). For example:

- The standards for Qualified Teacher Status under 'Other professional requirements' require teachers to 'understand the need to keep up to date with research and developments in pedagogy' (DfEE 1998: 16:D(e));

- The TTA has a scheme to fund teachers' own small-scale research projects;
- A major government funded research initiative (ESRC 2000) on teaching and learning is encouraging increased partnership between researchers and practitioners in the attempt to learn more about how we learn;
- The Curriculum Guidance for the FS places a high value on teachers giving children scope to demonstrate their creativity and ideas. The principles for early years education include 'Practitioners must be able to observe and respond appropriately to children, informed by a knowledge of how children develop and learn . . .' (DfEE 2000:11).

Many different kinds of observation are used by researchers such as:

- Large-scale studies to provide normative information about classroom processes (e.g. Galton *et al.* 1999);
- Long-term case studies of children's learning during their school careers (Pollard with Filer 1996; Pollard and Filer 1999);
- Detailed analysis of how children and teachers negotiate meaning and develop understanding (Mercer 1995; Alexander 2000).

As teachers and trainee teachers we can adapt and use these in our own classrooms, as shown in the cameos that open the chapter. There, observation enlightened the teachers involved or disabused them of certain assumptions. They show also that observation includes *listening* to children as well as *watching* them because listening (*without* joining in) offers teachers unrivalled access to investigating and understanding children's concepts, learning and behaviour. In addition, once qualified, although teachers might now observe children closely, they have relatively few opportunities to observe other teachers. Student teachers therefore are strongly encouraged to observe how their teacher-mentors work, and their effects on the children, as in cameo 2. The results can inform both the student and the mentor.

In the rest of this chapter, we will consider the purposes, methods and value of planning for observation as well as for teaching.

Looking and observing: what is the difference?

On visiting a school, people quickly begin to form impressions. Certain signals such as the sound of rapid arpeggios on a clarinet, children's laughter, silence, litter in the playground or artwork displayed on every surface, attract their attention. Such impressions can have a lasting effect, and tend to reinforce rumours about a school, for example that it is 'good for music'; 'has a happy atmosphere'; or 'is untidy and run-down'. Unfortunately it is human nature to screen out signals that do not fit

Observations should be written down so that they can be interpreted, analysed and reflected on

one's theories and remember those that do, and that is where observation is important.

On meeting a new class of children, teachers form impressions of the children: Jodie is *always* talking; Mark *never* listens; Claire won't try. It may be that the negative impressions are formulated quickly because the teacher feels that something must be done about these things. Unfortunately, these impressions can sometimes persist and can influence the teacher's expectations of a child and judgements of the child's work. This could have a significant and long-term effect on a child's progress in school. Planned observation is a vital check on this process, as shown in cameo 1.

Observing in classrooms

Unlike impressions, observations

- are made for a *purpose*, for example, to assess a child's skills or to see how a certain resource is used;
- have a *specific focus*, for example, to record the level of a child's motor skills or oral skills or how children interact in a group;
- are made at set times including times when the child is *not* interacting with the teacher, as well as times when he or she *is*.

In addition and very importantly, observations should be written down so that they can be interpreted, analysed and reflected on, away from the bustle and quick decision-making atmosphere of the classroom. To achieve this, however, time to observe, perhaps as little as *one whole minute*, needs to be included in the teacher's planning, along with *what* to look for, *who* to look at, and *when* and *where* to look. Answers to these questions depend, of course, on *why* the observation is taking place.

Why should teachers make observations?

Observation gives information about what actually happens in the classroom so that teachers can base their judgements and their planning on the *process* as well as the *products* of classroom activities (see Chapter 6). It can be used:

- to provide 'before and after' evidence to show what *progress* a child has made as a result of some teaching or simply over a certain time period.
- to *compare* the effects on children's behaviour of different teaching approaches, different ways of grouping children or of managing the class;
- as *feedback* for the teacher in the evaluation of classroom activities, for example, if an activity was set up with the aim of getting the children to practise formulating questions, or explore colours by mixing paints, an observational record would help the teacher to find out whether it *actually did* encourage question formation or experiments in paint mixing.

The ultimate aim of classroom observation is to improve the children's opportunities to learn and to ensure that they get the best out of those opportunities. So, for example, a teacher might observe:

- one child to find out about that child's way of working or 'learning style';
- a group of children working together, to identify the cognitive skills and social skills used by the children through their interactions with other group members;
- the whole class, by scanning the room at regular intervals, to see who is engrossed and who is flagging, or by videoing the children's faces during a whole class teaching session to see who answers the questions, or who volunteers but gets ignored;
- other teachers in order to develop a range of styles suited to different teaching and learning objectives;
- themselves, by making a video or audio tape and (bravely) studying it critically afterwards, to study their own mannerisms, distribution of attention, use of praise, clarity of instructions, 'catch phrases' and so on.

Classroom observation is especially valuable for beginning teachers because they usually have more to learn about children than their more experienced counterparts, and they have a classroom partner, either another trainee, or their teacher-mentors, to help them make and interpret the observations. Moyles (1989) provides a very useful summary of ways to observe early years children, which are equally applicable at any stage of schooling, and there are several other accessible sources that can provide more detailed information about observational methods, for example, Simpson and Tuson (1995), Denscombe (1998), Hopkins (1993) and Wragg (1999).

What kinds of observations and recordings do teachers make?

The many different methods of making and recording classroom observations include long-hand continuous accounts of classroom events, the use of video and ticking categories on a checklist. The various methods are based originally on two different research traditions:

1 *Participant or ethnographic* observation is derived from anthropological research where it involved taking open-ended, longhand fieldnotes over a long enough period of time for the observer either to become accepted as a participant in the group or to become so familiar as to be ignored. Class teachers already are participants and can make notes about teaching and learning situations with some confidence that they understand them, although any newcomers to a particular class should take care to check their interpretations of any observations made with the teacher or children concerned.

2 *Systematic* observation, used in psychological studies, requires observers to record systematically on grids or checklists, which have been set up – or pre-coded – before the observations begin (Morag Hunter-Carsch describes some of these in Chapter 12). Systematic observers are concerned with how much or how often specific behaviours occur in certain settings and, perhaps, at certain times or phases of an activity or lesson. By pre-specifying the range of behaviours to be recorded in this way, the researchers try to minimize the level of inferential judgement about what is happening and so obviate the need for extended immersion in the culture of each classroom observed. Good examples of primary-phase research based on systematic observation include the ORACLE project (Galton *et al.* 1980, 1999).

What kind of observation is best – open-ended or structured?

The answer to this question depends on several factors, but most importantly on the question that underlies the observation, the reason why the observation is being carried out, and what kind of information. It depends also on what is feasible in the time and space available in a classroom situation (see Wragg 1999). If the aim is to find out what the children say or do in certain situations, longhand notes will be most useful. So, for example, to find out exactly how two children set about a co-operative task, one might take notes for a few minutes about what the children do in the opening phase of work on the problem. If, however, teachers already know what types of behaviour they are looking for, then the use of a checklist will be the most efficient observation method. Having set a problem to solve, the teacher might want to observe the children's spontaneous or existing levels of use of 'entry' and 'attack' procedures, before planning teaching on problem-solving. A checklist, or grid like that in Figure 3.2, can be used, with 'entry' procedures heading the columns, such as:

- explores the problem;
- makes guesses;
- defines terms and relationships;
- organizes the information; and so on (see Burton 1984).

Both traditions have something to offer classroom teachers and the examples which follow draw on both techniques.

Using open-ended observation

Longhand notes are particularly useful for individual child studies, provided that a factual account without value-laden terms is kept and this needs practice. For example,

> S wanders lazily to get book from drawers and strolls back to seat – flicks idly through pages to new page and gazes at blank page

presents a particularly negative view of what S actually did through the choice of words such as *lazily*, *strolls*, *idly* and *gazes*. What S actually did was:

- walk slowly to drawers and get book out;
- walk back, looking around;
- turn pages to find place and look at blank page.

Open-ended observations are ideal for individual child studies and can be kept to a simple format so that observations over a similar period of time can be made of other children, or of the same child in a variety of situations, such as during a craft activity, when reading alone, when playing and when working in a team.

The *Individual Observation Record Sheet* (Figure 3.4) combines a simple, structured format with spaces for longhand notes to be taken. This type of record is particularly useful to provide evidence that might support or refute a teacher's initial impressions of a child. A child's behaviour in a

Child's Name: .....Simon....(S)...........................

Activity: ...Science : circuit with batteries and buzzers........

Sitting/working with: .....Katie....(K)......................

Each row is for 30 or 60 seconds' observation. This could be organized as a five minute block, 1 minute every 5 minutes, 2 x 5-minute periods or 10 observations spread over a session, day or half-day.

Time	What is target child *actually* doing?	Child interacts with:	Resources/ equipment being USED
9.30	Simon attaches wires by holding it place. Presses buzzer. "mine's working!"	Katie	battery wires buzzer unit
9.31	continues to press buzzer demonstrates to 3 children	3 children and Katie	''
9.32	watches other children doing theirs. Tries buzzer again no buzz. Partner tries t	Katie	''
	attach wires —says 'We have to 'tach them'. S. 'Do we?' Try t manipulate croc clips	''	and crocodile clips
9.34	Katie tries t attach clips but they come off the terminals K: "It's not going to work"	''	''
	Simon works buzzer again by holding wires on. Katie says 'Clip the black one on'	Katie	.
9.35	Tries t clip π to battery. It falls off " Ha! ha! ha! "both Boy(R)comes over to watch.	Katie R.	''
9.36	S. 'ugh it's hard'. K. "should we ask Mrs. P.? (S. ignores) Boy (R) watches. "Is it hot?" — S is holding wire on battery.	R	''
	S 'No it's cold' carries on buzzing. Puts buzzer to face (to test for hot?) K. "we've got to clip them on" How do we clip them on?		''

NOTES: Simon seems to see getting buzz as aim – he is not interested in making a circuit.
N.B. clips difficult for children to use. Too stiff?.

Figure 3.4 Individual observation record sheet

Participant or ethnographic observation is derived from anthropological research

variety of different settings such as working alone, working in a group, playing in the playground or taking part in an expressive activity such as art (as described by Gill Robinson in Chapter 8) could be recorded to furnish a rounded picture of the child's work and social styles.

Structured observation

Cameo 3 uses a format for a structured observation system, based on a checklist or grid used when observing a small number of children at the same time. There are many areas where the teacher knows in advance what skills or behaviours he or she is looking for. These might be cognitive skills, or the problem-solving example above, or co-operative skills. If several teachers are going to observe the same aspects of children's behaviour, a checklist, with shared definitions and examples of the behaviour, will be most valuable. Checklists are also quick to use because there is no need to write notes and because a time pattern such as observing events during every third, fifth or tenth minute, or recording what is happening every 30 seconds can be imposed.

In Figure 3.5, the teacher has noted each time Louise showed any of the actions on the checklist during the time that Louise was being

GESTURES	Louise
smiles	///
nods	/
faces/looks at speaker	////
frowns	
turns away	
VERBAL BEHAVIOUR	
asks a question	
listens to other(s)	////
offers own opinion	
praises another child	/
interrupts speaker	
asserts self	

Figure 3.5 Individual checklist showing social skills

	Clare	Jack	Mark	Louise
GESTURES				
smiles	/	/		/
nods in agreement	/			/
faces speaker	/	/		
frowns			/	
turns away			/	
VERBAL BEHAVIOUR				
asks a question	/			
listens to other(s)	/	/		
offers own opinion		/	/	
praises another child	/			
interrupts speaker		/		
asserts self		/		

Figure 3.6 Group observation grid of social skills used

observed. This is called a category system and it shows the relative frequencies of Louise's various social actions.

In Figure 3.6 the teacher has observed four children and simply noted each action once. This shows the minimum number of times each action occurred but it shows which children did or did not use these actions. The pattern of ticks shows different social styles for the children. It suggests that Louise participated positively non-verbally but did not speak and that Jack was more self-assertive than the others. Mark did not listen to the others and Clare was more supportive of the others, in this situation.

The Groupwork Observation Grid (Figure 3.7) can readily be copied and the column headings can, of course, be changed to suit the focus of the observations.

	(skill 1)	(skill 2)	(skill 3)	(skill 4)
(child 1)				
(child 2)				
(child 3)				
(child 4)				

Activity/topic ....

Resources in use: ....

Notes:

Figure 3.7   A group work observation grid

Alternative methods of observation

Video and audio recordings – especially digitally produced video and still photography – are especially useful for emphasizing detail, for example, to record children's work in physical education, dance and musical composition or children's actual words in an oral task. They can be used to assess individual or group progress if repeated after one or two months, as well as for class evaluation of a composition or performance in the making. For example, a series of short video recordings of a sample of children made, say, twice a term of children's gymnastic skills, throwing and catching skills can show marked developments which, because they are gradual, might not be fully recognized on a day-to-day basis. In music, children's appraisal skills can be developed as they listen critically to their own singing or playing: in effect they are observing themselves. Stored on the computer, they can be revisited without the usual problems of hunting out the original tapes.

Making the most of video
To make the most of using a video camera a few points need to be con-

sidered, otherwise the video record can become no better than one's initial impressionistic view of a classroom, in which the camera simply follows the action, and moves rapidly from one scene to another.

1 Acknowledge that children and teacher might need time to get used to being videoed, so allow that this might affect behaviour at first. If videoing young children, invite them to greet the camera in some way at the beginning of the session but to pretend that it is not there during the session.
2 Be sure to focus on the appropriate source of information. If the aim is to study children's responses, the camera should point towards the children. It is a natural tendency to focus on the teacher, because he or she is usually the centre of attention, but the result will be that the children's reactions can neither be seen nor heard, whereas teachers' voices are usually loud enough to be picked up from quite a distance, even if their faces cannot be seen.
3 Keep the same children in view for a reasonable period of time, such as 5 minutes, so as to see an extended period of interaction.
4 Remember that videos cannot record everything. They omit a great deal of contextual background and some notes about the context will be needed.
5 Analysis will take at least as long as it did to make the recording itself, and requires similar principles to those that apply to making live observations, such as having a specific focus and sticking to it. It makes sense to select one or more short extracts, say 5 minutes, and study those in detail.
6 Storing the information on computer, allows it to be used for a variety of purposes.

Although it can be embarrassing to watch one's self, once this is overcome, it can be particularly useful to watch and discuss what is happening in the video with another student or teacher. Some teachers have shared their videos with the children and asked them to talk about the lesson, too.

Maps and plans

A map type observation was used in cameo 5 – this kind of record is ideal when children are likely to be moving about over a large area, as in PE, drama, or play activities, or when getting resources. It can be very instructive to track the movements of an individual child over a period of time, and to ask questions like these:

- Which activity did the child stay with for the longest period?
- Did the child return to the same activity several times?
- Does the child avoid certain types of activity?

A classroom plan can also be used as a record for:

- the results of *scanning* the room at regular intervals and noting how many children (boys/girls; younger/older) are in each area during an activity session to find out the relative popularity of the various activities;
- to mark out the *teacher's* movements as he or she moves from group to group, one could plot:
  - his or her movements about the class when children are working individually and requesting help;
  - how long he or she stays at one table;
  - which tables get the longest and shortest visits;
  - whether every table gets a visit in the time allowed.

It can also be used to plot how a teacher's or other adult's attention is distributed across a class. In a classroom where the children usually sit down at tables, a 'map' of the classroom with circles or 'blobs' to represent each seat as in Figure 3.8 can be used to record various aspects of classroom action and interaction as suggested by Hopkins (1993). In a classroom plan like the one suggested by Hopkins (see Figure 3.8), which can be photocopied several times if the children sit in the same places for most sessions, observations of which children answer questions in a class discussion or which children are on- or off-task, can be recorded easily. In Figure 3.8 each blob represents a child. By marking a tick in the blob when a child is on-task, or answers a question, one can begin to find out:

- Which children participate most in a whole-class discussion or question and answer session?
- Is it always the same children who volunteer answers?
- Do some volunteer but are not asked?
- What are those who are not taking part actually doing?
- What is the difference between the participation rates of higher and lower achieving children, or those who speak a different language at home?

Croll and Hastings (1996) have shown that very different levels of engagement exist at different tables in the same classroom ranging, for example, from being on task for 90 per cent of the time at some tables, to being on task 20 per cent of the time at others. After some practice with the 'blob' plan, a code to show whether the child is a boy or girl (b/g); whether they volunteered or were named (v/n); whether they offered but weren't asked (t = tries) or got the chance to give a long response (s = stars) could be made. Use + or − if the child receives praise or admonition. The code can be extended according to what we want to observe.

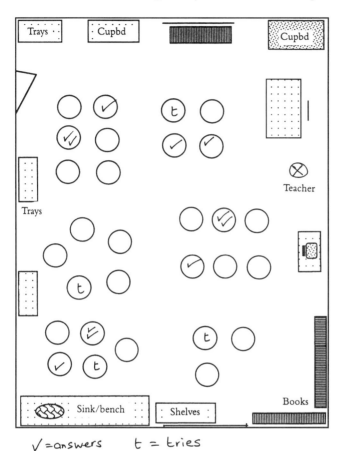

√ =answers   t = tries

Figure 3.8 Using a 'blob' plan to record participation in a teacher-led discussion

Observing teachers

In this last part of the chapter, several ideas for observing other teachers are presented. These will be very useful from the earliest school visits to observe other teachers' classroom styles, but later they could be used by students to evaluate their own teaching for the purposes of identifying standards and competences as indicated by Neil Kitson in Chapter 4. A tape recorder, a colleague, the tutor or a teacher-mentor could record the teaching session. The most well-known and widely used method for the observation of teacher talk is Flanders' Interaction Analysis Categories (FIAC) (Flanders 1970). Although inappropriate in a typical primary classroom, FIAC combines what can be described as 'managerial' and 'information-giving' talk by the teacher. These two functions of teacher talk are described below.

Two types of teacher talk

Beginning teachers soon discover that a normal conversational style can be relatively ineffective in gaining the attention of a class of children. Experienced teachers, on the other hand, can talk to the children in an apparently natural way and still command their attention and co-operation. They make it look easy and *because it looks so easy*, it is easy to overlook *exactly* what the teacher is saying and doing. It is very useful, therefore, to observe closely what teachers say and how they say it.

The first type to observe is *managerial talk,* when teachers are managing the children through a changeover of some kind and are, for example:

- gaining the children's attention;
- starting off the activities;
- changing children from one activity to another;
- clearing up and ending an activity session;
- sending children to play, or to another room.

The second is *teaching talk,* when teachers are maintaining the children's attention and actually teaching and are, for example:

- introducing a topic;
- asking children questions;
- answering children's questions (without being side-tracked);
- giving information or instructions;
- inviting children to make suggestions;
- dealing with, perhaps by ignoring, interruptions or attention-seekers;
- summing up a session.

Just one session spent observing (*not* just watching) an experienced effective teacher do such things will be invaluable. It will be even more useful to talk over the observations with the teacher after the session.

Using the teacher observation sheets

The teacher observation sheet (Figure 3.9) can be used to record both managerial and teaching talk but will be most useful for the former.

Column 1 – Time: There is no need to record this for every utterance; just note the beginning and end of each episode.

Column 2 – Teacher's location: Note where the teacher stands or sits: at the front, side or back of the class: at one of the children's tables; at the teacher's table/desk.

Column 3 – Teacher's actual words: Try to write down exactly what the teacher said, noting particularly how she or he (a) begins a question or a statement; (b) responds to a child's suggestion.

Time	Locat-ion	Teacher's words	Aud-ience	Non-verbal behaviour

ACTIVITY/TOPIC AREA.......................................

Phase of session (underline): beginning   middle   end

Notes about session: (any special features?)

Figure 3.9 Teacher observation sheet

Column 4 – Teacher's audience: Note down who is expected to listen to the teacher – the whole class, one group, one child, one child or group addressed but so that the class can hear.

Column 5 – Non-verbal behaviour: These aspects of teacher talk are so easily overlooked that it is worthwhile to observe them on their own, without noting the words. Note the teacher's:

- position and posture relative to the children;
- arm and hand positions;
- eyes – are they scanning the room? focused on one group? sweeping and stopping? inviting interaction – or not?;
- mouth/facial expression – smiling, dead-pan, expectant, frowning;
- style of speech – pace, pauses, tone.

Three phases of observation will be useful; one for the introduction or first 5–10 minutes of the session, one for any change-over or check-up time in the middle, and one to record from the *very first signs* that the session is ending to when it is over.

Reflecting on the observations

After making these observations identify how the teacher manages to:

- get the children's attention – through actions, words, or movement;
- keep the children's attention – a change of tone of voice, questioning, simple direct phrases, and so on, and how did the teacher encourage, speed up or calm down the children's behaviour;
- end the session – general announcement, quiet instruction to individuals, proffering a 5-minute warning. How did the teacher organize and control the children leaving the room?

Observing teaching talk

At a later stage, try to observe a teacher working with a whole class *and* with a group so that you observe an expert demonstrating these *actual processes of teaching*. Sometimes teachers themselves do not recognize what they are doing as a skilled performance, so the beginning teacher may need to ask to observe an experienced teacher working with a group or individual children.

At first, it can be difficult to disentangle the different constituents of the teacher's talk. Wragg (1999) suggests that a good way to start is by simply writing down verbatim two or three of the teacher's questions and the responses given to them by the children. Discussion with the teacher after the session can include the nature of the questions, why they were asked and, if applicable, why they were directed at certain children.

After some practice at identifying different types of talk, a checklist of the different types like that shown in Figure 3.10 might be used to look at how they are used in a teaching session. The checklist could be used for, say two 3- or 5-minute sections of teaching. Note the opportunity to use a 'don't know' category so that rather than panicking that the 'right' category cannot be found, the teacher's utterance can be placed somewhere and the observation can continue.

Type of teacher talk date ...... topic .... times: start ...... ends	1 number of uses in 3 min	2 number of uses in 3 min
QUESTIONS asking for a recap. of previous work asking closed questions (facts, recall) asking open questions (ideas, suggestions), other question (make note)	/ /// /	
TEACHER RESPONSES listening to a pupil (for 10 seconds minimum) positive feedback (more than just 'good') negative feedback other response (make note)	/ /(+++)// /	
STATEMENTS giving information (telling facts) giving instructions (how to do something), other statement (make note)	///	
ROUTINE TALK keeping control small talk, jokes, chat other	/ //	
Help! don't know what type of teacher talk	//	

Figure 3.10   A tally of types of teacher talk

Points to consider: hints and stumbling blocks

As cameo 1 showed, it is possible to teach and observe at the same time but the beginner teacher should not expect to be able to do this immediately. Observing should become a natural part of teaching for all of us so that we are consciously *making* observations – even if that means noting the observations down as soon as we can after the events – and not relying on general impressions. These observations are an important part of teacher-based, formative assessment to help in the identification of a child's, and teacher's, needs. They contribute to evidence-informed practice.

When first starting to use classroom observation, there are a few points about which we need to be aware:

1 Observation is selective. Like a magnifying glass, it will help the teacher to see one area of classroom life more clearly, but it cannot cover other areas at the same time. Other aspects have to be reserved for another observation session.

2 Observation requires practice. It can be frustrating and difficult to concentrate on one aspect of the classroom for even a short period when normally the teacher tries to be very vigilant and repeatedly scans the whole room to pre-empt problems arising.

3 In the early stages of using any timed observations and/or a checklist, the time between observations often seems too short to find the appropriate place on the checklist or grid. This feeling of being rushed soon disappears as the observer learns the way around the checklist with practice.

4 For teachers, observation is particularly frustrating because of the urge to intervene and teach, especially if the children are missing the point of the activity. Self-discipline is vital here, because by not intervening, the teacher-observer can see how the children deal with the problem. By intervening, he or she would (a) prevent the children from sorting it out for themselves; and (b) miss the expression of any further misunderstandings.

5 The children need time to get used to being observed and have to practise being self-sufficient when their teacher is observing. Teachers, who observe regularly, usually tell the children that they are observing, and the children soon get used to it and do appreciate some feedback from the observations.

Final comment

If, after reading this chapter, you feel that classroom observation sounds too onerous, please remember that even a few minutes of focused observation of a child or another teacher is very worthwhile. It will almost certainly reveal an alternative or surprising view of that person in the classroom. We all have everything to gain by giving observation a try!

Things to think about

1 How would you use observation to investigate:
   (a) how high and low achieving readers behave during the literacy hour?

(b) whether boys and girls get different kinds of attention from the teacher?
2 What strategies could you use to create short periods of time to observe the children?
3 What are three advantages and three disadvantages of structured over open-ended observations?

References and further reading

Alexander, R. (2000) *Culture and pedagogy: International Comparisons in Primary Education*. Oxford: Blackwell.

Ashton, P., Hunt, P., Jones, S. and Watson, G. (1980) *Curriculum in Action: Block 1: An approach to evaluation*. Milton Keynes: Open University Press.

Burton, L. (1984) *Thinking Things Through: Problem-Solving in Mathematics*. Oxford: Blackwell.

Cavendish, S., Galton, M., Hargreaves, L. and Harlen, W. (1990) *Observing Activities*. London: Paul Chapman.

Croll, P. and Hastings, N. (eds) (1996) *Effective Primary Teaching: Research-based Classroom Strategies*. London: David Fulton.

Denscombe, M. (1998) *The Good Research Guide*. Milton Keynes: Open University Press.

DfEE (1998) *Standards for the award of Qualified Teacher Status in England*. Circular 4/98. London: HMSO.

DfEE (2000) *Curriculum Guidance for the Foundation Stage*. London: HMSO.

Everton, T., Galton, M. and Pell, A. (2000) Teachers' perspectives on educational research: knowledge and context, *Journal of Education for Teaching*, 26(2): 168–82.

Flanders, N.A. (1964) Some relationships among teacher influence, pupil attitudes and achievement, in B.J. Biddle and W.J. Ellena (eds) *Contemporary Research on Teacher Effectiveness*. New York: Holt, Rinehart and Winston.

Flanders, N. (1970) *Analysing Teacher Behavior*. New York: Addison Wesley.

Galton, M., Simon, B. and Croll, P. (1980) *Inside the Primary Classroom*. London: Routledge.

Galton, M., Hargreaves, L., Comber, C. and Wall, D. with Pell, T. (1999) *Inside the Primary Classroom – 20 Years on*. London: Routledge.

Greig, A. and Taylor, J. (1999) *Doing Research with Young Children*. London: Sage.

Hastings, N., Schwiieso, J. and Wheldall, K. (1996) A place for learning, in P. Croll and N. Hastings (eds) *Effective Primary Teaching: Research Based Classroom Strategies*. London: David Fulton.

Hopkins, D. (1993) *A Teacher's Guide to Classroom Research* (2nd edn.). Buckingham: Open University.

Mercer, N. (1995) *The Guided Construction of Knowledge: Talk Amongst Teachers and Learners*. Clevedon: Multilingual Matters.

Moyles, J. (1989) *Just Playing? The Role and Status of Play in Early Childhood Education*. Milton Keynes: Open University Press.

Oates, J. (1991) The Competent Adult, in *Working With Under Fives* (Resource Pack). Buckingham: Open University Press.

Pollard, A. with Filer, A. (1996) *The Social World of Children's Learning: Case Studies of Pupils from Four to Seven*. London: Cassell.

Pollard, A. and Filer, A. (1999) *The Social World of Pupil Career: Strategic Biographies through Primary School.* London: Cassell

Simpson, M. and Tuson, J. (1995) *Using Observations in Small Scale Research: A Beginner's Guide.* Edinburgh: Scottish Council for Research in Education (SCRE).

West, N. (1992) *Classroom Observation in the Context of Appraisal: A Training Manual for Primary Schools.* London: Longman.

Wood, D. (1988) *How Children Think and Learn: The Social Context of Cognitive Development.* Oxford: Blackwell.

Wood, D. and Wood, H. (1996) Vygotsky, tutoring and learning, *Oxford Review of Education*, 22(1): 5–16.

Wragg, E.C. (1999) *An Introduction to Classroom Observation.* London: Routledge.

4

Identifying the positive within yourself: action planning for competence

Neil Kitson

Cameo 1

Claire is a young student teacher. Throughout her ITE course she, and her colleagues, are asked to reflect on their practice and consider in what areas they feel proficient and then what they wish to develop and improve. Claire reports: 'I think we captured the children's interest during the time in school with our theme of "pirates", particularly with the drama work, and when I dressed up and took on the role of a pirate and the children asked me questions. I have become aware that in order to engage the children the activities have to be interesting.'

Cameo 2

Jackie, in thinking similarly about her teaching, expresses an all too common anxiety relating to classroom control: 'I am still a little unsure about maintaining order and discipline. I managed it in the first teaching placement and I know that I can be firm with the children, but I think I am maybe a little apprehensive about the next teaching practice and a new group of children. I do feel that I am capable of it, I just need to prove it to myself.'

Introduction

Using a list of statements relating to the task of teaching known as 'competences', both of these students are able not only to take stock of their developing role as teachers but they are also able to see where best to direct their energies during the following weeks. As Jackie goes on to say:

> Through the next few weeks of the course generally I intend to concentrate on developing:
> My ability to plan long term, to develop a progression of understanding in children.
> My ability to review and evaluate my own work regularly and *realistically*.
> My ability to maintain discipline and order through positive reinforcement.

What can be recognized is that Claire and Jackie are both making statements about what they want to achieve and, in Jackie's case, how she intends to set about it.

Much has been written about the use of these statements of competence within teacher education (McNamara 1990; Baird 1991; Bennett *et al.* 1992; Carter *et al.* 1993) and what Houston and Howsam described back in 1972 has become increasingly significant today for teachers in training such as Claire and Jackie, as the schools, and the educational system within which they operate, experience major and unremitting change:

> In changing times, unchanging schools are anomalous. Competency based [teacher] education promises the thrust necessary for adaptation to meet the challenge of a changed and changing society. The emphasis in competency-based teacher education on objectives, accountability and personalisation implies specific criteria, careful evaluation, change based on feedback, and relevant programs [of learning] for a modern era.
>
> (Houston and Howsam 1972: 2)

This chapter will examine the rationale behind 'competency-based teacher education' and show how it can help both teachers in training and those recently qualified. It will do this by considering:

- what is meant by competence?;
- competences within teacher education;
- how this approach can help teachers and in particular student teachers;
- a model for a competence-based approach to teacher education;
- case studies examples of how the model has been used.

What do we mean by 'competence'?

The notion of competence was originally developed by industry and the world of employment from the ideas developed by behavioural psychologists. What they attempted to do was break down specific activities relating to a job into their basic component parts – the basic skills, if you like – which will enable an individual successfully to carry out the job. It initially considers all the elements that would be needed and then groups them into specific manageable skills. By working through these skills the individual learner, be they a surgeon or an electrician, can assess what they have already achieved, what they have still to do, and then what they must begin to work on next. It means that the learner can focus on those areas that are important to them and pay less attention to those where improvement has already taken place or those areas that the individual brings with them from another part of their previous learning. In this respect it is more like real life learning as opposed to traditional academic learning where all students must follow the same set of instructions and be presented with the same body of knowledge to ensure that they all have received the same and equal instruction. This 'traditional' method clearly fails to take into account the fact that everybody is different and their life experiences vary considerably. Competence-based learning attempts to be more efficient by acknowledging the strengths of individuals and allowing the greater expending of energy on those areas where development is needed.

Unlike the traditional models of teaching/learning, which concentrate on the transmission of a body of knowledge, kept secret until the point of transfer, here the skills needed to complete the task are presented at the outset. The individuals have knowledge of the range of skills and understanding that is required. They are able to become active participants within the learning process; no longer the passive recipients. They are enabled to identify their previously acquired strengths, their areas of deficiency and then engage in the process of selecting new skills that they wish to develop. In this way not only are they aware of what needs to be covered but they also have a responsibility for their learning. No longer can they blame their tutor alone for being ineffective! If competence-based learning has been correctly established then the learner has the responsibility to ensure that they are gaining access to the knowledge, skills and understanding that they require.

How do you think this way of learning can help you develop your skills as a teacher? Think for a moment before we move on.

Competences within teaching and teacher education

Teacher education is the process for the preparation of those individuals who want to practise in the teaching profession. In common with the majority of professions, this preparation involves:

- The acquisition of knowledge and the ability to apply it;
- The development of a specified repertoire of critical behaviours and skills.

To the extent that the knowledge, behaviours, and skills can be identified, these then become the competence objectives for the training of teachers. Learning objectives are commonly classified according to one of five criteria that can be applied in the assessment of performance, which in our case is teaching. These criteria are:

- cognitive objectives;
- performance objectives;
- consequence objectives;
- affective objectives;
- exploratory objectives.

But what are these objectives and how do they relate to teaching?

1 *Cognitive objectives* specify knowledge and intellectual abilities or skills that are to be demonstrated by the learner. In teacher education such objectives need to include the knowledge of the subject matter to be taught, knowledge of pedagogy, ability to analyse the curriculum area being taught, etc.
2 *Performance objectives* require the learner to demonstrate an ability to perform a given activity. One must not only know what should be done but also how to do it. For intending teachers such an objective could be identified as the development of higher order reading skills, the control of children during a PE lesson, or taking the register.
3 *Consequence objectives* are seen as the results of the learner's actions. For us in teacher training these are usually seen in the resulting work done by the children in the class under our care. The teacher may need to develop a programme of phonics to help an individual's reading progress, or show that he or she can get the class to engage in independent collaborative group work. Students need to be able to demonstrate the *effect* of their teaching not simply have *knowledge* of it.
4 *Affective objectives* deal with the area of attitudes, values, beliefs and relationships. Difficult to define, but these normally relate to the social health of the group; that is, the way in which the children interact with, and relate to, each other.
5 *Exploratory objectives* seen as self-learning or investigation. In teacher education the student might make a visit to a local place of worship or watch an experienced teacher working with a class. Such experiences may lead to the realization that the student needs to find out more about the community prior to working with children from a minority group and by so doing set up further competence objectives to work towards.

All five of these learning objectives are important in the development of professional teachers who are flexible to meet the challenges of today's teaching. When we look at competences for teaching we must make the greatest possible use of the *consequence objectives*. The knowledge alone of how to do something is only of limited use (McNamara 1990). What one must strive towards is the *knowledge*, the *skill* of being able to put it into practice, and *ability* to evaluate its effectiveness through the result seen in the children's work.

Characteristics of competences for teaching

'Teaching acts are an observable performance' (McDonald 1974: 27). Such performance is linked to situations that vary in terms of the underlying purposes of the teaching, the materials used, the children being taught and how they are responding to the specific situation. Such 'performance' has two main elements: (1) a behavioural component; and (2) a cognitive component. The first of these, the behavioural component, is a set of observable actions: the second is a combination of perceptions, interpretations and decisions. Proficiency in both areas is needed in order to produce a competent performance.

Any set of competences that might be established needs to take these components into account. Learning to teach is an on-going process and not one that can be achieved in a single year nor by attending a number of lecturers. Rather it is a process of developing knowledge skills and understanding, of appraisal and re-evaluation. Teachers need constantly to examine their practice, assess and alter their approach with every new child and every new situation that they meet. To this end teachers need to become reflective practitioners (see Chapter 13). This sense of reflection is built into the competence model for it looks at the training of teachers as an ongoing process, which has begun before students start their course and will go on a long time after the course has ended. Individuals will bring with them a wide range of knowledge, skills and understanding into the training situation and this needs to be taken account of. While you might not have formally stood in front of a class in order to teach them you may have had experience of running a swimming club or have been responsible for running a department with a sales team. In both of these you will have acquired skills that will be of great use to you in the classroom. It is important that we begin to recognize those transferable skills that are brought to the learning situation so that these can be built on. You should be given credit for those things that you can do and feel good about them before you begin to consider those areas where work is needed. As a result you will create a greater degree of ownership in your learning. It is you who will set the agenda for learning and you who evaluate what progress has been made.

For this to be effective the point of entry into the professional training needs to be recognized and the competences that the individual already possesses acknowledged and valued (an example of which we shall see in a moment). This will begin to indicate the markers by which the learning development can be plotted. It is from this point that you will begin to understand what needs to be looked at and what has already been achieved; at how one might best go about acquiring the new knowledge, skills, or understanding. It is not possible to learn all that is necessary to become an efficient teacher at once. The learning has to be gradual and focused so that specific aspects can be considered, questioned and built on. As McNamara (1990) shows, it is not enough just to have the facts necessary to teach, you also need to know the best ways of putting those facts across. In order to help children learn effectively, we need to identify attainable goals. We, too, need to feel that we are succeeding; not that we are being constantly de-skilled by discovering that there is more and more that we do not know. When using a competence approach we are given the range of skills at the outset and it is the responsibility of the learner to select those areas on which to work. It is then clearly implicit within the structure of the competences approach that the learning will never be complete, only that a higher level will have been achieved.

Standards and their relation to competences

This recent interest in competences has been reflected in the way that students are now assessed on initial teacher training courses and also at the end of their induction year. The notion of being competent has been translated into what are now referred to as standards. Here the basic skills of a teacher have been considered both in terms of generic skills and specialist teaching skills and a series of specific attainable standards have been defined. Again, as with the general concept of competences these standards are seen as a level that the individual should be able to attain in order to gain professional status. These may be attained at any point in the training but they are most frequently seen as being exit requirements. This means that the individual student teacher may come with a wide range of experiences that can relate directly to the standards but during the course and more specifically by the end of their training course they must demonstrate that they have met all the relevant standards. The standards for the award of qualified teacher status currently used in teacher training cover the spectrum of professional skills needed by a teacher working in schools of the twenty-first century.

Within this structure of standards there are four main sections. The first section concentrates on knowledge and understanding. Here the trainee teacher is asked to consider in very general terms the nature and scope of the National Curriculum and to show that they have an under-standing of the key stages and of the primary core and foundation subjects and RE. They are asked to have a secure knowledge of English, math-ematics and science, irrespective of the subject in which they are speci-alizing, and to have a secure knowledge of foundation subjects to at least level 7 of the National Curriculum. For those working with the early years children, the second section of the standards applies. Here trainee teachers must also demonstrate that they have an understanding of the early learning goals and how these can be provided for within the Foun-dation Stage (as Nansi Ellis points out in Chapter 1).

From this basic understanding of the curriculum and how to deliver it they must also consider issues of planning, teaching and classroom man-agement. They must be able to plan their teaching in order to achieve progression in pupils' learning through identifying clear teaching object-ives and content and be aware of how these will be assessed. It is here that the trainees are being asked to recognize the need to set targets for the children in their classes and to have high expectations of them. It encourages them to build on prior attainment and ensuring that the pupils are aware of the purpose of what they are being asked to do. They are asked to identify pupils with special needs and those who are especi-ally able, as well as those who are not yet fluent in English, and to be able to access help in order to give positive and targeted support (see Jenny Lansdell's discussion in Chapter 15).

There are a number of standards within this section on teaching and classroom management. The trainees must demonstrate that they can teach both whole classes, groups and individuals and make the best use of their teaching time. They must ensure a purposeful working environ-ment and know when to intervene in the classroom in order to maintain sound learning discipline. They must know how to pace lessons; sum-marize key points; and use effective questioning so as to ensure that the pupils are kept interested and on task. Here the focus is on the develop-ment of good teaching skills, which will also contribute to sound dis-cipline of the class. If the children are working effectively at a level of high expectation, and if they are supported and encouraged, then they have a much greater chance of becoming effective learners.

The final section of the standards concentrates on monitoring, assess-ment, recording, reporting and accountability (see also Chapters 3 and 12). This section looks at how targets and objectives are set by the trainees and how the work of the class and of individuals is monitored to ensure progression. It encourages students to look at different types of assessment and to make these an integral part of the children's work. What is asked of trainees is that there is an effective planning cycle (see Chapter 6) that sets out objectives which are then implemented, reviewed and finally revised as a result of these assessments. It requires the trainees to be aware of the national tests and forms of assessment and to be able to make a range of comparisons between classes within a school and between schools locally and nationally.

There is also a focus on the trainees' professional role as a teacher. This takes them outside a specific classroom and asks them to consider their role within the broader context of the school. New entrants to teaching must have an understanding of the current School Teachers' Pay and Conditions, as set out in the Pay and Conditions Act in 1991 and be aware of their legal rights and liabilities relating to such issues as mentioned in the Sex Discrimination Act 1975, Race Relations Act 1976, Health and Safety at Work Act 1974 and to understand what is reasonable for the purposes of safeguarding children's welfare as set out in the Children Act 1989 (Chris Curran helps understanding of some of these aspects in Chapter 17). The standards demand that students consider how to organize the classroom for learning and maintain a working environment (see Chapter 6), how to assess and evaluate what they and the children have learned and to make sense of this in a wider context.

Students must also show they can establish effective working relationships with professional colleagues, set a good example to the pupils they teach, be committed to ensuring that every pupil is given the opportunity to achieve their potential and to understand the need for them to take responsibility for their own professional development. A very tall order indeed, especially on a one-year PGCE or School-Centred Initial Teacher Training (SCITT) course!

As with the other forms of competence assessment mentioned earlier in this chapter, the Standards for QTS are to be met by each trainee teacher. It would be inconceivable that they should all be met at one time, rather they should be seen as progressive. The student needs to demonstrate an awareness of the standards and be moving towards them throughout the ITE course. Students will meet each standard at different times and no two trainees will meet them in the same way. As a result of this it is important that the trainees begin to take responsibility for their own attainment within the standards as soon as possible. This means being aware of the work that they are doing as part of their training and show how this is supporting the meeting of the standards.

While these standards might look daunting, and one might wonder how they can ever be achieved, when taken one at a time and related to real classroom practice, they become much more understandable and manageable. The next part of this chapter looks at the link between the standards and how student teachers might begin to think about demonstrating such competences. Each section raises a number of issues about which we, as teachers – and certainly new teachers – will need to think as the basis for our own learning and development, as well as what this might contribute to meeting the standards.

Standard A c. Understand how pupils' learning is affected by
their physical, intellectual, emotional and social development

Identify from either your work with children or your own recollections
of being at school what effects physical development might have on a
child's learning. Spend a few moments thinking about a child who is
large for their age and still in KS1. How might size affect others' perceptions? How might this affect the way in which that child might be
expected to behave? Now think of that child engaged in playground
activity with friends. What problems might result from their size? How
might this effect social and moral development?

Now consider a child who is at KS2 but small in comparison to peers.
Think about the effects using similar questions to those posed above.
How might you now demonstrate your understanding of this aspect as a
teacher? Do you think that it would be best done through lesson commentaries or could you show it in other, more formal ways?

Standard A d.viii. Trainees are familiar with subject-specific
health and safety requirements, where relevant, and plan lessons
to avoid potential hazards

Imagine that you are going to teach a science lesson at KS2 on changing
states. You have decided that you should use boiled red cabbage water as
a chemical indicator so that the children can see how it changes different colours when you add acids or alkalines. You use simple substances
such as lemon juice, vinegar and bicarbonate of soda to make your
teaching points and you want the children to have 'hands-on', practical
experience. How could you organize this, keeping safety of the children
as one of your key concerns? What might the lesson look like? Would
you have to compromise your desire to let the children be as active as
possible? Why and in what ways?

When you have done this think how you would be able to demonstrate an understanding of this standard.

Standard 4.a iii Setting appropriate and demanding
expectations for pupils' learning, motivation and presentation
of work

You are teaching a year 5 class. The children are looking at developing
creative writing and you have chosen a story for them to write about.
You have shown them the stimulus picture of the monster Beowulf and
read some of the story of the Norse legend. You have some very able
children in your class as well as some less able. Can you think of a range
of writing activities that you could set up so that the more able would be

challenged, the less able would be equally challenged at their level and the group in the middle would also be stimulated? (Chapter 10 offers some support here!)

How might you be able to demonstrate that you have attained this standard? Would it be through paper evidence or a practical example of teaching?

How then are these standards used by students?

In order to make sense of this it will help to look at an example of how these standards are used within an actual training course. Throughout the training year, students on the Primary PGCE Course at Leicester, for example, are given a number of opportunities to make formally recorded statements relating to their perceived level of competence. This is done through discussion with a tutor or with a 'critical friend' – someone with whom the student feels comfortable to talk through examples of practice and progress and who will give constructive feedback. Having identified development needs in terms of knowledge, skills or understanding, the student then makes decisions as to how to improve on these particular competences in relation to the experiences they expect to have next on the course.

When does this identification of competences take place?

There are three significant stages to the process of identification of standards and the development of an individual action plan as outlined below.

Entry phase
At this stage, it is like a baseline assessment as students look at what they bring with them to the course. Many competences – knowledge, skills and understandings – will have been developed through previous employment, be it full-time, part-time or raising a family, involvement in leisure pursuits or pastimes and on other academic courses. These must be acknowledged and noted.

Intermediary phase
This will be an on-going process by which individuals are reflecting on their practice. As new experiences arise so the competences will need to be re-appraised. This will be constantly changing and evolving as development of teaching competence emerges. Developing competence is not just restricted to the training course. For example:

• What was seen as effective management of behaviour in one class may not be effective in another.

- Communicating with parents may not be possible until later on in the course so will not be relevant until then.
- Certain of the standards may well be met in one school and the student may have gone a long way towards establishing it. In another school it might be necessary to start working on them again (behaviour management is often a case in point where there are significant differences between schools).
- Conversely, identifying and reflecting on experience is a skill that can be developed over time and is not dependent on the teaching situation.

Exit phase
This comes at the end of the course and marks the transition from training to newly qualified status. It is the time to take stock, to identify what learning has occurred and to look to the learning that will take place in the induction year and how to ensure that access to such opportunities is created by the individual new teacher. It is here that the Standards for Newly Qualified Teacher Status must be seen to be met and linked to the Trainee's Career Entry Profile. This document, completed by the trainee, is taken into their induction year school and is used as the basis for setting and establishing new targets for the first year of teaching. This will assist in NQTs meeting the additional requirements of the induction year.

Students engage in these three stages with a growing degree of confidence. What is at first a rather tentative approach to the activity becomes a powerful tool that enables the students to assess their individual strengths and plan their future professional development.

How do students respond?

Let us now look at one or two entry phase responses to the standards. These students were only a few weeks into their course and had just begun to realize what was going to be required of them as teachers and also what they had to offer to the profession. In the first example Anna quite naturally focuses on what she can't do but begins to identify some of her potential strengths. The statements following in brackets are taken direct from the standards.

There are two particular areas under presentation and management on which I wish to concentrate.
(C4k.v clear instruction and demonstration, and accurate well-paced explanation)

I have only had very limited experience in this area, and then only with small groups. Consequently, I wouldn't describe myself as being competent in this area.

(C4k.iv clear presentation of content around a set of key ideas, using appropriate subject specific vocabulary and well chosen illustrations and examples)

I often struggle to find the basic wording which I think is due to three years of university training in essentially pretentious writing.

At the moment I assume I am able to fulfil most of the basic standards, but more time and responsibility in school might disprove this! I have chosen to put the preparation section aside for the moment as this is the area in which I feel most confident as a result of the work I did for my first degree.

Cathy also starts off with a positive approach but quite clearly she is fully aware of what she can and cannot yet do. This honesty and self-appraisal is very typical of the responses:

I'm a fairly well-organized person and bringing up a young family has made me more so. I think I will be OK in planning and preparation and record keeping.
   I have chosen three main areas of competence to look at.

1 Management and organization of the classroom. (Standard C4h.) Matching classroom organization to meet the different needs concerned with how to cope with a slow worker, or a non-worker. How do I develop a non-nagging approach.
2 Presentation and management of activities. (Standard C4k.iv) Giving clear explanations and instructions to children. I think I can usually deliver clear explanations, but I need to develop adaptability and quick thinking to enable me to offer alternative explanations and different methods of solving questions and problems.
3 Reflection, analysis and evaluation. (Standard D f.) I find evaluation hard. I'm much more a 'Well that didn't go very well but tomorrow's another day' sort of a person!

Part of the strength of the competence model is that it recognizes previous experience. Gill had previously worked in marketing before deciding to train as a teacher. In her job she had acquired a wide range of professional skills that she was able to identify and relate to her new role as a teacher through the statements of competence. Here she has matched the work she previously did to the standards.

I had experience of making presentations to groups of people numbering from 2 to 200. Through the presentation an agreement usually had to be made, so it was vital that the presentation was correctly focused, it was professionally presented, and it covered all possible aspects and eventualities. I feel that this will greatly help when I'm working in a whole-class situation and working in the class generally as it is important that one makes oneself clearly understood. This experience will also be useful when working with other teachers and parents.

I am used to working in a highly pressurized environment and under strict time deadlines and know the importance of prioritizing my work. These skills are easily transferable and as teachers are under increasing pressure in and out of the classroom to produce work within time constraints this skill will be useful. Also, time management with respect to classroom organization.

Preparation and planning – my previous work taught me that success within any environment depends on it. I used to work within a team to reach common goals as quickly and efficiently as possible. When in school especially as a new teacher, it is essential to co-operate with other members of staff to tap into their experience. Don't be too proud to ask!

Changing perception of the demands of the standards

As students progress through a particular course and gain a range of experiences, perceptions of themselves will change. The standards will remain the same but students' response to them will alter. Those things that, as a student, you were concerned about may have been worked on and no longer seem so important; that is, you now feel competent in them. Those skills that were not an issue may well have assumed a much greater significance as you find yourself in different teaching situations.

Following on from this is the *intermediary phase*. In the example below, Rachel is part way through the course. With one teaching experience behind her, she expresses her very real and understandable concerns as she reflects on her focus for the next few weeks in school.

I need to look at giving children more ownership of tasks, e.g. monitoring work covered, checking maths work using calculators, increased self-esteem and confidence. I gave praise and recognition where appropriate and tried positive management techniques, e.g. to gain class control praising those paying attention; those not, took notice and listened, rather than shouting.

Careful planning with clear expectations from each party produced a good working relationship during teaching practice. Communications with children: need to make what is implicit more explicit. I need to work on aspects of my personality.

Influence others and assert myself in an indirect manner, e.g. prefer to resolve conflicts through diplomacy and harmony, prefer to negotiate rather than to argue/debate and tend to ask rather than

Trainees recognize the need to set targets for the children in their classes and to have high expectations of them

tell. Therefore I found open displays of conflicts in the school situation, especially situations of open intimidation, stressful.

In responding to people I tend to be reserved. I need to express my enthusiasm and energy. Open up body language, eye contact and express feelings more readily.

Pace of action and decision making tends to be steady. Therefore, I find frequent interruptions stressful.

Being precise in structuring of dealing with details find ambiguity, lack of organization and poor planning stressful. Therefore I must make sure that I continue to plan effectively and discuss my plans with the teacher.

Using the statements of competence she can identify areas where attention needs to be focused and then set a clear plan of action in order to address these issues. She can share her plan with tutors and teacher-mentors so that they can offer appropriate support.

It would be helpful now to look at some examples of how the students used the competence statements to improve their teaching. The following are examples of competences that students have wished to develop in relation to the standards, strategies for action and, finally, illustrations of what was done.

Standard C4b.

Provide clear structures for lessons, and for a sequence of lessons, in the short, medium and longer term, which maintain pace, motivation and challenge for pupils.

Strategy

Seek out an individual teacher within a school – the subject co-ordinator for example, or a tutor – to help with a specific question.

Example

If you're not sure about the school plans for History or the ethos relating to PSHE then ask!

Standard C4k ii.

Matching the approaches used to the subject matter and the pupil being taught.

Strategy

Use the literature in order to extend understanding.

Example

If you are unclear as to what is meant by 'collaborative group work' use the library and find out.

Standard C4d.

Plan opportunities to contribute to pupils' personal, spiritual, moral, social and cultural development.

Strategy

Set up specific situations within the classroom in order to gain experience not yet covered.

Example

If you haven't been able so far to engage the children in real life, first-hand experience, arrange a visit, bring the resources into school or invite someone to come into school to talk to the children.

As the personal competences develop the standards will be achieved and the student will be able to look at the process of teaching in a different light. Throughout the course the individual trainee has the responsibility to take from those experiences being offered – from either formal learning opportunities (lectures and seminar), informal learning opportunities (tutorials and discussions with teachers), and individual learning opportunities (library and personal research) – to build up the knowledge, skills and understanding necessary for them to be competent teachers. It is the statements of competence that help them know what is required and against which they can plot their development.

The final stage and beyond

This brings us to the next stage of the process: the exit phase, which is the transition between the training course and the first appointment taking the trainee from student to NQT. It is here that the level of attainment against the standards can be assessed. You can assess which competences and skills have been achieved and which ones could be developed further, as in the case of, say, your curriculum strength/specialist subject area. It becomes an action plan for the individual to take into the induction year school and builds towards the induction standards to be met by the end of the the first full year of teaching. It sets in place a process of critically appraising one's practice that should continue throughout the professional career of each teacher. Indeed as Early (1991) shows, there is growing interest by schools in the competence approach for staff development. Students may indeed find themselves in a school that uses the action plan from college to set out continuing professional development plans, linking in, perhaps, with the school's development plan. Now that performance-related pay is a reality in schools, the process is on-going and should ultimately become seamless.

In this final extract Simon not only looks back at what he has learnt but he looks ahead to where his learning will take him next:

> I feel that I have developed considerably during the past year. I didn't realize just how much there was to learn about teaching but I feel that I have begun the process! In terms of planning and evaluation I am aware of my own short-comings and also aware of what needs to be done. I still feel uncertain or rather unconfident about aspects of the maths curriculum but I've already talked to the Head of my new school about this and we have set up some meetings with the maths co-ordinator. It looks as if I'll be taking on some responsibility for music and drama so feel that I need to find out what courses are on offer in the LEA and see about getting on them. The Head has said she will try too.

Concluding remarks

In conclusion what about those students who have gone through the process? How do they feel about using competences? The overwhelming response has been extremely positive. Quite clearly what is offered is not the open-ended behaviourist model alluded to at the beginning of this chapter but what has resulted is a positive approach to each individual's learning. Having used this process, several were asked what advice they would like to pass on to others wishing to use the competency-based model. It is perhaps fitting to end with their thoughts and advice:

Using competences let us know what was expected of us and gave us something to work towards.

Identify the positive skills within yourself. Say what you can do and don't concentrate on what you can't do.

Using the standards helped me to focus on what was important for me to learn and build on my strengths.

Take responsibility for your own learning. At the end of the day only you will really know what can be achieved.

The skills of self-evaluation that I learned as part of the competency process will set me up for my on-going professional development. I think it's more effective in the long run.

References and further reading

Baird, J.R. (1991) Individual and group reflection as a basis for teacher development, in P. Hughes (ed.) *Teachers' Profesional Development*. Melbourne: ACER.

Bennett, S.N., Wragg, E.C., Carré, C.G. and Carter, D.S.G. (1992) A longitudinal study of primary teachers' perceived competence in, and concerns about, National Curriculum implementation, *Research Papers in Education*, 7(1): 53–78.

Carter, D.S.G., Carré, C.G. and Bennett, S.N. (1993) Student teachers' changing perceptions of their subject matter during an initial teacher training programme, *Educational Research*, 35(1): 89–95.

Department for Education (1993) *The Initial Training of Primary School Teachers: New Criteria for Courses*. Circular 14/93. London: DfE.

Early, P. (1991) Defining and assessing school management competences, *Management in Education*, 5(4): 31–4.

Houston, W.R. and Howsam, R.B. (1972) *Competency-Based Teacher Education*. Chicago, IL: Science Research Associates.

Kitson, N.G. (2000) *Inset for NQTs. An In-School Course for Teachers in the Primary School*. London: Routledge.

McDonald, J.F. (1974) The rationale for competency based programs, in W.R. Houston (ed.) *Exploring Competency Based Education*. Richmond, CA: McCutchan.

McNamara, D. (1990) Reaching into teachers' thinking: its contibution to education student teachers to think critically, *Journal of Education for Teaching*, 16(2): 147–60.

Pollard, A. and Tann, S. (1993) *Reflective Teaching in the Primary School* (2nd edn). London: Routledge.

Teacher Training Agency (2000) *Supporting Induction*. London: TTA.

5

Inside the learning mind: primary

children and their learning potential

Roger Merry

Cameo 1

Julie is six. She is working through a sheet of basic addition problems, using Unifix cubes. Given '3 + 2' she confidently takes three cubes from the box, counting each one aloud as she removes it, then counts out a further two in the same way. She then counts the total, reaching five, and writes '2' on her worksheet. The next problem is '5 + 2', but instead of beginning with the five cubes already in front of her, she returns them to the box and starts again from scratch. Nor does she notice that her figure 'five' is different from the five printed a few centimetres away.

Cameo 2

It's half way through the literacy hour, with the whole class sitting on the carpet. The teacher has carefully gone through what the groups working independently will be doing, and has asked if anybody has any questions. No one has, and the children return to their seats. She is about to start work with her chosen group when Martin comes over. 'What do I have to do?' he asks plaintively.

Introduction

Such incidents are so much a part of hectic, everyday classroom life that busy teachers normally have no time to stop and think about them. Yet they raise many questions, which could be of interest to psychologists as well as to teachers themselves. For instance, why doesn't Julie use the five cubes already in front of her, or correct her own figure when she sees a five written correctly? What do her actions suggest about her concept of number, her perception of the problem and her strategy for solving it? Why does Martin need to ask what to do when it has been explained so carefully and the children have been asked if they understand? What does his behaviour suggest about his attention, memory, understanding or motivation? In brief, what's going on inside these children's heads and how might teachers try to help them? These two basic questions lie at the heart of this chapter, and are discussed in more detail in Merry (1998).

The first part of the chapter presents a brief outline of what cognitive psychologists have to say about attention, perception and memory, along with some implications for teachers. The second part of the chapter focuses more on cognitive development.

Attention, perception and memory

Cognitive psychologists propose a view in which learners are not merely taking things in in a passive way but are, in fact, highly active, often making use of fragmentary and incomplete information by supplementing it with past experience and predictions, which they then check and modify in the light of new data. Because the learner is seen as actively constructing knowledge, this view is known as 'constructivism'. For example, research on attention has shown that, although we can scan the complex events going on around us, we can really only concentrate on one thing at a time in any depth. If you are driving along a familiar route, for instance, you may occasionally have had that sudden and frightening thought 'how did I get here?' Experienced drivers sometimes unintentionally let their attention drift after a while, scanning the road ahead only very lightly while they concentrate on something else in their minds. However, a red light or pedestrian stepping off the kerb is picked up immediately and their attention returns to their driving – hopefully.

Even when we do manage to attend to something, our attempts to perceive or make sense of it rely on equally fragmentary information. As you read this text, for example, it may seem to you that your eyes move quite smoothly from one word to the next along the lines, taking everything in. But in fact, your eyes focus on one small area for a fraction of a second, then jump rapidly to another spot, all the time, whatever you are looking at. The information received by your brain is therefore very piecemeal and fragmentary and you rely on your past experience and knowledge to fill in the gaps. Perception is not a passive taking-in of our surroundings, but a highly active process in which the information supplied by our brains is at least as important as the information received by our senses.

Similarly, remembering something does not simply involve retrieving it from storage. As with attention and perception, what we have available to us from memory is usually only partial and fragmentary so that we again have to supplement it by using our knowledge of the world – memory, too, is partly a constructive process. For instance, you could not possibly remember every single word of this chapter so far, but if you were asked if it had contained the word 'custard' you would be able to answer with a confident 'no' because you know that such a word would not occur in this context. However, if you were asked if the word 'car' had appeared, you might answer 'yes' because you recalled a paragraph about driving earlier on and guessed that the word had appeared. (To save you checking, it didn't!) What might some of the implications of such a view of human learning be for teachers?

Paying attention

Teachers are highly aware of the importance of attention because some children seem to have real problems with it. It is very tempting to blame Martin's problem on his inattentive behaviour, or to see Julie's reversed figure 5 as the result of a lack of attention to detail but, as we shall see, there could be other explanations. Some of the points below will suggest ways of trying to get through to these children but we should also be careful about interpreting poor attention as a problem entirely 'within the child'. We need to be aware of the difficulties we can inadvertently create for children – in a piece of writing, for example, expecting a child to concentrate on being creative, neat and grammatically correct all at the same time is actually making cognitive demands that many professional writers, let alone 6-year-olds, would find a challenge.

Attention and distractions

Picture in your mind a 'good' primary classroom. The children are working in several groups on a range of lively activities, discussing the tasks with each other. The walls are festooned with colourful displays. A gerbil thrashes round in its wheel inside its cage. A computer screen flashes and makes funny noises. Although many children will thrive in and enjoy such a setting, for some children this 'good' classroom may, in fact, be a very difficult learning environment, full of distractions. Not surprisingly, a lot depends on the nature of the task and the potential distractions – given 'verbal interference' such as other people talking, it is harder to perform a task requiring lots of language than one requiring only a little.

This is not to say, of course, that teachers should rip down their displays, unplug the computer and have the gerbil put down. But it does mean that some children, some of the time, might learn better in a less stimulating environment. This need not be impractical or expensive – one early years teacher, for instance, set up an 'office' consisting of a large cardboard box fastened to the wall like a phone booth, and found that her children actually competed to spend a few minutes working in this seemingly boring but 'grown-up' environment, relatively free from distractions.

Attention and failure

Unfortunately, it is not always that simple. Understandably, as teachers we sometimes tend to see learning failure as a result of not paying attention, but it could equally be the other way round. Children who find it hard to cope with failure (as many of us do) may deliberately 'switch off' when confronted with a task at which they expect to fail on the grounds that if you do not try, you cannot fail. In the second cameo, Martin may well have deliberately only half listened to the teacher's instructions, hoping that he will get the extra one-to-one help he likes simply by asking what he has to do. 'Learned helplessness' is a phrase sometimes used to describe such behaviour and it can appear to the child that deliberately not paying attention is a good strategy for avoiding failure and getting extra help. In such cases, trying to encourage children to feel more positive about themselves as learners will be at least as important as using lively, attention-grabbing materials, and the aim of this chapter is certainly not to suggest that cognitive processes and strategies should be emphasized at the expense of attitudes and feelings. See Sotto (1994) for a discussion of how attitudes and cognitive skills interact.

Attention span

It is difficult to get an accurate idea of the length of time that an adult can go on attending to the same stimulus without letting attention wander. It is quite likely that, fascinating as this chapter is, your attention may well already have drifted away at least once, perhaps without you really being aware of it. For most children, the span of attention will be even shorter, probably only a few minutes at a time. This does not mean that we can shorten the school day to ten minutes, but experienced teachers are well aware of this potential limited span of attention and take measures to get around it. Variety and change are the key here. If good teachers are reading a story, for example, they will automatically build in some variety: a range of voices or gestures to avoid monotonous delivery; stopping to ask a question or pausing to show an illustration. They may well bring in discussion so that, although the activity is still 'reading a story', the children will be presented with different sorts of input and will be actively involved in different ways all the time.

Attention grabbers

What sorts of things 'grab' your attention? If you made a list, it would probably contain specific items such as 'a fire alarm' or 'my name' and more general ones such as 'bright lights' or 'something unexpected'. In fact, 'attention-grabbers' can be roughly divided into two categories. Some things grab our attention automatically – sudden loud noises, movements or pain, for example. Others are things that we have learned about and which involve our experiences, expectations or interests, like hearing our own name or seeing something bizarre or new to us, just as you probably noticed this row of xxxxxxxxxxxxxxxxxxxxxxxxxxxxxxxxxxxxxxxxxxxxxxx well before you actually got to them in your reading. If you watch an hour or two of children's television, you could probably learn something from other experts in grabbing children's attention, even if it is rather disheartening to see what you are, in a sense, competing with as a teacher. This is not to suggest that you dress up as Bart Simpson (though that would certainly capture the children's attention!) but that you note how children's cartoons, for instance, make use of bright colours, rapid movement, bizarre events and very short scenes in order to grab and maintain children's attention. Similarly, if you want to quieten a whole group of noisy children, it is usually better to call out a few names of the noisiest individuals rather than just say 'shh' to the whole class in a vague and optimistic way. Teachers also develop lots of techniques like 'hands-on-heads' to grab a whole group's attention, perhaps turning it into a game so that the children actually want to be among those who are attending to you.

Teacher's attention

One of the greatest compliments I was ever paid as a classroom teacher was by a child who told me, 'You must have eyes in the back of your head, Mr Merry!' Experienced teachers have actually developed different attentional skills in order to manage a group of children and such skills can sometimes be difficult for beginners to learn. A new teacher, going round helping individuals or groups, may get commendably involved with them only to realize ten minutes later that the other children have demolished the furniture. An experienced teacher, on the other hand, will constantly glance around the rest of the room, particularly at individuals or activities that their experience tells them could become disruptive, nipping likely problems in the bud, and letting the children know that they are being watched. Such monitoring of the rest of the room would, of course, be highly inappropriate, if not downright rude, in a staffroom conversation but in the classroom it is a vital attentional skill which often marks out experienced and effective teachers.

Seeing is believing

If perception involves a great deal of 'imposing meaning', using our past experience to supplement fragmentary information, it follows that when children's experiences do not match those of the teacher, they will literally perceive things differently. The classic 'visual illusions' like the two heads/candlestick show how two people can look at the same thing and actually see something totally different, and one of the biggest problems for teachers may be to see things from the child's point of view, or to understand why they don't understand. Such different perceptions help to explain Julie's behaviour at the beginning of the chapter. If her notion of the symbol '5' was something like 'that's the one with the two straight lines at the top and the curly bit at the bottom', she simply would not notice that hers was the wrong way round because her 'internal model' would describe her version just as well as the correct one. Watching how children actually write letters and numbers can sometimes give a clue to understand their perceptions – if a child forms both a 'b' and 'd' by drawing a 'ball and stick', for example, they are likely to get the two symbols confused. In such cases, teachers obviously need to draw the child's attention to the different orientation and encourage them to form the symbols in a different way, avoiding them becoming mirror images of each other.

'Advance organizers'

Apart from being aware of such different perceptions, teachers can sometimes actively intervene by preparing the children beforehand, especially if the material is complex or introduces new ideas. The idea is to tell them what they are going to see and direct their attention to the important bits even before they see it. In one classic study, for example, Bransford and Johnson (1972: 68) gave students a rather odd passage, which began:

> A newspaper is better than a magazine. A seashore is a better place than the street. At first it is better to run than to walk. You may have to try several times. It takes some skill but it's easy to learn. Birds seldom get too close. Rain, however, soon soaks in.

Although they understood each sentence, people found the passage difficult to comprehend and remember, but if they were told beforehand

Building up curiosity is a strong attention grabber and can help arouse children's interests

that it was about flying a kite, it was much easier. Hopefully, similar 'advance organizers' can make children less likely to concentrate on irrelevant features or to jump to faulty conclusions, which then have to be corrected. Building up curiosity is also a strong attention grabber in its own right and can help arouse children's interest in the first place.

Modality preferences

Although we are not usually aware of it, adults differ quite dramatically in their preferences for having information presented in some ways rather than others and in the way they tend to process that information. Visual imagery is a good example. For instance, try to picture a car in your mind's eye. What colour is it? Which way is it going? Can you imagine Long John Silver driving it? People vary considerably in the vividness of the images they can form, including ones they could never have actually seen and are often surprised when they compare notes with friends. This, too, has important implications for teachers, who will under-standably present material in ways that they find interesting or easy to use, not realizing that their children may have different preferences.

Some teachers of dyslexic children (who can be seen as having particular processing problems), therefore, deliberately use 'multi-sensory' presentation, and we should all consider using, for example, pictures, diagrams, writing and speech in combination wherever possible, to get across the same message in different ways, rather than automatically choosing the one that we think is easiest because we prefer it.

Understanding and remembering

It will have become clear that 'attention' and 'perception' are inextricably linked, and similar links are apparent if we go on to consider learning and remembering. If we can perceive something in a meaningful way, it will be much easier for us to remember it. Take, for example, this series of letters:

ecnetnes a etirw ot yaw ynnuf a si siht.

Once you have recognized what it is – in other words, once you have 'perceived' it – you would be able to remember it and write it down quite easily. However, you would not simply be recalling what you had seen, but would use your understanding to re-create what was there. You would, for instance, probably start at the right-hand end and work towards the left. If the same letters had been presented in a random sequence, such as:

ehiyw iwtfo nrte iau e asnye nnsta stc

the task of remembering it would have been virtually impossible because you would not have been able to make sense of it in the first place. A major implication for teachers is, therefore, simply to recognize that children's perceptions, in differing from ours, often mean that the material we give them may be much harder for them to remember than it is for us.

Learning strategies

Although it is very difficult to find out exactly what strategies children might be using, this has been a popular topic for psychologists to study. Later in the chapter, we consider briefly how strategies may develop but, as teachers, we understandably tend to concentrate on content – on what is to be learned rather than exactly how children should learn it. Even when we do try, we may still not give enough help. A popular and effective spelling technique, 'look, cover, write, check', for example, does seem to provide children with an overall strategy for learning spellings, but many young children still are not sure what exactly to do when we ask them to 'look at' something in order to learn it. Very simple strategies, which adults take for granted, can be surprisingly effective. For example:

- shut your eyes and try to picture the word in your head;
- repeat the letters several times over;
- actually practise writing it out a few times;
- see if the word reminds you of any others which you can spell;
- compare your version with the correct one and, if yours is wrong, concentrate on the bit you got wrong;
- if you haven't got access to the correct spelling, write your version down and see if it looks right;
- if the word is familiar but spelled in an unusual way (for example, with a silent letter) try deliberately mispronouncing it in accordance with the way it is spelled.

In general, research suggests that even very young children or those with quite severe learning difficulties can improve their learning dramatically by being taught appropriate strategies, though they often do not spontaneously continue to use them for themselves. (For a review of research into 'educationally relevant' mnemonic strategies see Levin 1993.)

The first part of this chapter has looked briefly at what cognitive psychologists could suggest to teachers about processes such as attention, perception and memory. Such processes are not static but are developing in children and this next section looks at some of the major ideas of psychologists interested in how these changes occur.

Cognitive development

For those who trained to be teachers some time ago, one name more than any other will still be associated with their notions about cognitive development – Jean Piaget. Piaget had a huge influence not only on developmental psychology, but indirectly on what goes on in the classroom. Certainly when I was a psychology undergraduate in the 1960s, he was accorded an almost god-like status equalled at that time only by Eric Clapton. A detailed summary of his theories is clearly beyond the scope of this chapter but almost all standard educational psychology texts will have a summary of his work. (See, for example, Fontana 1988; Gage and Berliner 1992.)

Very briefly, Piaget proposed that there were several discrete stages of development through which all children pass, rejecting previous concepts as they come to realize that they are inadequate or misleading. He used demonstrations to show how children have to learn, for example, that the amount of liquid is unchanged even if it is poured into a different container, or how young children find it hard to see things from a different perspective. He also showed that young children behave in 'egocentric' ways, unable to see things from a different point of view. This can often result in apparently selfish behaviour. In the second cameo, for instance, Martin expects the teacher's personal support whenever he wants it, and children like him may find the independent group work of the Literacy and Numeracy Hours particularly difficult.

There were criticisms of Piaget's theories and research, however, with a particularly important contribution made by Margaret Donaldson in 1978. Her book, which includes a summary of Piaget's work, reviewed evidence suggesting that some of Piaget's ideas were faulty and that, for example, some of the results he obtained were because children had not under-stood the situation or the questions asked, or were unable to relate them to their own experiences. In sum, Piaget had underestimated the social aspects of learning (Faulkner *et al.* 1998).

In fact, one of the most important recent developments in psycholo-gists' ideas about learning has been an increasing emphasis on the social contexts in which it takes place, emphasizing that almost all learning is mediated by culture in some way. A book, for example, is a product of a particular culture, and although reading it may seem a solitary activity, it involves unspoken rules about layout, text, and meaning implicitly shared like a conversation between writer and reader, which children have to learn. For instance, you would probably find it quite annoying if I suddenly decided to omit every third word, or write from right to left! This is even more obvious in classrooms, and there has been a great deal of research on how children and teachers interact with each other (see, for example, Pellegrini and Blatchford 2000) In fact, many psychologists would now see learning not as an individual activity, or even as some-thing that usually involves other people, but as actually determined by its social context (see, for example, Salomon and Perkins 1998).

A few other alternative 'general theories' about cognitive development have also been proposed, taking social factors and the teacher's role more into account. The American psychologist Jerome Bruner was much more interested in teaching than Piaget was: his ideas about how children 'represent' the world were actually embodied in some learning materials that he helped to produce. For teachers, one important idea was the 'spiral curriculum', in which the same topic could be revisited in increas-ingly sophisticated ways as the child developed. Another was the notion of adults providing 'scaffolding' or temporary support to help the child move on to more complex learning.

Such ideas emphasize interaction with other people more than Piaget did, and this recognition of the social contexts of learning has become particularly apparent through increasing interest in the work of the Rus-sian psychologist Vygotsky. Vygotsky was interested in social factors in children's development, showing how adult intervention can enable the child to move into what he called the 'zone of proximal development' (ZPD). This involves skills or understanding where the child can succeed only with support, which is gradually withdrawn as they become more independent. (For a detailed discussion, see Lee and Smagorinsky 2000, and for a comparison of Vygotsky, Bruner and Piaget, see Wood 1998.)

Apart from these major theories, psychologists have also noted some general trends in development to which we now turn.

Some general trends in development

In terms of attention and perception, there seems to be a gradual shift towards greater control and awareness. The attention of even very young babies seems to be grabbed by many things that we also attend to as adults, but as they grow older, children generally exercise increasing control, selecting on the basis of experience what will be most relevant for them. Such control also enables them to concentrate for longer on the same thing if they wish. As children's concepts become more sophisticated, they are increasingly able to make up for inadequacies in what is available to them from their senses.

General changes in their whole approach to solving problems usually accompany these developments (Tina Jarvis and Lee Woods discuss investigations in a practical sense in Chapter 7). Many young children tend, for example, to react 'impulsively' by accepting the first solution that looks more or less right, often on the basis of what has worked in the past whether that response is actually relevant or not. Older and more successful learners are more reflective: they are able to hold several possible ideas in order to consider them, at the same time accepting that they do not yet know the answer because the problem may be a complex one and there may not be one simple answer anyway. Resnick (1987) describes the characteristics of such 'higher order thinking' in which the children are able to regulate their own mental activities, analyse complex situations and impose meaning using nuances of judgement.

Similarly, children become increasingly able to 'de-centre', to see the problem from different points of view and, in a sense, to step outside themselves and to suspend their previous assumptions. Donaldson (1992) discusses how the capacity to think in terms other than just the 'here and now' goes hand in hand with the growing ability to deal with more general and abstract ideas rather than simply with concrete objects and events in the current context. Another term used to describe this development is that their thinking becomes more 'decontextualized'. Going back to the first cameo, Julie will become increasingly able to recognize that the five cubes she ended up with in the first sum represent the same number that she needs for the second problem.

Bruner summed up another major trend when he proposed that children develop through three different ways of 'representing' the world around them. Their earliest thinking involves what he called 'enactive representation', where they have to have the physical objects and manipulate them. Thus Julie needs to 'enact' the problem by taking the cubes out of the box and counting them out loud. Later, she will be able to deal with 'iconic representation' when simply seeing a picture of five cubes will be enough, though she may still have to touch the picture and count aloud at first. Finally she will be able to deal with abstract concepts or 'symbolic representations' like the arbitrary symbol '5' which has absolutely no visual similarities to five objects at all.

At the same time as they are developing the ability to think at different 'levels', children are also developing a range of strategies – ways of dealing with information. It has already been suggested that young children simply often do not know what to do when presented with a learning task and that any form of instruction can help, at least to solve the immediate problem. So how do such strategies develop?

Children's developing strategies

Once they have realized that they do actually need to do something in order to learn (itself a major step), the earliest strategies to emerge involve simply trying to prolong the information. To understand this, look at the random digits below for five seconds, then shut the book, wait for ten seconds, then try to repeat the numbers:

485270391

What strategies did you use? You may not have bothered with the task at all, of course, deciding that it wasn't worth the effort. This can be a legitimate choice and in some ways it is uncomfortably like Martin's decision not to listen to the instructions in the first cameo. If you did try the task, for a start, you almost certainly repeated the numbers to yourself, in your head. Adults do this because we know that the information will rapidly 'fade' or disappear but many children simply are not aware of this basic fact, so that simply discussing such basic 'rote' or 'rehearsal' strategies can sometimes be helpful, even with children at the top end of the junior age range.

Even on such a basic task, however, you probably did other things too, perhaps without even realizing it. You may have pictured the numbers in your mind's eye, bearing in mind from what has been previously said that some people find this much easier to do than others. You perhaps repeated the numbers but in groups of twos or threes rather than one at a time, cutting down the load from nine single digits to three or four

People vary considerably in the numbers of the images they can form

larger 'chunks'. (You may even have said 'forty-eight, fifty-two', etc.).
Even though you were told that the digits were random, you may also
have expected some kind of trick (this chapter is about psychology after
all!) and spent your five seconds desperately looking for some sort of
system. (If you did this it is also likely that you 'cheated' by spending
longer than five seconds!) This 'search after meaning' has already been
discussed as a crucial factor in human thinking, and we do it as adults
because we know that if we understand something, it will be far easier to
learn and remember. Again, children need to be helped to recognize this
in order to improve their strategies.

What do all these strategies have in common? They all involve some
form of transformation or elaboration of the initial information presented – not just looking at it passively or even repeating it but actively
changing it and adding to it in ways to make it easier to learn. These
'elaborative' strategies are a major hallmark of children's cognitive development. We should also note that such strategies probably involve a
growing awareness of our own thinking. We learn, for example, what sorts
of materials we find easiest to deal with, to correct our mistakes, or to
predict what strategy will be most effective, and then plan accordingly.

This ability to think about our thinking is referred to as 'metacognition' and it represents a major development that is very much in keeping with the other general trends outlined in this section.

Conclusion

An understanding of such processes as attention, perception and memory, and of how they develop in children would appear to be very useful to teachers. Yet cognitive psychology seems to have had very little direct impact on classrooms (Merry 1998). Richardson (1992) notes that even those who actually teach cognitive psychology to students make little use of its principles to inform their teaching! Perhaps part of the problem is that these processes are so much a part of us that we are rarely even aware of them, let alone willing to consider changing them: we are unlikely to decide to try a bit of 'perceiving' because we have a few minutes to spare! If so, then even the brief discussion in this chapter may help to raise that awareness a little and to give some insights not only into our own minds, but also into the minds of the thousands of children like Julie and Martin whose problems confront teachers every day.

References and further reading

Bransford, J.D. and Johnson, M.K. (1972) Contextual prerequisites for understanding: some investigations of comprehension and recall, *Journal of Verbal Learning and Verbal Behaviour*, 2(7): 17–26.

Bruner, J.S. and Anglin, J.M. (1973) *Beyond the Information Given*. London: Allen & Unwin.

Donaldson, M. (1978) *Children's Minds*. Glasgow: Fontana/Collins.

Donaldson, M. (1992) *Human Minds*. Glasgow: Fontana/Collins.

Faulkner, D., Littleton, K. and Woodhead, M. (eds) (1998) *Learning Relationships in the Classroom*. London: Routledge.

Fontana, D. (1988) *Psychology for Teachers* (2nd edn). Basingstoke: British Psychological Society/Macmillan.

Gage, N.L. and Berliner, D.C. (1992) *Educational Psychology* (5th edn). Dallas, TX: Houghton Mifflin.

Lee, C.D. and Smagorinsky, P. (2000) *Vygotskian Perspectives on Literacy Research: Constructing Meaning through Collaborative Inquiry*. Cambridge: Cambridge University Press.

Levin, J.R. (1993) Mnemonic strategies and classroom learning: a twenty year report card, *Elementary School Journal*, 94(2): 235–44.

McNamara, S. and Moreton, G. (1993) *Teaching Special Needs*. London: David Fulton.

Merry, R. (1998) *Successful Children, Successful Teaching*. Buckingham: Open University Press.

Pellegrini, A.D. and Blatchford, P. (2000) *The Child at School: Interactions with Peers and Teachers*. London: Arnold.

Resnick, L.B. (1987) *Education and Learning to Think*. Washington, DC: National Academic Press.

Richardson, J.T.E. (1992) Cognitive psychology and student learning, *Psychology Teaching Review*, 1(1): 2–9.

Salomon, G. and Perkins, D.N. (1998) Individual and social aspects of learning, *Review of Research in Education*, 23: 1–24.

Smith, F. (1982) *Writing and the Writer*. London: Heinemann.

Sotto, E. (1994) *When Teaching becomes Learning: A Theory and Practice of Teaching*. London: Cassell.

Wood, D. (1998) *How Children Think and Learn* (2nd edn). Oxford: Blackwell.

Part 2

Teaching to learn

6

What shall we do today? Planning for learning – children and teachers!

Janet Moyles

Cameo 1

Response from a newly qualified teacher when asked by students what had been her most successful strategy for dealing with children's learning: 'Planning lessons thoroughly in writing over the day, week and half-term. This gave me the confidence to know where I was trying to head. It also meant I could let the children in on what they're supposed to learn and that made it all suddenly much easier! It also meant that I could give the children some information to start and then add details later in the lesson – otherwise they would have got swamped and switched off.'

Cameo 2

The beginner teacher had just finished reading a story to a class of 4-year-olds about some children going to the seaside. To engage the children in reflection about the story he asked 'Why do you think the children enjoyed going to the seaside? Who can tell us some of the things they did?' Several children put up their hands as was the custom and the teacher chose Melanie who immediately exclaimed 'My Gran's cat got a bird in the garden and ate it!' In jumps Gita with 'There was a dead dog outside my house tomorrow [*sic*]!' at which point several children joined in gory tales about deceased animals. The teacher tried again: 'Yes, that's very interesting but what about the children in our story. They were at the seaside doing all kinds of things. Tell me about some of them.' By this time, few of the children had any interest in the seaside story but had plenty to say about . . . guess what?!

Cameo 3

From a student's journal: evaluation of a history lesson, Year 5:
'David T is convinced that our present Queen Elizabeth was born in
the 1500s when she was called Elizabeth 1st. When pointing out the
differences between the two, I mentioned that Elizabeth 1st had red
hair, to which David replied, 'Yes but it's all grey now, isn't it! I saw
her on tele yesterday.'

Cameo 4

Pip, a student teacher working with a class of 5-year-olds, is dreading
today's plenary section of the literacy hour. Last time she tried it,
the children all shouted out at once and the whole thing ended in
disarray. Worse still, the teacher had tried to be nice to her and tell
her that everyone has 'failures' and it was 'not too bad'. The trouble
is, that she can't think of any other way to plan the plenary so she
crosses her fingers and tries again. For this literacy hour, and to save
a bit of time, Pip has used history as the focus of the literacy work
and she has been relieved to see that this appears to have worked
well and the children have enjoyed describing, drawing and labelling
the artefacts, for example, the bed-warmer. Now comes the plenary
and three pairs of children are given the opportunity to explain what
they did. The student teacher notices that the second of the pairs
treat the descriptive task rather like a quiz and the children give the
rest of the class clues like 'I'm thinking of a word that begins with B'
and 'The word sounds like red and you go to sleep in it'. All the
children are entranced by this presentation and the plenary goes
smoothly. This becomes planned into the plenary session as a key
feature solving Pip's earlier problem. She almost looks forward to the
plenary after this.

Introduction

It may seem that the NC and the Literacy and Numeracy Strategies
determine all of children's learning and our teaching in the key stages
and that there is little left for the teacher to do except follow the documentation. What other planning can possibly be needed when many
schools have translated the curriculum into schemes of work from which,
each term, the teacher 'lifts' the next set of activities? These outlines
represent longer term planning and are useful as starting points for
ensuring that all aspects of the curriculum are considered. However, they
are in reality just an overview of what should be taught in general
during a term or year and it is the teacher's job to translate them into
learning activities for the particular children in a class bearing in mind
what they already know and can do. This applies whether the children

are subject to the NC or the FS guidance. The result is what are usually called medium- to short-term written plans, which break down what it is possible to cover in a week or two and then daily. These are the nuts and bolts of teaching and learning and hold together the relationship between what is taught, what is learned and the required curriculum. They build on what has gone before and allow teachers to link the assessment of one or more aspects of learning with the next set of teaching and learning activities. This fundamental link – planning→assessment→planning – is part of the cycle of evidence-informed teaching (further outlined in Morag Hunter-Carsch's chapter).

Although time-consuming, planning in writing is eminently worthwhile for the teacher and child, as the new teacher in the first cameo explains, because it means that we think through clearly what is needed and correlate our own and the children's interests and dispositions to the overall curriculum. As we saw in cameo 4, all planning should be flexible so that new ideas can be absorbed and used when something triggers a useful change.

Primary teachers usually plan the programme of activities (or lessons) with three specific things in mind:

1 children's individual and collective existing knowledge and interests (often specific to the age group);
2 curriculum intentions (the FS, NC and the school's guidelines);
3 the teacher's own interests, motivations and professional responsibilities.

These are closely linked, as is evidenced in the cameo situations. Each operates to both support and yet equally constrain the others. For example, whatever the teacher's curriculum intentions, the children often have their own agenda, as both cameos 2 and 4 show, and making as good a match as possible between them is a crucial yet challenging planning feat. It involves teachers in:

- having a good knowledge of a particular class of children as well as an understanding of children's development (including cognitive as discussed by Roger Merry in Chapter 5);
- detailed and thoughtful planning and implementation of activities based on knowledge of children and curriculum;
- undertaking interpretation and analysis of children's experiences and responses and evaluating outcomes, often occurring through observation as Linda Hargreaves explains in Chapter 3.

These three areas are the focus of this chapter and they are approached from the practical angle of offering a range of different kinds of thinking about planning. One other dimension is briefly mentioned; that of support staff and planning their involvement within curriculum learning activities. First, however, we need to clarify what is meant by 'curriculum'.

Curriculum

Very broadly, it could be said that the curriculum is everything the child experiences in the context of schooling that is intended to foster learning. But 'everything' is a very tall order and clearly there is a wealth of knowledge in the world that would be impossible to transmit to every child everywhere. The school curriculum tends to operate first on thinking about subjects, such as English, science, geography, technology, art and the rest, and then within these subjects there are certain concepts, such as form and structure, grammar, change and so on. The 'subject' curriculum, therefore, is only a part of a broader overall curriculum intended to ensure that children are required to think about and 'know' some of the major influences we experience and have experienced in the everyday world.

Schools also have a 'hidden' curriculum, which centres around those aspects that children and teachers cultivate within their more informal relationships but which contribute to the general ethos of the school and through which incidental learning often occurs; for example, children learning games from each other in the playground (Bishop and Curtis 2001).

Curriculum processes should involve the children in many learning experiences of which knowing, thinking, doing, communicating and remembering are some main features. We know that any curriculum 'works' when, as Bennett *et al.* (1984) suggest, children can give evidence that they are:

- acquiring new knowledge and skills;
- using their existing knowledge and skills in different contexts;
- recognizing and solving problems;
- practising what they know;
- revising and replaying what they know in order to remember it.

What we attempt to do as teachers is to ensure through our planning that all of these processes are engaged in by children during most of the school day in balanced proportions. This will be achieved through planning activities to develop particular skills, for example, around individual subjects such as science, or around predetermined structures like the NLS and NNS. The balance comes through ensuring, for example, that children do not spend all day practising something they can already do, which is often the case with activities like worksheets, when investigating a problem might be a better way of exploring a concept (as Tina Jarvis and Lee Woods explain in the next chapter). Bennett *et al.*'s five-point list above is a very useful checklist for examining a day's or week's plans in relation to the quality of children's experiences and is worth remembering.

Planning for learning

In some schools, planning is undertaken strictly in relation to the subject being taught, something that tends to happen most in the final two years of KS2. In other settings, particularly nursery situations, a number of subjects or areas of learning can be incorporated into 'themes', such as 'Weather', 'Travel Agents' or 'Light'. This is a way of planning that teachers who believe in holistic forms of learning often embrace. (One example of this type of planning is shown in Figure 6.1.) There is a danger that themes will become rather too broadly based and the learning opportunities shallow, so with activities planned in this way, close attention needs to be paid to ensuring that children understand the key concepts involved and can apply their understanding to new situations.

Of course, there is similarly the danger that ten curriculum subjects, general curriculum aspects such as citizenship and personal/social education and assessment procedures, will mean that the children's understanding across all of these will be equally shallow and superficial as we rush them and ourselves into the next focus. This only emphasizes the need for medium- and short-term planning to be clear and realistic and to consider the key concepts that need to be taught and learned (Willig 1990).

Many schools attempt to make sense of the curriculum by specifying themes for particular year groups across the school, balancing out subject

Figure 6.1 An example of a cross-curricular topic plan

and other curriculum aspects, for different ages of children. Primary aged children bring their own perceptions to bear on learning (as we saw in previous chapters); therefore, the *processes* through which they acquire experiences assume greatest importance. This is part of the reason for the children's response in Cameo 2 where something (or nothing!) in the story suddenly triggered a quite different train of thought. It is interesting to speculate on how *you* would have reacted to this situation.

In Cameo 3, the child's current grasp of the concept of time – notoriously difficult (what do *adults* really understand of times past?) – means that comparing the two Elizabethan periods is beyond his present level of understanding. He will need many more process experiences of, for example, ordering pictures of distant past, recent past and present objects or events plus many stories and role play opportunities about other times in order to develop his concept of time past and present.

There are a few 'golden rules' for planning medium- and short-term curriculum experiences whether the basis of the planning is subjects or themes. With all children in the 3–11 age range, it is as well to remember the ancient (probably Confucian) saying:

I hear and I forget:
I see and I remember:
I do and I understand

1 Start with something from which children can have an immediate experience – something to *do*. (Torches and a darkened area of the room or a 'Colour Walk' around the local area could lead into much useful science teaching with older children and coverage of knowledge and understanding of the world with younger children.)
2 Children must be given opportunity to offer their suggestions to the planning – it gives them some responsibility from the outset and the teacher has the security of knowing that activities will be within the children's interests and experiences. For example, knowing that your quiz approach to the plenary has been taken up by the teacher, as in Cameo 4, will both motivate the children and enhance their self-esteem as well as make the learning more memorable and enjoyable.
3 Relate the activities to children's lives and experiences as far as possible. It is well known that children learn from a basis of things that make 'human sense' to them (Donaldson 1993); things which are meaningful and relevant to their lives. Teaching about the Aztecs or Ancient Egypt will require a great deal of work *from the teacher*, yet who is it who is supposed to be learning? In the very least children need to access relevant sites on the Internet, see plenty of pictures or videos of people and places, handle artefacts and have drama/role play opportunities. These are not frills but key ingredients to effective learning.

4 Include within curriculum plans:
  - content – subject and wider curriculum, including reference to attainment targets and outcomes;
  - skills and processes children should use and develop;
  - the main concepts to be covered;
  - points at which assessment will be undertaken;
  - the adults who will be involved.

  These may be done all on one large plan, or different smaller plans done showing how subjects or concepts integrate with each other. One example of this would be something like 'time', which is integral to history, mathematics, geography and science curricula.
5 Pin weekly and daily plans on the wall – this constant reminder to children and others who enter the classroom, often prompts the appearance of relevant books, pictures, artefacts, Web sites and so on. It allows children the opportunity for prediction and gives an indication of what they are intended to learn and the subjects to be covered.
6 Try to introduce the focus of any new plans at the end of a week, then spend time talking over the potential learning with the children. Children may well use the weekend to seek out useful books or internet resources and talk it over with adults and older siblings. It is also your starting point for what children already know and can save a lot of unnecessary time and planning in teaching aspects that are already within the children's understanding.
7 Involve the children in constantly *reviewing* progress: what they have learned and what more there is to do and understand in the time available. This not only ensures everyone remains focused but means that planning each day's activities is simpler.
8 Allow children with specific interests to follow these within the planned work and mark these on your overall plan. This is particularly important where some children's interest may be waning and some personal motivation is needed.

An example of a medium-term plan is given in Figure 6.2. How far does it appear to meet the requirement of the list above? What might be added in order to make it more comprehensive?

Support staff

The employment of support staff has been rapidly growing since the mid-1990s and is set to rise further (DfEE 2000). Some CAs work specifically with individual children to support their learning and personal needs. Others are employed as general support mainly for literacy and numeracy teaching (see Moyles and Suschitzky 1997a, b). Such staff are usually welcomed by busy teachers because it means that within the

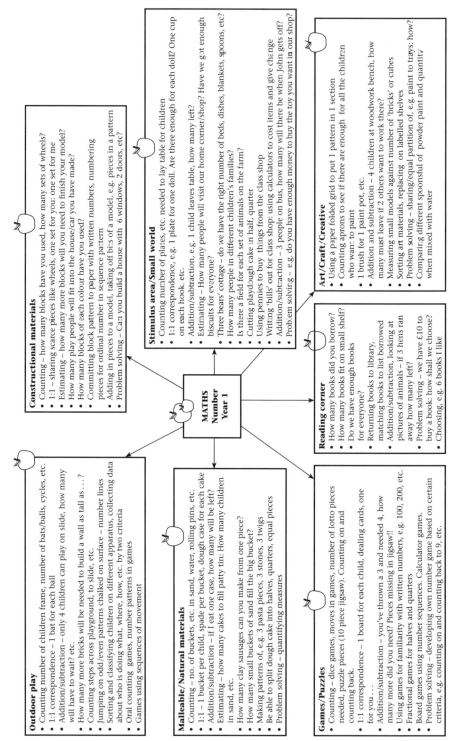

MATHS Number Year 1

Constructional materials
- Counting – how many blocks have you used, how many sets of wheels?
- 1:1 – sharing scarce pieces like wheels, one set for you: one set for me
- Estimating – how many more blocks will you need to finish your model?
- How many play people will fit into the house/car you have made?
- How many blocks of each colour have you used?
- Committing block pattern to paper with written numbers, numbering pieces for ordinal number in sequence pattern
- Adding in pieces to a model, taking off bits of a model, e.g. pieces in a pattern
- Problem solving – Can you build a house with 6 windows, 2 doors, etc.?

Stimulus area/Small world
- Counting number of plates, etc. needed to lay table for children
- 1:1 correspondence, e.g. 1 plate for one doll. Are there enough for each doll? One cup on each hook, etc.
- Addition/subtraction – e.g. 1 child leaves table, how many left?
- Estimating – How many people will visit our home corner/shop? Have we got enough biscuits for everyone?
- Three bears' cottage – do we have the right number of beds, dishes, blankets, spoons, etc?
- How many people in different children's families?
- Is there a field for each set of animals on the farm?
- Cutting playdough cake in half, quarter
- Using pennies to buy things from the class shop
- Writing 'bills' out for class shop: using calculators to cost items and give change
- Addition/subtraction – 3 people on bus, how many will there be when John gets off?
- Problem solving – e.g. do you have enough money to buy the toy you want in our shop?

Art/Craft/Creative
- Using a paper folded grid to put 1 pattern in 1 section
- Counting aprons to see if there are enough for all the children who want to paint
- 1 brush for 1 paint pot, etc.
- Addition and subtraction – 4 children at woodwork bench, how many must leave if 2 others want to work there?
- Measuring small models against number of 'bricks' or cubes
- Sorting art materials, replacing on labelled shelves
- Problem solving – sharing/equal partition of, e.g. paint to trays: how?
- Comparing different spoonsful of powder paint and quantity when mixed with water

Reading corner
- How many books did you borrow?
- How many books fit on small shelf?
- Do we have enough books for everyone?
- Returning books to library, matching books to list borrowed
- Addition/subtraction, looking at pictures of animals – if 3 hens ran away how many left?
- Problem solving – we have £10 to buy a book: how shall we choose?
- Choosing, e.g. 6 books I like

Outdoor play
- Counting number of children frame, number of bats/balls, cycles, etc.
- 1:1 correspondence – 1 bat for each ball
- Addition/subtraction – only 4 children can play on slide, how many will have to wait? etc.
- How many more bricks will be needed to build a wall as tall as ...?
- Counting steps across playground, to slide, etc.
- Jumping on odd/even patterns chalked on surface – number lines
- Sorting and classifying children on different apparatus, collecting data about who is doing what, where, how, etc. by two criteria
- Oral counting games, number patterns in games
- Games using sequences of movement

Malleable/Natural materials
- Counting – no. of buckets, etc. in sand, water, rolling pins, etc.
- 1:1 – 1 bucket per child, spade per bucket, dough case for each cake
- Addition/subtraction – if I eat one case, how many will be left?
- Estimating – how many cakes to fill patty tin: How many children in sand, etc.
- How many clay sausages can you make from one piece?
- How many small buckets of sand fill the big bucket?
- Making patterns of, e.g. 3 pasta pieces, 3 stones, 3 twigs
- Be able to split dough cake into halves, quarters, equal pieces
- Problem solving – quantifying measures

Games/Puzzles
- Counting – dice games, moves in games, number of lotto pieces needed, puzzle pieces (10 piece jigsaw). Counting on and counting back.
- 1:1 correspondence – 1 board for each child, dealing cards, one for you ...
- Addition/subtraction – you've thrown a 3 and needed 4, how many more did you need? Pieces missing in jigsaw!!
- Using games for familiarity with written numbers, e.g. 100, 200, etc.
- Fractional games for halves and quarters
- Board games using number sequences. Calculator games.
- Problem solving – developing own number game based on certain criteria, e.g. counting on and counting back to 9, etc.

Figure 6.2

Children must be given opportunity to offer their suggestions to the planning

school day, groups and individuals can receive additional support which the teacher would not have time to give to 30 or more children (see also Smith and Langston 1999). Student teachers – who are not always confident about their own expertise – may not always be so sure about having other knowledgeable adults around! Yet with a little additional thought, CAs can become a student teacher's greatest allies in offering consistency for children and in being another pair of eyes, ears and hands in a sometimes overwhelming situation. Having such support, however, does add an additional planning dimension, in as much as if CAs' time is to be used effectively, the support they are intended to give needs to be known in advance and it needs to be clear to everyone what outcomes and achievements are intended. Strategies such as *planning diaries*, which pass between the teacher and the CA, are useful in keeping both busy people focused: the teachers may well write into the book the names of the children with whom the CA will work and the learning intentions for the session. In turn, the CA will make notes on how individual children respond to the task and the extent of their achievements and understanding, which supports the next stage of the teacher's planning.

Specialist teaching

Some schools, particularly with children in Years 5 and 6, are now operating specialist teaching time, when the school's subject co-ordinators work with different classes or groups of children. Many primary schools, operate practices such as 'setting' for maths, English or Science, which is a way of ensuring that children of different abilities receive specific teaching. However, many primary schools still operate a one-teacher/ one-class system with teachers being required to teach all subjects to all abilities. The jury is still out on the values to children's learning outcomes of setting and streaming (Sukhnandan and Lee 1998).

Detailed planning and implementation

The emphasis on children 'doing' and playing, is particularly vital with children aged 3–7 years and for older children should only gradually be replaced by less active learning approaches (see Moyles 1994). The active curriculum is well represented in Figure 6.3, which also gives clear guidance on what detailed plans need to include in relation to processes and skills.

Primary children occupying too much time being told or working at pencil and paper activities will soon get bored and may, at best, simply not learn and, at worst, may generate discipline problems. Children presented with too much too soon (as in the case of the travel agency

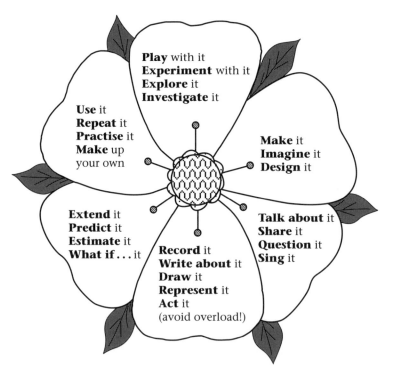

Figure 6.3 Curriculum flower power

Session:		Date:	Time:	Curriculum Area:
Plan	**Comment**			
Aim				
Objectives				
NC links				
Resources				

Activity structure	Timing	Teacher activity	Children's activity
Introduction			
Development			
Conclusion			

Evaluation – continued overleaf

Figure 6.4 Structuring the day

cameo in Chapter 2) may be so busy exploring new materials that the teacher's intentions are, albeit temporarily, lost. Worksheet activities and continual exposition, rarely enable children to be actively engaged in their own learning processes. Rather they often teach children how to fail; search for the 'right' answers; be passive recipients; hate written work; learn by 'rote' without understanding; be a spectator in one's own learning; wait to be told; find learning painful and/or boring and expect others to control their learning. Most teachers do not really want this for children and yet get drawn into this mode of working mainly to try to 'fit everything in'. There are other ways.

Long-term plans offer information about subject or theme and include the concepts, processes and skills we are aiming for, but the heart of day-to-day teaching is to undertake some quite detailed planning of each particular activity to be undertaken by the children. The chart shown in Figure 6.4 is one found helpful by beginner teachers to structure their activities, giving as it does opportunity to comment on both the children's activities and also on what the teacher or other adult will be doing. Students often need to recognize that children *can* learn without a continual adult presence but that if you do want to work with individuals or groups this must be incorporated into the planning. As indicated in the Bennett *et al.* model earlier, activities will need different levels of teacher attention:

Finding a wide range of ways of analysing and evaluating what children know is vital

- teacher intensive – when children are undertaking new learning or the teacher is assessing existing learning;
- teacher hovering – when children are engaged in applying knowledge and may need occasional teacher support;
- teacher monitoring – when children are practising skills and knowledge in relatively familiar situations requiring little teacher involvement;
- teacher available – when children are engaged in absorbing their own mastery and may need the teacher to tell or show an outcome at some stage.

The planning chart also ensures that you remember that each activity will need a specific introduction, something that develops it further (as the new teacher found in the first cameo) and a conclusion. The evaluation gives the basis (as explored by Morag Hunter-Carsch in Chapter 12) for making decisions on who has learned what and what is needed for progression to the next stage.

Remember with such planning charts that your *aims* are related to things you wish to achieve in the *slightly longer term*; for example, 'Children should enjoy science and learn a number of key concepts.' In contrast, *objectives* are *short term*, related to what the children should have learned and done by the end of that activity; 'Children should be able to use their knowledge of light in order to explain how the beam falls on an object.'

Ready to teach?

The final level of planning is how you and the children are actually going to work together in the learning context. There are several phases in this interaction, summed up under the following headings and questions:

1 *Entering strategy*
   What will be your starting point(s)? Introduction?
2 *Exploration mode*
   What exploration will the children undertake? What materials/resources will be available? How/by whom will they be set up?
3 *Content*
   This will be as in your planning, but how will you tell the children what you intend them to learn as well as to do?
4 *Ownership and responsibility*
   What level of ownership will the children have? What responsibilities? How will the children know what they are supposed to learn? How will these aspects be conveyed?
5 *Teacher strategies*
   What will your role be? What will the role of the CA be? How will you and your CA interact/intervene in the activities and sustain/extend them?
6 *Evaluation and analysis*
   How/when/who will you observe to see what children were learning in relation to concepts covered and the objectives set? Will other adults be involved in observation and recording? Who? When during the activities?
7 *Reflection/review/plenary mode*
   What opportunities will you provide for children to reflect on their learning and be part of its review/evaluation/analysis?
8 *Justification*
   What quality and standard of outcomes will you expect? How will the value of these be communicated to others (for example, through display, Web site, records)?

Using the chart shown in Figure 6.5, why not have a go at plotting how you would approach the task indicated in the light of the above statements. Doing this task will mean that it's necessary to consider different kinds of organizational strategies, for example, whether you introduce something to the whole class, give tasks to groups or pairs, or allow children free choice to explore materials for themselves. Figure 6.6 suggests a range of activities that might take place in the classroom and asks you to make decisions as to what you would organize in which way.

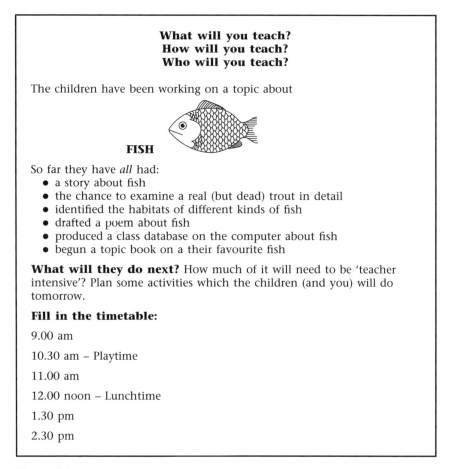

What will you teach?
How will you teach?
Who will you teach?

The children have been working on a topic about

FISH

So far they have *all* had:
- a story about fish
- the chance to examine a real (but dead) trout in detail
- identified the habitats of different kinds of fish
- drafted a poem about fish
- produced a class database on the computer about fish
- begun a topic book on a their favourite fish

What will they do next? How much of it will need to be 'teacher intensive'? Plan some activities which the children (and you) will do tomorrow.

Fill in the timetable:

9.00 am

10.30 am – Playtime

11.00 am

12.00 noon – Lunchtime

1.30 pm

2.30 pm

Figure 6.5

Having undertaken these activities with children, it is vital that you and the children reflect on what you did and the success or otherwise of the outcomes.

Interpreting, analysing and evaluating children's experiences

What we are essentially assessing is to what extent the children (and we as teachers) have been able to:

- reach the objectives set for them in planning;
- develop appropriate attitudes and opinions;

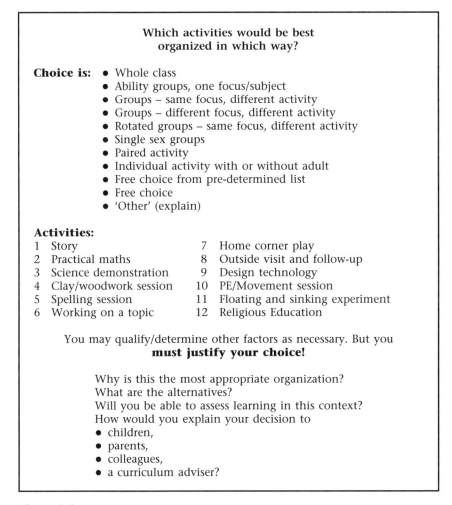

**Which activities would be best
organized in which way?**

Choice is:
- Whole class
- Ability groups, one focus/subject
- Groups – same focus, different activity
- Groups – different focus, different activity
- Rotated groups – same focus, different activity
- Single sex groups
- Paired activity
- Individual activity with or without adult
- Free choice from pre-determined list
- Free choice
- 'Other' (explain)

Activities:

1	Story	7	Home corner play
2	Practical maths	8	Outside visit and follow-up
3	Science demonstration	9	Design technology
4	Clay/woodwork session	10	PE/Movement session
5	Spelling session	11	Floating and sinking experiment
6	Working on a topic	12	Religious Education

You may qualify/determine other factors as necessary. But you
must justify your choice!

Why is this the most appropriate organization?
What are the alternatives?
Will you be able to assess learning in this context?
How would you explain your decision to
- children,
- parents,
- colleagues,
- a curriculum adviser?

Figure 6.6

- reach high standards and offer quality outcomes;
- deal with the rates at which they learn;
- find out about their strengths and weaknesses;
- understand what learning should take place next for children to progress;
- know what activities or experiences should now be provided or repeated and what differentiated experiences are needed for which children.

We then evaluate these against longer term aims to see what adjustments are required in planning. This process involves us in much interpretation of evidence and collection of data for written evaluations and records. Be careful that your interpretations are as value-free and objective as possible. For example, look at the following two written fieldnote observations from a FS activity, one highly subjective and the other much more objective.

> This went really well. Sam was having a wonderful time playing with the sand tray; she really enjoyed playing with Surekha and Amrit and they all seemed to get a lot out of it. They didn't communicate at all but just enjoyed playing alongside each other and doing things together.

> Sam was using a bucket and spade in the sand with Surekha and Amrit, filling and emptying the bucket for a full 10-minute period. There was no verbal interaction between the children but Surekha watched Sam on three occasions and then attempted to emulate Sam's actions. (Would Surekha benefit from more opportunities to learn from a peer model?)

It is quite obvious that the second written observation is a much more appropriate diagnostic and informative tool for the teacher in working on the next phase of planning. Next time you are in a classroom, make a brief observation like this of a particular activity or group of children and see how objective (or otherwise!) your fieldnotes appear.

Finding out about children's learning

Another main strategy for finding out about children's learning has to be through talking to them or getting them to write down what they did and what they think they learned. However, in analysing, interpreting and evaluating learning capabilities in this way, we need to remember that children's ability to understand things is not always matched in their written performance. Children who can *give* an extensive oral explanation of an exciting science experiment often then write 'I put it in the cup and it disappeared. the end' [*sic*]. (Marilyn Foreman and Nikki Gamble, in Chapter 10, offer more guidance on writing for different purposes and with different outcomes.) This happens right across the primary school particularly where fine motor development is slow and a child actually finds writing really difficult if not actually painful! Just those very processes of *active learning* discussed in detail above, are nearly always more important to primary children than writing about tasks! After all, would you always want to write about what you had done, or would you rather move on to the next exciting learning adventure? No wonder the word 'boring' often appears in the vocabulary of KS2 children!

Finding other ways of analysing and evaluating what children know is vital, not least through planning classroom activities in such a way that you have time to *observe* in the many ways described by Linda Hargreaves in Chapter 3.

It is in active situations that children frequently illustrate more of their knowledge. For example, I well remember a boy who stood on the edge of a group of children, in a design technology lesson, attempting to make a pulley out of various items of 'found' materials (sometimes called 'junk' though very precious in the primary school!). He chose to watch, despite the evident enjoyment of other children, and flatly refused to explain his reticence to become involved. After a half-hour the group still had not managed to produce a pulley. Almost at the end of the session, the boy walked up to the table, picked up three or four items and rapidly and ingeniously made a working pulley. It would have been easy to have thought of him as dull, lazy, insecure, sullen or downright obstinate! This is just one example of how we must be sensitive to the different ways in which our pupils' learn and perform.

We must also be mindful that children's apparent knowledge is not always 'secure'. Children can, for example, readily declare that the earth is round but then draw a picture of it flat-topped in order to show themselves standing on it! Young children can 'parrot' information, such as counting from 1 to 10, but when asked what number comes after 6 they haven't a clue (see Chapter 5).

Other ways in which children can demonstrate learning

As well as oral and written language outcomes, children could be expected to show different aspects of their learning in several other ways (though none of these should be overused – variety is imperative!):

- drawings;
- poems (and other different forms of writing, for example, acrostics);
- diagrams and charts;
- mind maps (see Buzan 1993);
- composing lists;
- photographs, with or without children's captions;
- making booklets about different activities – 'This is what we learned when we *worked* with the sand'; 'This is what we found out about Ancient Egypt';
- explaining to other children what to do (see Chapter 10);
- developing web-based communications;
- camera/video/audio recordings of activities;
- undertaking drama/role play;
- doing demonstrations for others.

However assessment is undertaken, you need to ensure that children are given opportunities:

- to *make their own ideas explicit*. Starting from what children know is a must in on-going planning;
- to produce *an end result* in different ways and *with several* alternative solutions. Investigations and problem solving activities allow children to show physically what they 'know';
- to explore ideas with peers – it is much easier to argue your points with peers than with adults particularly as children get to Years 5 and 6;
- opportunities to question actively their own thinking and undertake explorations in order to learn about their own misconceptions;
- question their own outcomes through open-ended questioning 'What would happen if . . .'
- to be part of situations in which they need to generalize in order to use and develop concepts;
- to *observe for* rather than simply *look at* objects and artefacts and raise questions. Help children to detect relevant similarities as well as differences;
- to *achieve* by setting *goals for children* that are attainable with just the right amount of effort – this means knowing the children's capabilities well through all those – and tell them what they are intended to learn.
- explore materials before expecting them to do something specific with them;
- apply their knowledge in a situation where they can succeed;
- learn and use the appropriate vocabulary for each topic so that they have the means to explain their activities to you;
- to gather all the information they need in order to fulfil the demands of the activity. We don't have to wait for children to reinvent the wheel every time but, having been told, children *must* be allowed to 'prove' whatever the concept is for themselves (Sotto 1994);
- to be genuinely praised for achieving learning.

The teacher's role

You should also give yourself plenty of opportunity for interpreting, analysing and assessing what *your role* has been in the children's learning. The following questions will act as a conclusion to this chapter and also serve as a reminder of the kinds of things important for you, as a developing professional, in planning for children's learning on a daily and weekly basis.

1 How positive or otherwise do you feel about the curriculum activities you provided?
2 Did you present activities with enthusiasm and vigour?

3 In what ways did the teaching and learning appear successful/unsuccessful to you?

4 What did you learn – about planning, curriculum, children?

5 Was the atmosphere generated in the classroom pleasant, task-oriented and positive?

6 How did you handle any challenges?

7 Were you more involved with the children in relation to supervision of *activities* or the management of *learning*?

8 Were your teaching strategies congruent with the objectives you set? Did you offer a structured sequence of experiences?

9 Were your interactions with children 'professional' and did you give and receive appropriate feedback?

10 How well did you communicate with children? Did you pace your talk appropriately and were your instructions (verbal and non-verbal) clear?

11 Did you make effective use of your time and energy?

12 Did you use a variety of teaching styles and strategies – exposition, different groupings, discussion, play and active learning, practice tasks, problem-solving, investigations?

13 Have you marked, analysed and diagnosed children's learning errors and noted those who need help?

14 Have you made appropriate observations and evaluations of children's learning?

15 Have you and the children used the physical space and resources effectively?

16 Would you have enjoyed the activities if you had been one of the children?

17 Have you discussed your progress with a mentor and noted points for professional development?

18 Have you enjoyed the experience of teaching – and learning?

Acknowledgement

I am grateful to Barbara Garner for allowing me to adapt her diagram for Figure 6.3.

References and further reading

Bennett, N., Desforge, G., Cockburn, A. and Wilkinson, B. (1984) *The Quality of Pupil Learning Experiences*. London: Lawrence Erlbaum.

Bishop, J. and Curtis, M. (2001) *Play Today in the Primary School Playground: Life, Learning and Creativity*. Buckingham: Open University Press.

Buzan, T. (1993) *The Mind Map Book: Radiant Thinking*. London: BBC Books.

DfEE (2000) see range of resources about Classroom Assistants at http://www.dfee.gov.uk/a-z/TEACHING%5FASSISTANTS.html

Donaldson, M. (1993) *Human Minds: An Exploration*. Glasgow: Penguin.

Early Years Curriculum Group (1997) *Interpreting the Curriculum at KS1*. Buckingham: Open University Press.

Moyles, J. (1994) (ed.) *The Excellence of Play*. Buckingham: Open University Press.

Moyles, J. and Suschitzky, W. (1997a) *Jills of All Trades . . . ? Classroom Assistants in KS1 Classes*. London: ATL and University of Leicester.

Moyles, J. and Suschitzky, W. (1997b) *The Buck Stops Here . . . ! Nursery Teachers and Nursery Nurses Working Together*. Leicester: Esmée Fairbairn Charitable Trust/University of Leicester.

Smith, A. and Langston, A. (1999) *Managing Staff in Early Years Settings*. London: Routledge.

Sotto, E. (1994) *When Teaching Becomes Learning: A Theory and Practice of Teaching*. London: Cassells.

Sukhnandan, L. and Lee, B. (1998) *Streaming, Setting and Grouping by Ability: A Review of the Literature*. Slough: NFER.

Willig, C. (1990) *Children's Concepts and the Primary Curriculum*. London: Paul Chapman.

7

Fruit salads and wild gardens! Developing investigative thinking and skills in children

Tina Jarvis and Lee Woods

Cameo 1

The class had been asked to prepare afternoon tea for their parents. One group set out to design and prepare a fruit salad. They were told they could use three fruits from a choice of apples, clementines, bananas, melons and kiwi fruits.

During their work, the group carried out investigations in mathematics, design and technology, and science. Investigative skills are important elements in each of these subjects, although they are used in slightly different ways and for different purposes. This can be illustrated by considering how the group went about designing their fruit salad.

Initially, the children had to find out what combinations of fruits were possible in a mathematical investigation. At first they just wrote down different combinations in a rather disorganized way. After a while their teacher suggested a more systematic approach would be necessary if they were to find all the combinations possible. Eventually they saw a logical pattern of results emerging, which they used to ensure that they had found all possibilities.

In design and technology, it is important to test the properties of different components and how they might be joined. Consequently, the children also investigated different ways of cutting each fruit, examined their flavours and considered various colour combinations in order to create an attractive, tasty dish.

While engrossed in the task, one child noticed that the apple went brown very quickly making it less attractive. Someone commented that his granny said peeled apples had to be put in water. The group decided to test this out and placed some pieces of apple in water and some were left in the air. They discovered that only the uncovered apples went brown. The teacher asked the group if this always happened. After some thought the children recalled abandoned apple cores also went brown. When asked why they thought this happened, it was suggested that something in the air made the apple go brown and the water kept the air out. This was essentially a scientific investigation as it focused on explaining some physical or biological phenomena, albeit in very simple terms.

Cameo 2

A group of Year 5 children are given the task of setting up a wild garden. The first task is to fence off the chosen area using the 40m wire-mesh fencing already purchased. The children want to make the wild garden as large as possible. Prompted to find out what area would be surrounded by a square fence, the children are soon exploring other shapes, including shapes with an increasing numbers of sides. One child remarks that as the number of sides increase so do the number of squares counted. Another child observes that 'their shape (which had many sides) looks more like a circle'. At some point the image of a circular wild garden was created with general agreement that this would be the best and biggest wild garden that could be made – and it was!

Introduction

It can be daunting to give children the freedom to try out their own ideas, as there is always the worry that they will become disruptive or that they may come up with a question that the teacher cannot answer! Children are usually highly motivated by the types of activity described in the cameos, so are less likely to be difficult as long as the task is within their capability and every child in the group can be fully involved. In undertaking investigations, children are able to use the kind of 'higher-order' cognitive skills outlined by Roger Merry in Chapter 5 and you will be able to see evidence of thinking in the way children approach the tasks. In this chapter, therefore, I shall:

- examine what is meant by 'investigation' as a cross-curricular process but with examples particularly related to science concepts and skills, technology and mathematics;
- offer a range of examples of how these activities can occupy a major role in the primary curriculum and in classroom practices.

Investigations develop both creative and critical thinking that will assist subsequent academic studies

What is an investigation?

Investigations are activities in which pupils examine different ways of carrying out a task or explore the effects of making changes in situations. Although some investigations, as in the cameo, have a specific objective or solution, the means by which the goal is achieved is open-ended. Other investigations have no immediately obvious goal as in the case of the science aspect of the above investigation where the children had no specific aim or preconceived result in mind.

Why develop investigations in the classroom?

Investigations develop both creative and critical thinking that will assist subsequent academic studies as well as enabling people to cope more effectively with everyday problems. In order to think creatively, children need to move beyond their first ideas to suggest alternatives. These ideas should be critically examined to make reasoned choices. Creativity involves taking a risk that one's ideas might prove foolish or inappropriate. Critical thinking requires an open mind that is prepared to make decisions based on evidence that may challenge deeply held personal views. Neither are easy. (In Chapter 8, Gill Robinson takes up these issues in relation to art-based activities.) Children will only develop creativity and critical thinking within a secure, supportive environment provided by the teacher. As investigations are an integral part of science and mathematics, as well as design and technology, these subjects can provide both appropriate contexts, which are in the experience and interest of the children, and a structure to enable children to develop strategies for critically examining their imaginative ideas. That said, investigations offer a wide, cross-curricular experience for both children and teachers.

Science investigations

The way young children are expected to develop science investigatory skills in the NC provides a useful structure for developing investigations in a wider context, as they provide a way to test the applicability of different ideas. However, it is important to realize that teaching science investigative skills alone is not sufficient as these skills are the means to create and test scientific concepts, explanations or hypotheses.

Science concepts

The whole purpose of science is to explain the existing physical and biological world. Scientists attempt to create ideas or generalizations that fit all situations, anywhere in this world or even the universe. Scientific generalizations are being changed and refined all the time. For example, until the time of Galileo and Newton there was a general belief that the Earth was the centre of the universe. Scientific knowledge is still tentative, so even the most cherished theories can be challenged by new evidence. Therefore, the scientist must be creative in order to suggest new theories as well as able to test them logically. Scientific investigations provide one approach to evaluate existing ideas and test the value of new ones. Children can follow similar procedures to test and explain their own ideas and if necessary adjust them.

Even very young children have ideas to explain what is happening around them (see Chapter 6). In many cases these explanations are not the same as those given by today's scientists. For example, many children think that light comes out of their eyes when they see objects (Osborne *et al.* 1990); only one wire from a battery is necessary to make a bulb light (Osborne *et al.* 1991); and large blocks of ice are colder than small blocks because of their size. Therefore, the teacher should encourage children to articulate their own ideas, raise their own questions and test their ideas logically and, if necessary, adjust them. A practical investigatory approach not only develops the children's thinking skills, it also gives them a taste of scientific discovery and helps them to recognize that they can have a role in revising and improving current scientific ideas.

A practical investigatory approach develops children's thinking skills and gives them a taste of scientific discovery

Example: Saving the kittens – a class scientific investigation

A practical investigation was used to help children explain some of the factors that influence whether materials are good or poor insulators. It is important that the children's activities have relevance to them, so a story about some kittens provided the context of the lesson.

A student teacher told her class of 7-year-olds that a cat had given birth to kittens in a mountain cave. As the kittens needed to be brought down the hillside before the weather got too cold, it was important to wrap them up in a warm material. The children were asked to test different materials to find out which would be the best insulators for carrying the kittens and to explain why some materials were better than others.

The children were given a variety of materials including wool, fur fabric, cotton, foil and plastic. They observed the fabrics carefully and then predicted which they thought would keep the kittens warm the longest. The children were asked to give reasons for their predictions. Some thought the wool would make a good insulator because it was thick, whereas others thought the foil would be best because it was used when heating meat in an oven.

With guidance the teacher helped the children to make the test fair. Five plastic bottles of the same size were covered with the same amount of material and placed in a milk crate to stop them falling over. For safety reasons hot water was put into the bottles by the student teacher.

A thermometer was placed in each bottle and the height of the fluid was recorded every quarter of an hour. A kitchen timer was used, as this was easier for the children to use than reading a clock. The fur fabric and wool were found to keep the water hot the longest. The foil was the poorest insulator. This appeared to confirm the explanation that thick materials made better insulators. Those children who had predicted foil would be a good insulator had to rethink their ideas.

When talking about their findings the teacher drew the children's attention to the fact that the fur trapped a lot of air, which improved its heat retention capacity. She also told the children that the metal in the foil was not only thin but that the metal conducted heat away from the bottle. To help the children understand this idea, she reminded them that metal spoons become hot quickly when left in hot water, unlike wooden or plastic spoons which did not let heat move through them easily. Finally, the more able children wrote about the experiment, while the less able produced a series of annotated drawings. (Marilyn Foreman and Nikki Gamble in Chapter 10 give stimulating examples of several ways in which children can record the results of investigations of all kinds, while Jane Hislam in Chapter 9, shows how storying can operate as the basis of children expressing their imagination and learning.)

Developing science investigatory skills

In the fabric investigation the children used several skills including observation, measurement, setting up a fair test, predicting and explaining. In order to develop such skills, children will need some activities that focus on one or two skills only, as well as having the chance to carry out whole investigations. The teacher needs to help children to make their own choices about when and how each skill should be applied and encourage them to raise and test their own questions. How can these skills be developed with young children?

Observation

In the kitten experiment, the children had to choose which observations were significant for their test. The way the light reflected on the water might have been interesting but not relevant in this case. On other occasions, a more open-minded approach is necessary where as much detail as possible is collected to stimulate new questions and discoveries. Before the class carried out the kitten investigation, their teacher wanted the children to look at a variety of fabrics carefully. She gave pairs of children two squares of fabric to find as many differences and similarities between them as possible. The discussion and comparison prompted a

Prediction is an important skill to help plan an investigation

wide range of creative ways of examining their samples, including whether they felt or looked different when wet, could be cut or creased easily, were transparent or woven. This experience not only developed into learning about insulation but also provided the foundation for finding out why some materials were waterproof and others absorbent. (Observation is emphasized as a crucial factor in children's and teachers' learning in several of the other Part 2 chapters.)

Classifying and organizing data

Phenomena need to be sorted in different ways to help identify significant relationships. If children make a collection of things that stick to magnets they should find that these are all metals, although some different metals belong to the non-magnetic set. This activity should help them to recognize that iron-based metals are magnetic.

To help children make appropriate classifications teachers will need to suggest criteria for sorting. When the children were examining fabric they could have been asked to sort fabrics into those that are elastic (can be stretched but go back into their original shape) and those that are not. On other occasions the children can be asked to suggest factors for themselves. One group of children thought of sorting toys according to colour, presence of wheels, material and type of energy used. Subsequently each individual grouped the toys according to self-chosen criteria. One child sorted them into those she liked and those she did not like, which justifiably prompted the remainder of the class to complain that this was not fair! The teacher was then able to talk in general about appropriate ways of making sets including the fact that some classifications needed measurement; for example, dividing the toys into big and little would be too vague.

Recording and measuring

Observations should be systematically recorded. Tick sheets, charts and graphs are useful but have to be introduced carefully as very young children find them difficult to fill in. It helps to start with very simple charts that only records one feature, such as 'Does the toy have wheels – yes or no?' Once the children have mastered this they might be presented with several columns but which still only focus on one criteria. They might record the type of energy used by different toys into, for example, battery, spring, elastic, people's push or pull or wind. With experience more complicated charts can be used. In all cases it is helpful to design the chart *with* the children so that they can see how it works and they are given the knowledge to draw up their own charts later. Although this may seem time-consuming it pays off in the end.

Measuring equipment is often needed to distinguish between phenomena or actions. Initially children will require help to know how and when to use equipment like thermometers and force meters. Before any activity, it is important that you check whether the children are able to use the equipment for its intended purpose. For example, some children do not realize that the fluid in the thermometer rises as it gets hotter and falls when cooled. Without this basic understanding measuring temperature will be meaningless. In this case the children could place a large clearly marked glass thermometer in different locations to watch and talk about the changes.

As many thermometers have scales extending over 100 degrees, the numbers and related calculations can be too advanced for some children. It may be possible to avoid the use of the thermometer at all by letting the children feel differences by hand (remember to make sure that it is safe). Another approach is to use a matching technique. In the kitten experiment, the less able children drew around their thermometer and coloured in the height of the liquid at each reading. When they compared the series of drawings for each material they could see which was the best insulator. If a matching technique is used, you can use the experience to introduce mathematical skills such as reading scales and showing the children how to carry out the calculations involved. This will be facilitated if the more able children have had the opportunity to make the more accurate readings as their work can be used in the explanations.

Carrying out a fair test

As the children start trying out different investigations, the teacher should introduce the idea of fair tests. In the 'kitten test' it would not have been 'fair' if a lot of fabric was wrapped around some bottles and only a little around others. With guidance, the children will be able to identify the variables that might influence a result and recognize that they must only change one. Only the variable that is being tested must change, i.e. the type of fabric. Everything else should be kept the same – size of bottles, amount of water in the bottles, the way the fabric is fixed to the bottle, and so on.

Prediction and hypothesizing (generalizations and explanations)

Prediction is an important skill to help plan an investigation. When the children think about what might happen in a test, they will be helped to know what to observe and what to measure. Children (as well as teachers!) are often reluctant to predict in case they are wrong. You will need to provide a supportive atmosphere that encourages children to take 'risks'. Initially it is often helpful to ask the children to predict orally rather than writing their ideas down as this is less threatening. By asking children to give reasons for their predictions they can also begin to hypothesize, which is the ultimate aim of all science activity.

A scientific hypothesis explains why something happens by suggesting a cause for an observed effect: in the 'kitten experiment' the children hypothesized that materials were good insulators if they were thick. They could have tested this idea further by comparing a set of thick and thin fabrics of the same type. On another occasion, a class noticed some plants dying on a windowsill. The teacher encouraged the children to suggest why or how this happened. The explanations included: the plants had been in too much sun, they had not been watered enough and the soil was poor. All of these are simple *causal hypotheses* and are scientific because they can be tested by experiment. To test their first idea the children grew some plants in direct sunlight and some in a more shaded area.

Evaluating and drawing conclusions

The children need to describe and explain what has happened during their experiments but, do remember, it is not always necessary for them to do this *in writing*. You will need to introduce a range of reporting methods, such as oral reports, drawings, tables, graphs and model-making, so that children (many of whom may come from different first language backgrounds) can make their own decisions about how they can communicate their findings most effectively. The children should also evaluate their experimental procedure, suggesting improvements and commenting on the limitations of their results, so that they can carry out further investigations more effectively.

Applying knowledge acquired during investigations

In order to help children to consolidate new ideas it is useful to ask them to apply their knowledge. This may be in the kind of technological investigation now described.

Technological investigations

Technology is involved with changing products to satisfy human needs or wants, whereas science is concerned with explaining the existing world. Technology applies science concepts to make these products but also uses ideas from all other curriculum areas. Similar testing skills are used in technology as in science but they are not aimed at making generalizations. Rather, they are used for *testing* how good a product is, or which materials and methods would be best for making a new product. As examples, groups of children in different classes tested:

- a variety of mugs for stability, capacity, insulation properties, appearance, cost, comfort to hold and ease of cleaning in order to identify the best mug for a child;
- different ways of joining fabrics when they were making a model cloth coat of 'many colours' for Joseph;
- the reflective qualities of materials that could be used as a torch reflector.

Testing products and methods is only a part of design and technology: it is also concerned with evaluating familiar manufactured products, learning making techniques as well as designing, making and evaluating products for themselves. The procedure of investigating and producing a product to solve a specific need can be applied to other problems. Consequently, design and technology provides practical, relevant and manageable contexts to enable children to develop the expertise to tackle many kinds of problems. Occasionally, the children will suggest a project but most design and technology tasks will be introduced by the teacher. These should include open-ended assignments to allow for differentiation and individuality. For example, young children can be shown the skills in making a lift-the-flap book but the story line and illustrations should be individualized. Although children should be given this opportunity to be creative, they will need to be taught basic technological skills, such as using saws and cooking implements correctly, as well as strategies for clarifying and solving problems effectively as in the following example.

Example: Rescue from a well – a class technological investigation

A class of Year 6 children was challenged to build a model of a simple pulley system to rescue a 'child' who had fallen down a well. The model was to be made to lift a doll, which was placed at the bottom of a large cylinder, approximately 10 cm in diameter and 20 cm deep. The cylinder had a small platform around the top, which could be used to rest the model on. The teacher guided children through the design and making process as outlined below. (These are simplified as, in practice, there is a tendency to go backwards and forwards from one step to another.)

Clarifying the task

The children needed to be sure they understood the task. Children often rush into an activity without looking at the whole problem, so have to make adjustments later. In this case they had to solve two main problems: building a framework with a pulley that fitted on to the platform, and finding a way of picking up the doll.

Review of existing knowledge that may be helpful and how similar problems have been solved by them or others in the past

When making the model pulley system, the children were helped to recall how to join wood using cardboard squares and ways of making pulleys. They were also given a variety of books showing simple models and actual examples of pulleys. Using others' research is an important stage of the investigation. It is foolish to 'reinvent the wheel' when it is more appropriate to build on existing inventions. It is also important that the children have been taught the basic skills and knowledge such as how to use a framework with added triangles or diagonals in 'focused tasks'.

Collection of different solutions

In order to promote creativity, groups were encouraged to brainstorm several solutions. Brainstorming gives an opportunity to collect many ideas in a short time without evaluation, criticism or discussion. Some of the ideas may well be impractical but, at this stage, creativity is more important. For example, one group suggested using respectively a large magnet, a scoop and a crocodile as a way of lifting up the doll!

Comparing and evaluating different approaches

All the solutions were evaluated and a few chosen for detailed exploration. This stage may involve testing different materials and combinations of components. The testing approach should be carried out in a logical and fair way along the lines of scientific investigations. In this task, many of the groups wanted to use a cotton reel on a piece of dowelling as a pulley but it fitted too loosely so several methods of joining were tested.

Choosing an approach, identifying the different tasks, deciding on an order for action and carrying out the plan
Eventually each group decided on an overall approach bearing in mind the time limit and available materials. Groups drew basic plans after a lot of oral planning and testing. Each group made their models, which varied enormously: some were triangular structures, others rectangular; some were made of wood, others of corriflute; some had winding gears, whereas others did not. Inevitably, unanticipated problems arose, which involved going through this same series of steps again, albeit briefly, applying the same imaginative and investigatory approach.

Evaluation and review
First and foremost, each group had to demonstrate that their model could 'rescue the doll', as this was the problem to be solved. They were then asked to identify their successes and problems and to evaluate both the final product and methods used. Finally, the class were asked to suggest improvements. If the children are not clear about the original purpose of the product and the criteria to be satisfied, the evaluation is likely to be very superficial. It is important to give time to the evaluative process as this reflection is significant in enabling children to become independent creative problem-solvers.

It does take time for children to build up all these skills. Therefore, initially you will need to take a leading role by using class or group discussions to help the children through the problem solving process. As the children become more experienced they can be increasingly left to work through their projects independently.

Mathematical investigations

When young children come to school their mathematics may reach high levels of independence as they sort objects into different categories and investigate how to fit shapes together in order to come to their own conclusions. As they grow older, this independent thinking should not give way to a formula-based method of learning that is based wholly on the assimilation of received mathematical knowledge and whose test of truth is 'this is the way I was told to do it' (Cockcroft 1982: para 321).

Mathematical investigations that promote independent thinking can be those of exploring mathematics within itself. For example, the children might be asked to investigate the possible patterns that can be made out of five squares, such as pentominoes, or ways of dividing a square into halves. Other investigations relate to exploring the range of possibilities for solving a problem, such as ways of making a fruit salad (as we have seen) or finding different layouts for a classroom or working on the wild garden project as in Cameo 2. As can be seen below, the stages of a mathematical investigation are similar to those in design and technology but the emphasis is on using systematic strategies for finding *patterns* in phenomena. Here the creativity tends to come towards the end of the investigation when the child sees the possible relationships and suggests ways of describing them.

Understanding the task

We need to make sure that the child has a clear grasp of the intended task, what they need to do and how it will be evaluated.

Exploring the possible outcome

Initially, the children may have a disorganized approach but, by encouraging them to look for patterns and relationships, they may come up with a logical way of tackling the problem.

Developing a systematic approach

This will involve finding a methodical approach to ensure all possibilities are covered and recording ideas so that the same ideas are not repeated.

Recognizing a pattern in order to predict unknown or untried cases

For example, if children are investigating triangular numbers or growth in a staircase, they should find the cubes needed to make the stairs produce the following pattern 1, 1+2, 1+2+3, 1+2+3+4, etc. They may be able to predict that the next number will be 1+2+3+4+5 and the ninth step will need 1+2+3+4+5+6+7+8+9 cubes. Of course, if their prediction is not correct they will need to rethink their ideas.

Coming up with an explanation or pattern or generalization

In the above example, able children may be able to make the generalization that the *nth* step will need $1+2+3+ \ldots +n$. They then need to decide whether it will always work. If not their ideas may again need to be revised.

Concluding and evaluating

The value of an investigation can be lost unless the outcome and process is discussed by and with the children. Such discussion should include talking about not only the successful approaches but also reflecting on the false trails so that the whole experience can enhance children's ability to tackle later investigations and to improve their thinking skills in general.

Making it all happen – classroom management and ethos

Although slightly different, investigations in science, design and technology and mathematics all enable children to be both creative and logical. To develop these thinking skills it is important that children have the opportunity to make decisions for themselves in a secure positive environment. This means that you will need to:

1 *Involve pupils in some of the decisions* regarding how they set up their investigations and in what they will make or do.
2 *Provide easy access to mathematical and scientific equipment, tools and a variety of materials* so that the children are able to make choices for themselves. Ideally the children should be able to see what is available. Being able to scan the possibilities can help to stimulate the children's ideas.
3 *Encouraging small group discussion* as articulating ideas and negotiating procedures promotes creativity and provides mutual support.
4 *Providing time for children to make, and correct, mistakes in a supportive atmosphere.* There is a temptation to provide only those materials that are directly needed and give such detailed instructions that the children are guaranteed a good 'end product'. However, this will *not* be in the children's long-term interests in developing their ideas and imagination. The timing of the teacher's intervention is very significant, as children need to learn from their mistakes but must not become excessively disheartened. If children become stuck after trying, questioning by the teacher or sharing other children's solutions are useful ways to assist without actually giving the solution, although the latter may be necessary sometimes.
5 *Valuing a range of outcomes.* If the children have the opportunity to respond in different ways, their final products will range in quality and creativity. Therefore, each piece of work should be assessed with respect to the ability of the child concerned.
6 *Accepting some noise and mess is inevitable.* Working and talking in groups may well be noisy but this does not necessarily mean that children are being disruptive. The teacher needs to monitor the activity and conversations to check that the children are on task (Linda Hargreaves

describes several ways this can be done in Chapter 3). Although there will inevitably be some mess, this can be managed if the children are aware of the responsibility of using materials economically and of cleaning their working areas after use. If this expectation is developed by adults from the nursery and reception years, the children gain by having increased responsibility. It also has the advantage of releasing teachers to concentrate on *teaching* rather than on organizing and preparing materials.

7 *Answering the unanswerable question!* If the teacher has tried out activities that are presented to the children, it is unlikely that many unanticipated questions will arise, even if a child tackles the investigation in an unexpected way. However, occasionally questions will crop up that the teacher cannot answer. Some can be investigated later or researched by looking in books. But if this fails, the teacher should feel able to admit to not knowing. This is itself a good model for the children, who also need to develop the confidence to acknowledge when they do not know and need help.

Conclusion

As teachers we often find that even very young children, or those iden- tified as having special educational needs (such as are described by Jenny Lansdell in Chapter 15), are able to surprise us with the variety and imaginative approaches to problems, once they understand that we want them to be independent. 'Standing back and watching groups of highly motivated children using their own initiative and resources to extend their experiences and capabilities significantly is an experience that few teachers forget in a hurry' (Shepard 1990). Do try to ensure that you, as a new teacher, have this experience yourself.

References and further reading

Cockcroft, W.H. (1982) *Mathematics Counts*. London: HMSO.

Fisher, R. (1990) *Teaching Children to Think*. Oxford: Basil Blackwell.

Garrard, W. (1986) *I don't know: Lets find out: Mathematical Investigations in the Primary School*. Ipswich: Suffolk County Council.

Harlen, W. and Jelly, S. (1989) *Developing Science in the Primary Classroom*. Edin- burgh: Oliver and Boyd.

Jarvis, T. (1991) *Children and Primary Science*. London: Cassell.

Jarvis, T. (1993) *Teaching Design and Technology in the Primary School*. London: Routledge.

Johnsey, R. (1986) *Problem Solving in School Science*. Hemel Hempstead: Macdonald Education.

Johnsey, R. (1990) *Design and Technology through Problem Solving*. Hemel Hempstead: Simon and Schuster.

Kincaid, D., Rapson, H. and Richards, R. (1983) *Science for Children with Learning Difficulties*. London: Macdonald Educational.

Osborne, J., Black, P., Smith, M. and Meadows, J. (1990) *Primary SPACE Project Research Report: Light*. Liverpool: Liverpool University Press.

Osborne, J., Black, P., Smith, M. and Meadows, J. (1991) *Primary SPACE Project Research Report: Electricity*. Liverpool: Liverpool University Press.

Osborne, R. and Feyberg, P. (1985) *Learning in Science: The Implications of Children's Science*. Auckland: Heinemann.

Shepard, T. (1990) *Education by Design: A Guide to Technology Across the Curriculum*. Cheltenham: Stanley Thornes.

8

Mummy's face is green! Developing thinking and skills in art

Gillian Robinson

Cameo 1

Head down, and in a world of his own Martin, a six-year-old, is
drawing a picture. He has set the scene and now he wants to
include some buried bones. Motivated by his knowledge and love
of dinosaurs he knows exactly what these fossil bones are going
to look like and where he is going to draw them. Crayon poised,
he is about to create a site for the first bone when the teacher
interrupts. The timetable tells her that the session has come to an
end. 'Pack away please' she instructs, 'We are now going to have
a story'. The fossil picture is removed and placed in a pile along
with all the other unfinished drawings. Martin is bewildered and
devastated.

Cameo 2

Emma, a 6-year-old, is given a range of crayons and introduced to a
reproduction of a picture by Paul Klée which includes a small figure
divided into coloured geometric shapes. Later she returns having
drawn a figure divided into all colours and shapes. 'Is this real?' she
says. This presents Jenny the teacher with a dilemma. If she says 'Yes'
and Emma knows it's not, then her answer is not appropriate and if
she says 'No' and Emma is at the symbolist stage, then this is equally
wrong for her. 'What do you think?' the teacher asks. Emma replies
'I know it is not real. I can draw real things if I want but drawings
don't always have to look real do they?'

Cameo 3

The rain streams down outside, it is a typical wet playtime. Ten-year-old Sanjit is completely absorbed covering a sheet of paper with one small drawing after another, creating to all appearances a pictorial storyboarding effect. The bell goes and instructions are given to pack away. Automatically all traces of activity during the playtime period disappear. The series of sketched drawings vanishes into the bin. Only their small creator knows its significance and potential.

Introduction

As teachers we know that a vital part of our responsibility is the provision of a curriculum that is broad and balanced (see Introduction to this book). Somewhere within this provision is children's entitlement to an art programme, which is rich and multifaceted, motivating and challenging, and which takes account of the individuality of each child. It involves somehow, in a busy timetable, finding ways of respecting the time that Martin in Cameo 1 needs to engage fully in the imaginary world that he has created through his drawing, being aware of the strategies that he will use in art in the developing process of understanding his world. Importantly, too, we need to be aware of the reasoning behind Emma's understanding of reality in Cameo 2. In Cameo 3 Sanjit's spontaneous ability to think and create solutions pictorially also needs to be understood and harnessed. How do busy teachers achieve this? This chapter seeks to share some possible solutions.

Making time for art

Let us return to Cameo 1 where six-year-old Martin is drawing his dinosaur picture. There are two important issues here. The first is that Martin needs time to finish his picture and the second is the importance of the teacher's awareness of the stage Martin is at and what motivates him to want to learn.

First, the issue of time. Art has survived being mistaken as a 'wet playtime' or 'Friday afternoon' activity and now, in a climate that focuses on core subjects, there is a danger that art could become marginalized. Unless we as teachers remain aware of the value of art in education, can justify it and build it firmly into the curriculum, art could once again be threatened with becoming an endangered species. It is likely that those who really care about art will still find ways of sustaining the arts curriculum, although in cases where art is not seen as so important, individuals might find in the current situation some excuses not to do it. One thing is certain, however, time for art is ultimately organized: a quality experience of art as a subject in its own right must be ensured irrespective of whether art additionally derives from, or is seen to support, other subjects. For the child, as for the adult, art is a fundamental and unique way of experiencing the world, which has its own particular discipline. Within this discipline, the value that the teacher puts on input and mutual respect is crucial.

One of the greatest challenges in a structured timetable, which quite rightly includes demands for the teaching of literacy and numeracy, is to accommodate the needs of other key disciplines enabling enough flexibility to allow time for completion of tasks in hand leading to meaningful learning. In Cameo 1 Martin is suddenly interrupted and the world he is creating from his imagination is brought to an abrupt end. Naturally he is bewildered and disappointed. So how do we generate time for his art? As teachers we need to look carefully and critically at our planning, trying to build in flexibility in art wherever possible so that children like Martin are given opportunities to follow enthusiasms and complete work. A few strategies for approaching this might include considering time allocation, planning cross-curricular links, realizing aims and objectives and the issue of progression.

Time allocation

Some schools manage scarce art time by the block timetabling of art rather than the drip feed experience of art every day. This might mean that half the term the focus is on art and for the other half on design technology. This is not ideal but if it can provide more continuous time it ultimately might make for a more coherent programme and greater opportunities to develop levels of understanding.

Planning meaningful cross-curricular links

Additionally, there is the possibility of art combining with, and stemming from, other subjects. For example, in the half-term where there is ostensibly no art there might well be art-related activity derived from time, on paper, dedicated to other subjects, for example Science and History. This can be very positive if the relationship between the two subjects and the relevance and meaning of the combination is understood by the teacher and by the child.

Reflecting on a realization of aims and objectives

Some of the most meaningful and rewarding work in art results from an engagement with the process where children have been involved in first-hand experience and with experimenting and investigating prior to making a piece of work (see section on sketchbooks and Chapter 7). There is a danger that lack of time for art can sometimes result in 'one off' or product-led work rather than process-generated pieces. The product-led approach can lead to superficial work and at its worst, because they are easily administered and quickly completed, to the use of work sheets. This is to be avoided as, the outcome can be lost excitement, and portray art as a passive activity. It is most important that instead, children are given opportunities in art where they are encouraged to research and explore and are given ownership of their work by being offered relevant choices.

Building process into the programme of work

It's easy to lose sight of process in a product-focused climate. Art co-ordinators need to look carefully and critically at planning (Clement *et al.* 1998). Time for experimentation and the use of sketchbooks should be built into the programme and there should be evidence of continuity and development, which is an important factor if the art experience is to have any meaning for the child (see Robinson 1995).

Art is personal

Now let us look at the stage Martin in Cameo 1 is at and what motivates him to learn in art. Martin is using drawing both as a means of under-standing the world and as a way to create his own imaginary world. By interrupting his activity, the teacher is taking him out of this imaginary world. In order to be sensitive to the role that art plays for Martin, it is important to understand not just the stage Martin is at now in his drawing and what motivates him, but to be aware of the likely pattern of his future development. Children create their own vocabulary of images and most children go through a recognizable pattern of stages (see, for example, Cox 1997). First they enjoy motor movement through playing and experimenting with materials and tools; then they move on to working symbolically, developing and practising 'schema' and imaginat-ive symbolic images. Martin is at that stage now. Nonetheless, with an increasing awareness of the way in which images are represented by the media, and of the expectations of parents and friends that images should be representational, as time goes on Martin, who is a symbolist at heart, will begin to feel that he needs to make images that are representational. Soon he will feel that he can't draw. This feeling will be partly to do with natural development but will also possibly be due to a misconception about the purposes of drawing rather than any inadequacy on Martin's part (see Beetlestone 1998). However, the stages through which children are thought to pass are not entirely discreet. Rather they tend to overlap or operate simultaneously and older children, and adults, continue to experiment and work symbolically throughout their lives. (For more detail consult Morgan 1993).

Looking back at Cameo 2, we can address the notion of Emma's view of reality. Here it is necessary to understand that even the experience of looking and seeing is not only about drawing observationally in a visually real way, for the image is seen through the eyes of each individual and therefore should be a personal response. Seen through Emma's eyes it will bear the marks of her experiences that shape her view of the world. Without this realization and understanding there can be a danger of opening children's eyes, without opening their minds and extending their vision to realize that new realities can be created through art (Duffy 1998). Clearly, even at this age Emma realizes that there are different ways of drawing. Therefore, we as teachers should not be afraid to teach children that there are different but equally acceptable ways of making art. If the child has a very narrow expectation of drawing it may well lead to the child feeling that they cannot draw.

Fortunately there are ways to overcome this problem:

1 use a sketchbook in which to experiment and explore. At times this might be used prior to the main activity. This places the emphasis on the process rather than on the end product and provides a particular challenge and an unthreatening exploration space where it is acceptable to 'make mistakes' and try things out, as we see later in the chapter;
2 explore a range of tools and materials, for example, pencil, charcoal, chalk pastel, oil pastel, paint, collage materials and clay;
3 challenge children to respond to natural and made stimuli;
4 offer sensory and tactile challenges that provide opportunities to make things in three dimensions using tactile and observational response to stimuli;
5 isolate small areas of things to look at by means of small view finders cut out of card or use magnifying glasses to emphasize and focus on specific detail;
6 introduce children to examples of drawing by artists using a range of media from different cultures;
7 use unusual tools. For example make your own brushes or use sharpened sticks dipped in ink (Morgan 1993).

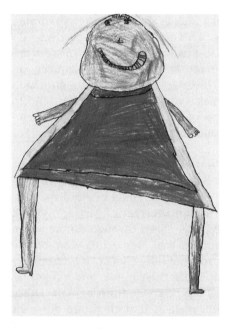

'My mummy's face is green'

Mummy's face is green

A parallel situation can be seen in painting. A wide range, variety and nuance of colour is also really exciting to a child. Young children first use colour freely and not representationally and colours are chosen for their appeal rather than for the way in which they might relate to reality.

For example, you might see several small children clad in yellow plastic aprons busily painting at easels. Jars of ready mixed brightly coloured paint, each supplied with its own brush, stand in a row. Jack reaches forward for the pink and paints a strip across the top of the page, the nearest colour to him is pale green and with this he paints a circle for a face. He is painting 'mummy'.

There is no doubt that if challenged Jack could tell you that the sky is blue and that mummy's face is pink, so why does he choose pink and green? The answer is that for this picture he is possibly choosing colours for other reasons than naturalistic representation. It could be because green is his favourite colour, because he intuitively knows that it will look 'right', or merely because it is the colour nearest to him and for the moment, if another child is reaching across, the most easily available. The solution is not to tell the child that they are wrong but rather to engage with him in conversations about colour and present opportunities for mixing colours as early as possible. Previous colour mixing experiments can then be built on and both imagination and first-hand experience used as starting points for colour work. Older children use general descriptive colours and, later on, they use colour for matching, but we still need to nurture and encourage imaginative approaches to a colour response.

Celebrate the process

How do we as teachers promote and nurture creative and imaginative approaches? Look again at cameo 3. Perhaps we should stop to think what might have happened if Sanjit's drawings had been made in a sketchbook and therefore stored, so that they could have been saved, talked about and possibly developed further.

One of the important ways in which we can encourage Sanjit's individual response, creativity and ideas is by giving him the skills, the stimulus and the opportunity to have something to say, and somewhere to record his experiences. This can happen in a number of ways. First, we can introduce him to the basic elements with which art is made – line, tone, colour, texture, pattern, form – essential to art in the same way that vocabulary is important in writing. Similarly it is important that he is introduced to a range of materials and techniques in art. For Sanjit, sketchbooks are an ideal place in which to explore the elements of art and sketchbooks can provide a space in which experimentations with techniques can be stored and revisited.

Ultimately, art education is not just about the teaching of skills. Along with the development of skills and hand control there is also a need for the development of feeling and response. Sketchbooks and notebooks are the ideal tool for this, offering a forum for feeding and developing ideas. Those of us who have already established them as a way of working will know how significant they can be in generating a situation where one thing leads to another, building up a sequence of work. Because they focus on and store processes they are also an effective way of generating creative thinking. Sketchbooks enable children to see the pattern of their thinking as it emerges and are therefore a forum for promoting thinking skills and metacognition. Sketchbook content might include drawing and annotation, graphic tools, paint, collage, experimentation with materials, brainstorming of ideas, observational drawing, recording of a technique (Robinson 1995).

We have seen that sketchbooks are a valuable tool to enable children to engage in meaningful art experiences and develop their creativity but as teachers what else do we need to offer? In this context, the importance of first-hand experience, which promotes real engagement, cannot be emphasized enough. Art concerns working with ideas and Martin, Emma and Sanjit all have something to say. We have seen that sometimes ideas come through the imagination or an experience at home but additionally they may come from stimulating experiences inside the classroom and on trips outside school. Without these starting points and meaningful experiences children sometimes have very little to say and their work as a consequence can be empty and without motivation or innovation.

The world needs divergent thinkers and art has the capacity to challenge individuals and create thinking minds if the opportunities are there to question, experiment, explore and reflect. One of the hallmarks of art is that it promotes divergence, encourages children to ask questions and to look for different ways of developing ideas, to explore and experiment. In many other subjects we are encouraging children to search for 'right' answers. Art above all subjects nourishes the unconventional and nurtures the unexpected by:

- respecting children's imagination;
- developing their creativity;
- encouraging adventurous and lateral thinking;
- recognizing the validity of a personal response.

Another way of giving children something to say is through challenges in three dimensions. Martin, Emma and Sanjit understand the three-dimensional world before the two-dimensional one. They enjoy touching, building and squeezing malleable materials. It follows that they should have many experiences in touching, looking at and naming forms from an early age. Even if there is no available working kiln, it is possible to give them opportunities to make things in clay that do not necessarily need to be fired. Playing with clay is important and hands are the best possible tools. Direct modelling is also important. Techniques can be learned also of making hollow forms and later slab pots and coil pots. If your school does have a kiln, do use it taking all the necessary safety precautions, of course. Then at a later stage there can be opportunities to decorate surfaces using brush on glazes, slip or oxides. The added benefit is that three-dimensional work naturally links to other curriculum subjects particularly design technology. Linked in with science, opportunities can also be taken to work with natural materials outside. Clay work too, for example reliefs and small pots, can sometimes be woven in with history topics such as the Greeks and Romans.

Artists' work in the classroom

Additionally, we can introduce Martin, Emma and Sanjit as young artists to the multifaceted world of artists and craftspeople. One of the objectives for doing this is to exemplify the variety of responses that art activity fosters, and it is vital to offer as wide a selection of images as possible from different periods and cultures and created in different ways using a range of materials. In this way we open up their minds to new freedom and new possibilities in art. This has particular relevance for any child who has reached the stage where they feel that they can't draw, because no two artists have the same vision or make the same image in response to an idea or a stimulus. By observing this children can learn that there is no 'right way to draw', just a range of different ways of looking and responding.

However, there is a caveat. If all that Martin, Emma and Sanjit see is the Van Gogh or Monet, then their experience will be severely limited, so a wide range of examples should be made available. These do not have to involve huge expense. Postcards can be collected and stored in a photo album, many shops now sell remaindered art books at reasonable prices, out of date 'art' calendars can be used and pictures can be downloaded and printed from the Internet.

Using art and artefacts in the classroom, or indeed in a gallery does have some problems. Teachers may not be artists or experts but it is nevertheless necessary to get the facts right. Our knowledge about art must be solid before we discuss an artist or a particular painting with the children. This does not mean, however, that we necessarily need to tell children these facts. Sometimes far more learning takes place if the children are able to talk freely and openly to us about what they see in front of them, offering their own perceptions and ideas. We as teachers can do the same!

Adults seem to have more problems with abstract art than do children. It is unlikely that Martin, Emma and Sanjit will understand fully the

Encourage children to ask questions to look for different ways of developing ideas

process by which the artist arrived at an abstract painting or, indeed, the context in which the abstraction occurred. However, this does not prevent the picture from becoming a good starting point for the exploration of colour and shape and the ways in which they can create mood and affect feelings. Very young children, if not over-directed into pictorial forms too soon, naturally create in abstract forms and not representational shapes and colour.

It is important for Martin, Emma and Sanjit to realize that to dislike a work of art is as valid as to like it. After all most of us know clearly what we like and don't like! The important thing is for them to be able to say why. It is necessary that our questioning skills allow children to have an opportunity to offer their own opinions when they engage with a painting or artefact and to question their own preferences. This requires an atmosphere of freedom and trust so that each child feels that his or her opinion, however different, is welcomed and respected. The main purpose is to extend children's experience and offer choice to enable them to understand that there are many ways of responding and making art forms.

Assessment

As art involves personal response, there is no doubt that the issue of assessment in art can be full of dilemmas and questions concerning what can be assessed, how it can be identified and the means by which it can be appropriately assessed. However, evidence of learning in art comes in many ways and there are very powerful means of assessment. Willingness to experiment, competence with new techniques and the development of ideas can all be assessed, especially when examining a sequence of children's work. Collecting selections of children's work or analysing the sequence of work in their sketchbooks offers two immediately accessible contexts. It is crucial to note that, while looking at both the successful and the unsuccessful to see where the problems lie, we always view whatever the child has produced for its positive qualities. One way to achieve a productive class discussion about a challenge and to encourage children to look for positive qualities in each other's work is through a 'pavement show'. This happens when, immediately after the lesson or even during the session, while the objectives are still fresh in people's minds, the children's work is laid out on a large surface, for example desks or the floor. Questions can then be asked related to the learning objectives, for example 'Who can point to a picture where there is colour mixing . . . and/or . . . imaginative use of collage'. Of course children's work should be respected and the questions should always be couched in positive terms to promote confidence and self-esteem.

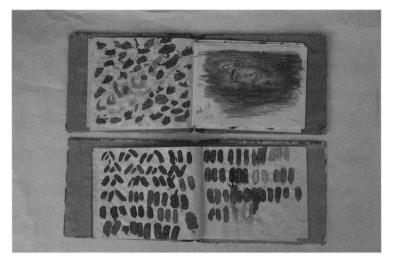

Analysing the sequence of work in children's sketchbooks is a powerful means of assessment

Consider the following assessment opportunities:

- consulting with children about selecting work for a record folder in art;
- talking to individual children while they are working and after they have finished about what they have done, why they did it that way and what they might do next;
- collecting selections of children's work or looking at the work in their sketchbooks in order to be able to observe and discuss the process and to identify the thinking skills that have been used;
- discussing outcomes with the class at the end of an activity to draw out teaching points and lesson objectives;
- displaying work and celebrating achievement.

Other opportunities are suggested in section which would link well to the art curriculum.

Display

From the minute we walk into a school it is possible to see if it is alive if what is displayed shows real exploration and celebration of learning. It is important that what is mounted on the wall represents what children have been working on and thinking about. Drapes and a potted plant, 'picture of the week' mounted in a crinkly gold paper frame is an all too familiar sight in the foyer of a primary school. But what is the display communicating? At its most trivial, display can be merely 'wallpaper'.

Think instead, how stimulating it is for the children, other members of staff and parents alike to see children's written work, painting, computer work, model making, maths books and photographs, all as part of the display. Think about the importance of process and the thinking skills that are involved. It raises the interest level and reflects the whole child's learning experience. It extends rather than narrows.

Unfortunately, many schools will have a policy of displaying only finished results. The stimulus or starting point, the process of learning, the thinking and questioning that went into achieving the displayed items is seldom visible. This needs redressing. It is vital for us to realize that the finished result is only a part of the working process. There should be evidence of starting points and stimulus. There is an excellent example in a project that involved observational drawing of a mother and child where initially the children explored what charcoal would do (Morgan and Robinson 1997). It was not scribble: it was exploration. The attempts were all put on the wall and underneath the teacher wrote 'We are exploring the marks which these tools will make'. This also demonstrates how important it is to annotate displays in order to explain the context. Sometimes small flaps with hidden questions can make the display more interactive and encourage the child to be more involved in, and more aware of, the display.

It is also good for children like Martin, Emma and Sanjit to know why their work is being displayed on the walls. At its best, display has to be about celebration and communication. Display speaks volumes and when it shows not only the product but, through draft material and annotation, the process by which it was achieved, it can be a means of explaining to the child and to a parent or casual visitor the nature and the quality of the learning that is occurring in school.

Display is cross-curricular and does not have to be limited to one or even two subject disciplines. Presentation and display are pertinent to all areas of the curriculum. For example, shape lends itself to maths, and form, structure and growth to science. It is also effective sometimes to combine subjects in one display. Annotation should be used to make meaningful connections and teaching points.

Conclusion

We have seen that making time for art in a way that offers a meaningful experience involves knowledge of children's development and what motivates them. We have also explored why in a particular painting 'Mummy's face is green' and why we need to be sensitive to the fact that what is perceived by the child to be 'reality' may not always match our own expectations and perceptions. Finally, through Cameo 3, we have explored the reasons why it is important to value the process in art as well as the product.

What are the main questions that readers, as new teachers, might need to address? Essentially:

1 Can we positively say that what we offer children like Martin, Emma and Sanjit as an art experience is one that spans and informs the whole curriculum and at the same time is a way of learning in its own right?
2 Do we offer a stimulating environment? Creating a school resource for example, shells, stones, bones, mechanical parts, toys, models, bringing exciting artefacts into the classroom, items from unusual places, a case full of exciting articles, taking children into the local environment, if possible organizing informative and stimulating school trips, working from word stimuli – descriptions, poems, stories.
3 Do we provide an art experience that has a capacity to address visual and sensory learning and utilizes both the intuitive and logical operations of the brain? Do we provide experiences that are a means of working and thinking other than in words and are no less intellectual for that? Do we provide experiences that:
   • embrace feeling and personal expression in common with the other arts that are a unique way of observing, imagining, interpreting, recording and making sense of the world?;
   • challenge children to be aware of process as well as product?;
   • provide a forum in which to think creatively and divergently?;
   • form valuable partnerships with other areas of the curriculum?

Do we offer a really stimulating environment?

To ensure that our children enjoy and maximize opportunities in art we, as teachers, should consider carefully the time we allow for art, how we structure that time and what kind of experience we are offering. A sound art education can be offered if the points mentioned above are taken into consideration. There can be no way round direct practical involvement and the build up of personal confidence.

References and further reading

Bettlestone, F. (1998) *Creative Children: Imaginative Teaching.* Buckingham: Open University Press.

Calloway, G. (2000) *Improving Teaching and Learning in the Arts.* London: Falmer Press.

Clement, R., Piotrowski, J. and Roberts, I. (1998) *Co-ordinating Art Across the Primary School.* London: Falmer Press.

Cox, M. (1997) *Drawings of People by the Under-5s.* London: Falmer Press.

Duffy, B. (1998) *Supporting Creativity and Imagination in the Early Years.* Buckingham: Open University Press.

Kenyon, P. (1999) *Creative Development.* Leamington Spa: Scholastic.

Matthews, J. (1994) *Helping Children to Draw and Paint in Early Childhood.* London: Hodder and Stoughton.

Morgan, M. and Robinson, G. (1997) *Developing Art Experience 4–13.* Oxford: Nash Pollock.

Morgan, M. (1993) *Art in Practice.* Oxford: Nash Pollock.

Morgan, M. (1989) *Art 4–11: Art in the Early Years of Schooling* (2nd edn). Oxford: Blackwells.

Robinson, G. (1995) *Sketchbooks: Explore and Store.* London: Hodder and Stoughton.

9

Telling the whole story: developing children's oral skills and imagination within the literacy hour

Jane Hislam

The child who has nothing to talk about has nothing to write about and the whole experience of hearing stories, using a wide range of talking and listening skills, can clearly stimulate the imagination and promote creative speech and writing as well as providing sheer enjoyment.

(Weir 2000: 66)

Cameo 1

Craig sat with his mouth wide open and his eyes wider still. When the teacher finished telling the story there was a small silence and then Craig drew in his breath and asked: 'How did you *do* that?'

Teacher: Do what?
Craig: Say it without a book. Where did it come from?
Teacher: Where do you think it came from?
Craig: From out your head?

Cameo 2

Joe, aged 4 years, is playing alone in his sandpit at home with a pile of bricks, some Play People, an upturned wastepaper basket and a toy fire engine with a ladder. The game is about a wolf who wants to eat people, so the people decide to put him on the roof until he can be trusted to come down. Joe narrates as he plays: 'We can get rid of him. How will we get him down? They pushed the button and the ladder lowered. Then out came the hose, right through the holes. He shouted I promise I promise I will not eat anyone. But the people would not listen. They put their fingers over their ears. Right if you promise never to eat anyone we will let you down. They heard the engine coming neee-naaa-neee-naaa-neee-naaa.'

Cameo 3
A group of Year 2 children is part retelling, part re-enacting, the story of 'The Greedy Goat'. Their teacher had previously told them a version of the story, and then subsequently read it to them from a big book, earlier in the week. The children use a variety of props including a bowl, an apron, and hats for the different animals. In group time, each group takes it in turn to retell the story in their own way with the support of the ancillary teacher, and then at the end of the literacy hour they act it out for the rest of the class in the plenary and talk about the story. On this occasion, the activity leads into a written version of the story, and the teacher comments on how the quality of the stories is noticeably better than usual.

Introduction

Many teachers, when first retelling stories to a class, remark on the fact that children expect stories to come from books and are surprised when they do not. This is understandable since, in children's experiences, the word 'story' is often closely related to the printed word.

In the first of the cameos above there was no book and the children were at first mystified and then intrigued. Previously, whenever teachers told them to gather round for a story, a book appeared. In these situations the teacher acts as mediator for the writer who is the creator of the story. The writer-storyteller is absent, almost invariably an adult and probably regarded as someone with special and creative gifts.

In the second cameo, however, Joe shows that in play even the youngest children are capable of producing imaginative commentaries, in themselves a kind of oral story. His narratives form part of an imaginary world, which is already rich with images from books, television and his own experiences. His own story making has almost certainly been assisted by the many stories he has been read and told (Wells 1986).

Some children enter school with wide experience of imaginative play. They will have heard stories told and read aloud and watched stories in visual forms. For others, these experiences may have been limited. In the third cameo above, the children's classroom teacher weaves oral story and dramatic re-enactments into the literacy hour, knowing that this is likely to enhance the pupils' understanding and ability to produce written story. She recognizes that not all pupils will be able to tell the stories they have heard without help from her and will need opportunities to rehearse in a variety of oral, visual and often physical forms.

Children need opportunities to experience and orally rehearse narratives

In this chapter I look at ways to develop children's capacity to use language imaginatively through storytelling, play and literature. I want to suggest that for the imagination to be given space to grow in the classroom it is important to create a context in which there is time to talk, to share stories and poetry, to play with language and for pupils to be listened to with attention and interest (Gill Robinson makes similar points about art teaching in the previous chapter).

The teacher's role as model in this process needs to be given particular attention. If children are to be encouraged to take up linguistic challenges, teachers have to show them the way by sharing their own pleasure in using language as readers, writers and talkers. In order to use their imaginations to begin to construct stories for themselves, both as oral and written texts, children need opportunities to experience and orally rehearse narratives in a variety of forms. What Helen Bromley terms 'narrative talk' (2001) is fundamental to children being able to make sense of stories for themselves, both in their own lives and in literary versions.

The power of the oral story

When children hear stories told, as opposed to read aloud from the printed page, and when they recreate and retell stories themselves, they are able to experience stories 'as a whole' in a way that more fully engages their imaginations. This is an approach that is needed more than ever in order to counter-balance an often fragmented experience of literature through the use of short extracts lifted from whole texts. (This is particularly likely to occur at KS2 in the literacy hour.) When children hear 'the whole story' they are given opportunities to reflect on, interpret and recreate the story experience for themselves. This allows children to access printed texts at a deeper level. Strong oral and visual experiences can offer a better sense of engagement with the thoughts and feelings underlying the story.

As teachers gain confidence in telling stories, they can begin to make explicit for children the particular pleasures involved, sharing with them the skills needed to become storytellers themselves. The essential message for children is that people tell stories because they want others to listen and because the story itself is enjoyable or interesting enough to be heard. This message can give a purpose to both oral storytelling, and also to writing, because it emphasizes the fact that stories are designed to get a response. Funny stories are meant to make you laugh. Sad ones may make you cry. The teller or the writer is in direct communication with their audience. The purpose is clear. This very simple message about the communicative nature of story can so often be missing in a classroom that is heavily focused on making judgements based on accuracy of presentation, spelling and grammar (however important these may also be).

Throughout this chapter practical examples are given of working with oral story at Key Stages 1 and 2. Approaches are described that rely on teachers acting as storytelling models, but which also allow children to develop their own skills as storytellers. At the same time, these approaches enable teachers and pupils to engage fully with the range requirements of the NLS.

The impact of the literacy hour

Making speaking and listening, including oral story, central to the literacy hour, has presented a challenge for teachers. Since the introduction of the National Literacy Strategy (NLS) Framework of Teaching Objectives (DfEE 1998), concerns have been voiced that, paradoxically, the framework may have restricted the opportunities for pupils to hear and work with stories in ways that allow them to experience the story as a whole. Grugeon and co-workers (1998) report that activities like oral storytelling may have been increasingly squeezed out by the perceived restrictions imposed by the literacy hour. Student teachers working with her to develop their own and pupils' oral storytelling skills commented on some of the practical difficulties they experienced in the classroom: 'It was difficult to make oral storytelling an important part of the curriculum because my teacher believed the proper time for stories was the last session in the afternoon, which lasted for ten minutes' (Grugeon *et al.* 1998: 52).

Teachers, too, have worried about the extent to which the literacy hour has decreased opportunities for the development of oral work alongside the study of texts. In particular, they have raised issues related to the lack of attention to oracy within the Framework of Teaching Objectives, as well as to the lack of flexibility afforded by the prescriptive structure of the hour. The term text has almost exclusively been interpreted as the printed word. What has often been lacking is a holistic experience of story, offering pupils diverse and personally meaningful ways of accessing stories. The emphasis on the study of sentence construction, words and parts of words, important though these are, may have detracted from a genuine engagement of senses, thoughts and emotions with the text as a whole.

At KS2, in particular, there have been concerns that pupils may rarely experience the 'whole story'. The use of extracts to illustrate teaching points gives pupils a fragmented experience of texts where opportunities to respond to the story as a whole become limited. The more flexible approach now being widely advocated, allows teachers to think more in terms of both oral and written texts, and the connections between them. This is made explicit in the First Steps *Oral Language: Resource Book* (Raison 1997), where 'narratives are produced in both oral and written contexts'. This practical set of teaching and assessment materials dedicates an entire chapter to developing children's own experience of oral storytelling through a variety of approaches and techniques including:

- teachers modelling stories;
- role playing;
- story reconstruction;
- circle stories.

A way forward

Grugeon is only one of a number of commentators who have argued strongly for the place of storytelling and drama within the literacy hour (Corden 2000; Grugeon and Gardner 2000; Toye and Prendiville 2000). She demonstrates that 'storytelling is more securely embedded in the curriculum' since the introduction of the NLS and the revised English NC. The NLS Framework, despite the fact that explicit mention of speaking and listening is sparse, places emphasis both on pupils' knowledge and experience of stories, and on their ability to 're-enact, re-tell to others, recount . . . in sequence'. Many of the objectives, in particular in Years 1, 2, 3 and 5 imply the need for children to hear and tell stories orally.

The QCA document *Teaching Speaking and Listening in Key Stages 1 and 2* (1999) strengthens the links between children's experiences of the range of literature and opportunities to work with, and extend, oral language. It emphasizes, for example, how oral storytelling can enhance literacy understanding and knowledge in all children, including those whose reading and writing skills are not yet well developed. In Year 2: term 2, practical classroom activities are suggested which allow the teacher to focus on the skills of the 'good storyteller'. This unit of work, while geared primarily to speaking for different audiences, meets NLS range requirements (traditional stories with patterned language) and illustrates a programme for developing an understanding of the features of effective oral storytelling.

The experience of listening to an oral story

The experience of listening to a story told, as opposed to read, can be qualitatively different. Craig's teacher (cameo 1) described him as 'not easily motivated'. When she was reading from a text, Craig would often work his way outwards from the group of children towards the edge of the carpet where he proceeded to see how many pencils he could snap or how quickly he could destroy Christopher's 'best ever' model. But, on this occasion, Craig sat absolutely still and 'spell-bound'. It seemed that, for those few minutes, he had entered the world of the story itself. The story he had heard the teacher tell was 'Sapsorrow' (a version of Cinderella). Craig was hooked from the moment the teacher, with no book in sight, began: 'There was once a king whose wife had died. He had three daughters. Two were bad. One was good.'

What is more, Craig was able to hold the story so clearly in his mind that, when several days later, he was invited to retell a story of his own choice, he picked this one. With an uncharacteristic degree of concentration, he elaborated on the story using elements of his own. He also talked about the story with confidence to his teacher and then to his 'talk partner'. He even told the story at home.

Why this story had such an impact on Craig, it is impossible to know. The story experience is highly personal and individual. Perhaps traditional folk and fairy stories have lasted so long precisely because they engage our imaginations and emotions so powerfully. Reading a story aloud can also create a powerful imaginative experience, but the fact that this story was told rather than read seems to have played an important part in its effect on the listener. For tellers, too, as initial teacher trainees with whom I have worked report, the experience is distinctively different from that of reading from the printed page. They have commented to me that they feel 'a much more direct connection with the pupils'; that 'eye contact and body language' create a sense of immediacy and tension, which brings the story alive; that they have experienced the power of holding the 'audience in the palm of their hands'.

Story sources and story links

Craig was impressed that the story just seemed to come from nowhere, 'from out your head'. In reality, of course, the particular retelling of this story, while personal and unique in that moment, was far from the work of an individual imagination. The teacher acknowledged and talked explicitly to the children about how her version of the story stood along-side countless others across time and through countries. The teacher read and told them other stories with similar themes and familiar objects – rings, shoes, rags to riches, joy to sorrow and back again. She brought in books and told more stories so that the children began to appreciate that there are versions of the Cinderella story in oral and written forms right around the world.

In Years 1, 2, 3 and 5 pupils are required to work with traditional tales. There are now many wonderful collections drawn from world literature. These provide a rich resource from which teachers can select stories to read, tell, compare and discuss. A Year 3 teacher with whom I recently spoke, was concerned that many pupils in his class (especially the boys) would be unlikely to show enthusiasm for the classic fairytales. It is perhaps significant that Craig and his classmates were drawn into a story without prejudice, little thinking at first that they were hearing an alternative version of Cinderella, a story they might well equate with Easy Read or Disney versions. In selecting stories to tell, it should always be a key concern that both teacher and pupil can engage imaginatively and emotionally with the story, that the story 'speaks' to them.

The role of the imagination

These moments, when the story 'speaks' to the listeners, give shared pleasure to children and adults alike. The storyteller and the listeners act together to create the story. For each participant the story takes shape in a unique way. Barton (1991) talks about the active involvement of the listeners. It is at these times that we are reminded of the power we hold as teacher-storytellers. It is essential not only that we choose our stories with care but also that we encourage children to feel actively involved in the imaginative process.

When children listen to a story with eyes wide open, they experience the fact that language has the power to make the impossible happen.

Student teachers who are prepared to take the risk and tell a story without the aid of a book are nearly always richly rewarded. If there are problems, usually a glimpse of the special relationship that storyteller and listeners enjoy is enough to prompt a further attempt.

Stories from books, pictures and oral sources can provide daily enrichment for the imaginations. They need to be chosen for the quality of the story itself. There has always been a temptation to 'exploit' a story thus overlooking its central themes or 'emotional core'. The need to find examples of texts for the literacy hour in order to 'deliver' text, sentence and word objectives has increased this risk.

Teacher as model

There are countless practical ways in which teachers can create a positive learning model for young children. First and foremost, they can make apparent their own pleasure in the written and spoken word and talk to children about the images that language creates. They can share in a wide variety of imaginative genres, through reading aloud, storytelling, drama and language play.

A first step is to rekindle that freshness of enthusiasm in the adult teacher that children experience when they first encounter stories and poems that are meaningful for them. This may involve recalling childhood experiences, or if these were less than positive, discovering them for the first time. Many student teachers have discovered their delight in stories quite late in life! Practical steps towards this could include frequenting local libraries and children's bookshops. Best of all, would be to take opportunities to listen to some of the professional storytellers who now frequently appear in theatres and story clubs.

Above all, children need opportunities to hear their teachers model the telling of stories with enthusiasm and commitment. This means choosing a story you like. Betty Rosen (1988) gives excellent advice in her book about oral storytelling *And None of it was Nonsense*. She explains that in preparing to tell a story you should:

- find a story you like massively; a story your imagination will relish, cherish and nourish.
- get all the facts and details together, even those you will later reject: there's a lot of lesson preparation involved, although, with luck, your pupils will never guess!
- decide what you are going to include, note it down in sequence and, in the process, consider particularly carefully how you are going to begin.
- visualize the start precisely; by this I mean allow the opening situation to occupy – take over – your imagination. This will go a long way

towards ensuring that you will speak with your own voice a story that has become your own.

Being a positive model for pupils means recognizing and acknowledging that the imagination is not a commodity which some children lack but a human quality that we all possess which can be strengthened and enriched.

Storytelling can engage children's minds and create a language context for imaginative talk and play. It provides a 'scaffold' for children to learn about language forms, structures and conventions. They will be able to internalize these features through teacher modelling, well beyond what they could generate for themselves in their own writing. In this respect, storytelling is closer to drama than to reading aloud, providing a whole context and a lived experience of the way the story works.

Storytelling in the classroom

Storytelling is probably the most comfortable and accessible way of promoting meaningful talk in the classroom. Apart from anything else, it is cheap on resources, highly flexible and can take place practically anywhere. Key features of storytelling are:

- it is a personal and individual act of imagination;
- it is essentially social and participative;
- it works for all age groups.

Storytelling can be particularly valuable for children for whom English is an additional language. The universal qualities of stories mean that cultural traditions from home and school can be brought together on an equal basis. Storytelling provides a natural context for the use of home languages. Stories with repeating words, phrases and actions, with call and response patterns, and where learners can actively participate can be especially beneficial for young children. Teachers can modify their approach to suit their audience giving support to pupils for whom English is an additional language. The universal images and themes of traditional tales from around the world are particularly well suited to bilingual pupils. In a section entitled 'Handing down the magic in Story', Gregory (1996) describes the powerful nature of story to provide a semantic, syntactic and lexical set of clues which scaffold the bilingual learner in particular. In fact, storytelling can provide this helpful framework for all pupils.

Stories immediately provide a shared and usually pleasurable experience, allowing pupils to talk in a non-threatening way about aspects of their own lives. The context of the storytelling should enable everyone's contribution to be acceptable. If teachers resist a prescriptive approach and are open to personal responses, children will be more likely to make a story their own, thinking about it, discussing it and picturing it in their own minds.

Practical examples of storytelling activities

In both key stages storytelling has a strong part to play in literacy learning. Apart from instances, such as those cited above, where it is an obvious means of meeting NLS and NC requirements, its strength lies in enabling pupils to experience the central communicative role of story. If explicit links are made between this process and that of creating a story in written and/or visual form (pointing out differences as well as similarities), pupils are likely to transfer this experience as they develop a stronger and more confident 'voice' in writing (see the following chapter).

Once it has been acknowledged that oral story has a legitimate place within the literacy hour the possibilities become endless. The main value of oral storytelling is that it provides a context for the story to be a focus for learning, both within and outside the literacy hour. For example, at the beginning of a piece of work on traditional tales, and in the context of shared work, the teacher can provide an initial whole-class experience of the story that is entirely oral – no written text in sight!

The Snowman

In the literacy hour a teacher of Year 2 pupils told an oral story about a little boy and a snowman that he built in the garden (based on the Raymond Briggs' book without words). Many children recognized the story having seen it on the television at Christmas and were spellbound by it, despite (in her words) 'a noisy open plan area'. In describing the work she did with her pupils she felt it to be important that it had also recently snowed, and stressed the need to link stories of all kinds with the pupils' own experience.

Using ideas taken from Bromley's work on storyboxes (2000), the teacher introduced a storybox to her pupils which they used to make up their own stories. The box was made from a shoebox covered with snowman wrapping paper and constructed so that one side flapped down to reveal an arena for the story to take place. In the shoe box were: cotton wool, a plastic snowman, two Play People figures, a cardboard cut-out house, a Father Christmas and a motorbike. Two children in particular, she felt, had need of these props to help them develop a storyline, which was then tape-recorded and later transcribed. In essence, she was providing them with the kind of context for narrative imagining that Joe (Cameo 1) provided for himself in his home play. Other pupils were able to write stories in guided writing time with different kinds of scaffolding from the teacher. The strong visual and oral experiences provided prior to writing profoundly affected, in this teacher's view, the quality of written response for all children.

This series of activities focused on the textual aspects of the story and its structure and narrative elements. But storytelling can also be a way into language activities related to vocabulary, to the ways words work in sentences and how language hangs together. In other words, pupils' attention can be drawn in a meaningful way to sentence and word level objectives, and more importantly perhaps, they can be encouraged to make their own language choices as they experiment with storytelling.

Willow pattern plate story

For example, in preparing to tell a story such as the willow pattern plate story in Year 3, pupils can be asked to do a visualization exercise that requires them to describe the garden in which the pagoda is set. They can explore the way adjectives work through 'experimenting', orally, with 'deleting and substituting adjectives and noting effect on meaning'. This can lead into a shared or guided writing activity, if appropriate, or might be an entirely oral activity linked to a spoken presentation. Story-telling can also link with work going on outside of the context of the literacy hour.

The Fire of London

In this example, the teacher linked her storytelling work to a history project. The first experience of the story came from her oral account of a family living in London at the time of the Great Fire. This was supported with pictures and artefacts to create a sense of the period. At a later point in the week, she set up a storytelling game where the pupils sat in a circle, and in turn were invited to contribute a few words or sentences to build up a visual picture just prior to the event described. The teacher modelled the first few sentences:

> In a street in London, a woman stood with a basket of flowers.
> Beside her a small child played in the gutter.

This activity allows pupils to build up a visual picture of the setting of the story, crucial when beginning to give the story imaginative life for both storytelling and writing. The children then retold the whole story in the circle using a pebble to pass from one to the other so that each would get a turn if they wished.

This type of storytelling makes it clear that there is no 'correct' version of the story that will unfold as a collaborative and joint construction.

This can be a creative releasing experience for pupils, who are both supported through the shared telling, but also 'allowed' to elaborate, add and refine ideas in their own individual ways. The teacher took this creative and individual approach further by asking pupils to act parts of the story before she finally moved into guided writing, which focused on diary entries for the day of the Fire of London.

The story game

This game would work very well in the context of group work, and following work on stories in whole-class sessions. This board game, which was devised and used by a student teacher in her final placement, aimed to give pupils practice at structuring questions and statements; give them experience of making up and retelling stories and help them listen and respond to each other. The game is set out as a track in a fairytale type setting (see illustration). The track is made up of squares with either speech marks, question marks or a golden book on them. There is a bag that contains small objects, such as a ring, a mermaid, a clock (dependent on the stories the children have heard). To play the game the children choose a traveller figure for their game piece and move it along the track by throwing a dice. If they land on speech marks they take an object out of the bag and have to make a statement about it. If they land on a question mark, they take an object out of the bag and make up a question about it to ask one of the other players. If they land on a golden book, they have to take two objects out of the bag and start to make up a story that involves those objects. This story is then continued by the other game players as they take out objects.

The student teacher used this game with Year 2 pupils in an inner-city school. Initially, she found that they struggled to frame questions and statements and to distinguish between the two. (This is in fact nowhere near as straightforward as it might appear, even for more experienced language users!) But as they played the game they became increasingly skilled at working out what sort of sentence structure was required because of the need for particular responses from the other players.

The stories the pupils told were (in the student's words) 'fairly pedestrian at first' and the pupils were disinclined to use 'fantastic ideas', preferring instead 'safer, more imaginable options'. They were very excited, however, by the freedom the game gave them to make up the story in their own way, and to include 'silly bits'! They listened well to each other's part of the story, although until they got used to the game, they were 'shy at getting started on their own part'. The student commented that 'their confidence increased noticeably even within the course of one game'.

Storytelling activities such as these, especially if used in a sustained and progressive way across year groups can build pupils' confidence to

As the children played the game, they became increasingly and noticeably more skilled at working out sentence structures

try out their own ideas, to be prepared to offer them in shared contexts, and finally to use ideas in their own independent writing.

What if . . . ?

This storytelling activity was used with a group of Year 3 pupils, as part of a whole raft of ideas working from personal storytelling out into flight of fantasy. (This is a step that many children – see above – are reluctant to take. It is worth pointing out to them that the way many writers work is to take events, characters or settings from their own personal experience and then imagine something unusual, strange or unbelievable on the basis of that.)

The teacher had been talking about the local geography of their town. The pupils orally rehearsed with her how the school related to other key places in the locality. Then, on another occasion she began the story:

What if . . . the carpet they were sitting on was a magic carpet and carried them out of the classroom, above the school, hovered over Sainsbury's, began to glide across the town . . .

She took the main narrative role herself at first, stopping at points in the story where the children could offer decisions about characters, places and events. It was therefore quite distinctly a piece of storytelling and not drama or role-play, since the narrative voice remained an essential feature of the story throughout.

The carpet took them over the land to the coast and Skegness; across the sea (some interesting insights along the way about the children's geographical understanding!) and at last to a giant's castle where they were deposited at the door. There was a feeling of high expectation about what was behind that door even though not a single person, at that point, appeared to have decided on what it might be. The story had taken on a life and direction of its own, and seemed almost tangibly to fill the circle of space between the children. One of the children became rather agitated in fact and the teacher decided to use her authority as main narrator to inject lightness and humour into her voice and so reduce the suspense a tone or two.

Not one child asked how it could be that everyone fitted on the carpet, or expressed any scepticism about the storyline or about the process of creating the story itself. Their story, like the magic carpet, had succeeded for those few moments in transporting them to other places and times in their imaginations.

Story as improvization

As the examples above illustrate, oral storytelling is to a large extent an improvizational and playful activity and draws on language that can be symbolic as well as literal. Certainly the language of story often attempts to create visual imagery in the listeners' minds.

In order to develop this sense of language as playful, evocative and visual, it is worth gathering together resources that give examples of:

- rhymes;
- games;
- songs;
- metaphors and similes;
- exaggerations – tall stories;
- jokes;
- riddles;
- proverbs;
- adverts.

Children need to experience a wide range of texts, both oral and written. As they learn more about the world and have the chance to play with its possibilities through storytelling and imaginative play, they will increasingly be able to express themselves and manipulate language in imaginative ways, given opportunities and encouragement to do so by the adults around them. (Writing is covered in the next chapter.)

In conclusion . . .

Try the following:

- Think back over childhood experiences of story and what gave you particular pleasure;
- build up your story repertoire starting with personal stories, well-known traditional tales and broaden your range to include stories of different kinds and from different cultures;
- seek opportunities to hear storytellers in action.

In the classroom you could:

- provide opportunities for pupils to hear stories both within and outside of the literacy hour (including stories specifically linked to subjects other than English);
- give children time to talk to each other in pairs and small groups and to retell stories;
- be an attentive listener;
- provide audiences who value children's talk;
- discuss and praise children's oral work and if rewards (e.g. stickers) are given for reading or writing do similar thing with spoken language;
- make tapes and videos of children's storytelling activities;
- recognize and acknowledge relevant sources of imaginative material for children (e.g. television, family stories);
- invite professional storytellers into schools, as well as 'ordinary' people who have a story to tell (perhaps about their work experiences).

Acknowledgements

I would like to thank primary PGCE students at Leicester University and the many teachers and pupils with whom I have worked, in particular: Alison Newman-Turner and the pupils and staff at All Saints' Primary School, Wigston.

References and further reading

Aylwin, T. (1992) Retelling stories in school, in P. Pinsent (ed.) *Language, Culture and Young Children*. London: David Fulton.
Barton, B. (1991) Bringing the story to life, in D. Booth and C. Thornley-Hall (eds) *The Talk Curriculum*. Markham, Ontario: Pembroke Publishers.

Booth, D. and Thornley-Hall, C. (1991) *The Talk Curriculum*. Markham, Ontario: Pembroke Publishers.

Bromley, H. (2000) The gift of transformation: children's talk and story boxes, *Language Matters*, Winter.

Centre for the Children's Book (2000) *Tales for the Telling: A Journey through the World of Folktales*. Education Pack available from the Centre for the Children's Book, tel: 0191 274 3941.

Colwell, E. (1991) *Storytelling*. Woodchester, Stroud: Thimble Press.

Corden, R. (2000) *Literacy and Learning Through Talk: Strategies for the Primary Classroom*. Buckingham: Open University Press.

DfEE (1998) *The National Literacy Strategy Framework for Teaching*. London: HMSO.

Dombey, H. (1992) *Words and Worlds: Reading in the Early Years of School*. NAAE/NATE.

Dunstan, M. (1997) *Speak Out Listen Up: A Storytelling Resource Pack for Teachers Key Stages 2 & 3*. Sidmouth: Devon County Council.

Grainger, T. (1997) *Traditional Storytelling in the Primary Classroom*. Leamington Spa: Scholastic.

Gregory, E. (1996) *Making Sense of a New World: Learning to Read in a Second Language*. London: Paul Chapman.

Grugeon, E., Hubbard, L., Smith, C. and Dawes, L. (1998) *Teaching Speaking and Listening in the Primary School*. London: David Fulton.

Grugeon, E. and Gardner, P. (2000) *The Art of Storytelling for Teachers and Pupils: Using Stories to Develop Literacy in Primary Classrooms*. London: David Fulton.

Hislam, J. (1996) *Story Clubs In Schools. Society for Storytelling*. Artisan series No 1. Combe Martin: Daylight Press.

Howe, A. and Johnson, J. (1992) *Common Bonds: Storytelling in the Classroom*. Sevenoaks: Hodder and Stoughton.

Mellon, N. (1992) *Storytelling and the Art of the Imagination*. Rockport, MA: Element Books.

Parkinson, R. (1999) *Three Angles to an Awakening Kiss*. Oracle Series no. 4 Society for Storytelling. Combe Martin: Daylight Press.

Qualifications and Curriculum Authority (1999) *Teaching Speaking and Listening in Key Stages 1 and 2*. London: HMSO.

Raison, G. (1997) *Oral Language: Resource Book*. First Steps. Melbourne: Rigby Heinemann.

Rosen, B. (1988) *And None of it Was Nonsense*. London: Mary Glasgow Publications.

Rosen, B. (1991) *Shapers and Polishers: Teachers as Storytellers*. London: Mary Glasgow Publications.

Toye, N. and Prendiville, F. (2000) *Drama and Traditional Story for the Early Years*. London: Routledge.

Weir, L. (2000) 'Miss, are you going to tell us a story out of your mouth?' in M. Medlicott and M. Steele (eds) *Eileen Colwell: An Excellent Guide*. London: Society for Storytelling Daylight Press.

Wells, G. (1986) *The Meaning Makers*. Sevenoaks: Hodder and Stoughton.

10

Getting it write! Supporting and responding to children's writing

Marilyn Foreman and Nikki Gamble

Cameo 1

David and Matthew are 7 years old. They are collaborating to compose a story. Two student teachers are acting as their scribes. The class has just enjoyed a storytelling experience in which the teacher has created an imaginary purpose for writing. In pairs, the children are embarking on a quest to write stories for George, a bear who lives in a kingdom where books are banned and life is impoverished as a result. The children have decided to put their own stories into print and read them to George. 'Verbal energy' (Crook 1996: 123) abounds as, without exception, pupils group themselves and identify with an expert writer with whom they can share the writing process. They are convinced that they can create and frame stories that have the power to transform George's life.

Cameo 2

Helen and Rosie are 6 years old. They are using a computer to compose their own versions of the traditional tale of Goldilocks and the Three Bears. Having had numerous versions of this tale read to them over a period of two weeks, and been positively encouraged to read them for themselves, Helen and Rosie are asked to revise the story and write it from the protagonist's point of view, an activity directly related to a learning objective from the National Literacy Strategy. They plan their story by engaging in storytelling. They are observed and recorded in the process of moving from storytelling to story writing. They are expected to work independently but are not bound by the structure of timing within the literacy hour. They plan and compose over a period of an hour, which allows for an extended period of time in which to write.

Cameo 3

It is the first half of the Spring term and a Year 6 class are writing in response to Walter de la Mare's poem *The Listeners*. At the beginning of the week in shared reading the children read and listened to different voices reading the poem. They experimented with variation of pitch, tone and volume and evaluated the effect these different readings had on their interpretative responses. The NQT guided their exploration, prompting them to consider ways in which de la Mare created atmosphere and evoked an emotional response by asking them to identify effective words, phrases and poetic devices. The emphasis in this introductory session was on oral activity.

In the second lesson, the class used drama strategies including hot-seating, freeze-frame, sound collage and thought-tracking to refine their appreciation of character, explore motivations and to consider ways in which the reader seeks to close gaps in the enigmatic narrative. Then, building on the whole-class introduction, independent groups arranged and prepared dramatic readings of the poem. In the plenary session the interpretations were performed and evaluated.

In the third lesson the children respond freely in writing to the poem; they are already experienced in making choices about the content or form of their written work. To aid those overwhelmed by choice, a menu of possibilities is brainstormed; the children do not, however, feel constrained by these suggestions. The class work individually but some share work in progress. Their responses are varied. For example, Kieran, aged 11 years, has chosen to write a letter from the traveller demanding an explanation for the failure to meet at the assigned time and place. Chloë, aged 10, is not usually an enthusiastic writer but on this occasion she has written a poem from the point of view of the 'deserted' house incorporating some of the techniques and devices discussed in the previous lesson. Others have chosen to write personally about the effect of the poem on them.

Introduction

What are the distinctive features of a good literacy classroom? Planning should be done on the basis of notes made about ways in which the writing environment can be enhanced. Classrooms should be attractive and well organized with easily accessible materials and implements (see Chapter 2). It is essential that an ethos is created where values are attached to literacy and children are immersed in print: where books are read for pleasure rather than mechanistic purposes and young writers are invited to talk about their reading (Cambourne 1988). Books in the class library should be regularly changed and new titles promoted. Themed and author displays should be used to introduce new writers and genres. Children's writing should be afforded the same respect as published work. Our attitudes and expectations are also crucial – children need encouragement to 'have a go', to experiment and to try out new ideas. They are more likely to feel safe to take risks if we participate in writing; learning implicitly from the modelling of processes, discussion about ideas and justification of choices.

The three cameos exemplify these features in practice and we will now explore each of the cameos in turn, drawing out the particular features of merit in each one.

Cameo 1

The trainees are experimenting with, and analysing aspects of, shared writing. Discussion has previously taken place around this concept and its place within the NLS and in this encounter they understand their role as supporting and extending children's writing by demonstrating the writing process and using their own knowledge of language to talk explicitly with children about the features of narrative genre. One can hear talk at all structural levels. Word, sentence and textual features of the emerging texts are prominent in the classroom discourse. Some groups are expressing thoughts in relation to how interest will be created in their story openings; others talk of using aspects of punctuation accurately. Alternative adjectival and adverbial words and phrases are offered for debate to find the most effective way of shaping meaning. Structural elements of language are not being learned in drilling and skilling contexts or as isolated, decontextualized exercises. These pupils are developing a knowledge and understanding of language in a manner that is enabling them to become 'confident, enthusiastic and competent readers, writers and speakers' (Wilson 1999). By the time their stories are published for the bear to read and have read to him, opportunities will have arisen for language knowledge to be fully explored at all structural levels.

Matthew and David use their knowledge of a variety of print, media and electronic texts in their new and original composition. Traditionally they open with:

Once upon a time there was a little rabbit.

The range of subversion in traditional stories that children know and enjoy today becomes apparent as:

> The rabbit met a bear. The bear was afraid of the rabbit and the bear ran away home.

and power relationships are explored.

> Then squirrel said 'Hi!' and he ran off to his friend fox. When the bear saw the fox he said, 'Everyone is scaring me'. Then the hedgehog came up and said, 'Why is everyone scaring you?' Then they ran home.

This scene replicates those found in countless tales of animals where the emotions of characters are explored as they repeatedly meet each other while journeying through forest and wood. The speed of action implicit in:

> They decided to pick some berries and have a war against some of the animals they met. Then they got a catapult and fired the berries at the animals. They went so fast that they hit each other in the middle and squashed the berries together. Then they got some big rocks and catapulted them at the animals. They shot honey at the bears. Bees came and stung them.

is a feature of the visual images experienced in cartoon and video games to which the boys have access.

> The bear and the fox said. 'OK, you've won!' and they never came to the forest again. They went back to their own forest and played with their toys – rocks for marbles.

appears to draw the story to an end as the boys return the bear and the fox to their own world in which playing with marbles is familiar. However, knowledge of fables, possibly Aesop's, manifests itself in the attached moral statement:

> Their father said they should not fight and they went back to say sorry.

A vicarious form of pleasure is achieved as:

> They went on their computer and got onto the Internet and talked with the animals – all sorts of things.

And so their story ends and in this final sentence we gain an insight into Matthew and David's perception of writing as being a shared experience. To these children the experience of talking to friends through writing using a keyboard and mouse is quite natural, usual and enjoyable. They have understanding of settings where humans collaborate to talk and write.

Shared writing is a collaborative act, which allows all participants to articulate, challenge and co-construct ideas. Matthew and David had a problem to solve and in voicing their ideas aloud they were able to gain

Shared writing is a collective act that allows participants to articulate, challenge and co-construct ideas

greater clarity about their opinions, predictions and interpretations through a joint reflective process with their scribe. The group setting demanded that they take responsibility for declaring and justifying their ideas. They were able to listen and learn from each other's strategic moves in the creation of the story and the more expert participant was able to prompt, elaborate and fill in processes allowing the boys to achieve what might have been impossible in a solitary setting.

A shared writing experience can take place during any phase of a lesson and is more about children as a community of developing writers than its position within a literacy hour. The experience described above formed the developmental phase of a lesson emanating in part from the privilege afforded by the wealth of human resources that the situation offered. The same activity could have occurred with one adult and a whole class collaborating to write a story. The literacy hour model is but one of many models of lesson delivery. Knowing when, where, how and why shared writing will benefit a group of children as writers is of greater importance than religiously observing a prescribed model of teaching. Imaginative, passionate and inspiring teachers will always reflect critically on their own and others' established practice in an effort to interpret curriculum in a way that facilitates learning for their pupils.

David and Matthew are in the process of creating a product with a real sense of audience and purpose. The teacher is fully aware of the importance of providing children with real audiences when they engage in writing and this sense of audience is essential in creating a purpose with which children can identify. Often this can be achieved through using real-life contexts for learning, for example writing letters to authors or joining e-mail discussion groups to share responses to books. Alternatively, imaginative contexts, created through drama and role-play, can be equally effective in inspiring and stimulating young writers. The affective nature of the imagined bear's response in this cameo is integral to the act of composition. Authors of any age need to have an intuitive feel for their readership and it is important that children, as authors, are not denied access to this.

With adults as scribes the elements of handwriting and spelling have been withdrawn. The boys are secure in the knowledge that they do not have sole responsibility for the secretarial aspects of writing, which they are at present seeking to master. Their imaginations have been released and allowed to fly. They are able to focus their complete attention on achieving their purpose and, as a result, motivation is high. For many weeks following this lesson, visitors to the classroom were able to witness children enthusiastically and competently reading and re-reading their stories to the bear whose residence had been firmly established in the book corner. Many children continued to compose stories for the bear at home and within a short space of time the classroom library expanded and children's publications sat equally alongside those of established and renowned children's authors. At other times in the day the children were engaged in consolidating their knowledge of the spelling patterns and conventions of the English language and memorizing these in a fluid and joined style of handwriting. Additionally planned guided and independent writing activities gave them the opportunity to integrate the multifaceted skills, knowledge and understanding that the process of writing demands.

There is no dichotomy between writing as a process and writing as a product in the shared writing context. The product is a necessary part of the process. The importance of what Matthew and David wanted to say was integral to the activity and they were fully aware that they were producing a first draft that they would be able to review and revise at a later date. The emphasis of the activity was firmly rooted in expressing meaning to a third person and they were involved in making vital decisions about content and form. They were convinced that they had a voice that would be valued. The scribing element eliminated intervention aimed at developing correctness and as a result creative thoughts were allowed to develop. The presence of the instructor in this shared writing added a further dimension to what was previously understood as beneficial in writing workshop approaches (Graves 1983). The discourse allowed for Matthew and David to be taught to recognize how their ideas could be organized into the structure of a specific genre; that is, narrative that the bear could understand and this happened in a way that did not value the product over and above the creative input essential to the process.

Preparation for shared writing involves teachers in two fundamental processes:

1 increasing our knowledge of a range of texts written for children;
2 engaging in the writing process ourselves.

As a collaborative experience, shared writing is not only concerned with the teacher scribing children's ideas but being a full participant in the structuring of joint mental activity. The success that children experience as writers is dependent on the nature and quality of our participation. Role modelling a fluent hand and spelling accurately on the whiteboard is insufficient. We need to be expert craftspeople who are able to articulate and share how we construct texts so that our pupils can be empowered to use language in a similar way.

Cameo 2

Helen and Rosie are accustomed to using both new and conventional technologies for writing and other purposes. They have been explicitly taught the functions of the computer and have been given opportunities to gain physical control of the keyboard and mouse and to explore a wide range of software. They both have access to computers at home. As readers they 'are shaped by the sum of their literary experiences' and 'our basics are not theirs' (Mackey 1994: 9). Both at school and at home it is likely that they will have encountered Goldilocks on television, film and video, in song and cassette form, as well as both traditional and sub-versive book-based versions. The rewind facility on their videos, cassettes and CDs will have given them countless opportunities to revisit and review. To them, this 'multiplicity of media' (Mackey 1994: 9) is com-monplace, and they are not daunted in the least by the opportunity to explore the text.

On this occasion they have been presented with a twin challenge; working at the computer and working alongside each other. They are not simply replicating an electronic alternative to a pencil and paper exercise. They have been thrust into a context where spoken language is an essential element. They are involved in 'a social mode of thinking' (Mercer 1995: 4). At different points in the lesson they both act as more able peers supporting and extending each other's learning. They intuit-ively apply strategies for learning, which they have encountered in previous shared reading and writing contexts with adults. They take turns to speak, ask many questions, make requests and frequently initiate ideas.

Gaining control of the mouse greatly influences the role children adopt in language and literacy events where the computer plays a mediating role. Helen and Rosie adopt anticipated roles. When manipulating the mouse they accept a secretarial position: their eyes constantly shift between the monitor and the keyboard. When relinquishing power over the mouse, they constantly monitor the screen, continually reading and evaluating the emerging text (see Chapter 11 for Nick Easingwood's extension of these ideas). Responsibilities within the writing process are implicitly, yet clearly defined.

The computer setting creates the conditions for spontaneous and immediate peer review because a published version of the text is apparent as writing is in progress. Traditionally, this has been the role of the teacher but it is easy for Helen and Rosie to take ownership of the monitoring and review process because they have immediate access to how their story might be received by others. Writers, especially those that are still novices, find it harder to detect problems in their own texts than in other people's. The computer setting creates the conditions for immediate peer review. Helen and Rosie are both readers and writers in this act of spoken co-authorship. The concept of multiple authorship implicit in collaborative and shared writing has the potential to improve performance by enabling the writer to get immediate feedback from another writer and, with the advent of the Internet in primary classrooms, multiple authorship will soon have no temporal or spatial bounds. Computers are providing opportunities for children as writers to come much closer to reading their own compositions with a critical eye. Helen and Rosie are reading and writing in an act of co-authorship. The computer is providing them with a powerful technological means to abolish the traditional distinction between writers as producers and readers as consumers.

The word processor is a public medium. It creates writing to be shared. It is easier for Helen and Rosie to see themselves as writers when they see their words in print. They are motivated to write because they realize the process of writing for other people. There is a real sense of audience. 'To be a writer is empowering, yet every word that a child forms on paper is confirmation of inferiority. However carefully and neatly a child may write, the result is a poor substitute for adult typeface' (Sharples 1985: 10). Through the use of a computer or word processor they are able to lay claim to the power of written language.

The girls' revisions focus on word level structural elements of the text. Spelling of key vocabulary dominates the spoken discourse. Their revisions are focused on the minor details or lower-structural levels of the text. Their different strategies for spelling become immediately apparent.

Rosie depends wholly on a phonic approach while Helen extends the range to include visual and analogical reasoning. The mediating role of the computer is serving to promote learning in relation to transcriptional elements of writing. The spelling of the word 'cottage', for example, is mutually acknowledged as a problem to be solved. Rosie suggests immediate use of the spell check but Helen, aware that it can only be operated once a plausible prediction has been offered, makes a phonic-based suggestion as her first move. She is confident in her knowledge of the first three phonemes, which she pronounces aloud. She then gives an alphabet-based offering of the more complex word ending. She suggests 'ig', but also offers 'ij' for scrutiny, typing both alternatives for visual discrimination. The easy eradication of the rejected offering that the delete facility provides, promotes risk taking. Rosie takes up the challenge and suggests the latter, consistent with her reliance on phonic strategies. Helen by now has made a decision using visual clues and writes the word correctly, hence dismissing Rosie's idea. Seeing the word in print has resolved the confusion between 'j' and 'g' and the modifying 'e' naturally falls into place. In her role as reader in this engagement, Rosie now reflects on the final spelling and confirms accuracy by using the spell check. This is a far cry from pupils standing in a line with wordbooks asking their teacher to write words for them.

Throughout the discourse Helen and Rosie consistently use the pronouns 'we' and 'they', the former representing their perception of this co-operative, shared experience, while the latter refers to unidentified others. Helen, at one point, is heard saying 'Sometimes it comes out right, because they think it is another word, don't they?' Her understanding of the writing process mediated through a computer is encapsulated in this single question. She does not see herself as having ownership of her writing. Unchallenged by Rosie, she holds a conviction that there are multiple authors whose identities are unknown. When asked a few weeks later whether they wanted to make changes to either this or any of their handwritten stories both girls expressed a desire to alter that produced on the computer only. Helen emphatically explained that she would be reluctant to change anything handwritten as that belonged to her. She took a more objective view of the computer-generated text reiterating her strongly held belief that it had been written by others. This perspective is of significant importance when planning for writing in classrooms and the appropriate use of ICT. Helen is taking a more objective view of her writing at the computer. The collaborative experience, in her mind, is extended to include significant, knowledgeable others who intervene between the typing of the work and that which appears in print. She is feeling the support of what she possibly perceives as teachers other than the one physically present in the classroom. She sees her work as being marked as it progresses and *without judgement*.

This factor alone could account for why Helen and Rosie are not fearful of making mistakes and are able to write with confidence.

Helen and Rosie are completely at ease with this process. Their discourse is punctuated with giggles, jokes and song. Learning to write in this setting is an enjoyable and affective experience. They are learning through play and their delight is apparent. They have been allowed to negotiate their own rules; to learn self-sufficiency; to take risks and to learn from their own mistakes. The blank computer screen has given them the opportunity to create something from nothing. Their talk is continuous, displaying their thought processes. It gives us clues to the features of their inner speech that develops into written text when children write in isolation. We need to make time to listen to children writing at computers.

Cameo 3

Organization and management are key issues in the success of the lesson. Objectives are to develop independence and to promote writing as a vehicle for the expression of ideas, thoughts and feelings. To this end the teacher has worked hard during her first term to establish a response-centred classroom where validation and refinement of children's ideas are paramount. To create a supportive environment it is essential to develop children's belief in the teacher and each other as a genuine audience by asking questions that open the response route rather than narrow it down (Chambers 1993).

The effective teaching of speaking, listening, reading and writing are closely integrated and although specific NLS objectives for text, sentence and word level work can be identified in this sequence of lessons, the approach is essentially holistic. An observer in the class is struck by the high level of commitment the children have to their writing. Significantly, for the level of engagement, there has been substantial opportunity for the children to talk before writing; their experience of the poem has been a multi-sensory one comprising oral experimentation, identification of visual patterns, and exploration of the affective domain through role-play.

Motivation is affected by the freedom to choose, which is also an important factor in moving the children towards taking responsibility for their own learning. Guiding them to draw on previous experiences of writing for a wide range of purposes and audiences, helps the children to make choices. This is likely to have a lasting impact where genuine contexts have been established rather than constructed for the purposes of practising different types of writing. The literacy environment is also an integral part of the teacher's strategy to encourage independence. A

Interesting writing usually breaks with convention

large collection of dictionaries and thesauruses is accessible to the children (including rhyming and etymological dictionaries). Suggestions for writing are pinned to a notice-board in a designated writing area where materials and implements are carefully stored and labelled and the children are responsible for maintaining standards of orderliness. The teacher fosters an interest in words and encourages delight in language play; a 'Word of the Week' is displayed and a notice-board of jokes, riddles and funny poems is maintained by class editors. *Aide-memoire* posters prompt children to follow procedures to help them spell unknown words and to edit their writing. Most importantly children's written work is attractively displayed and their stories and poems are bound and available for others to read alongside the collection of books in the class library.

The start of the independent writing session is characterized by a short period of silent concentration. The teacher notices that some children start writing immediately but others are slower to put pen to paper; while some children need this time to be quietly reflective, others require more support in the initial stage and she asks questions to encourage them to talk through their ideas and stimulate their thoughts (Graves 1983: 107–17).

Although Chloë participates well in discussion, has a good general knowledge and keen imagination, she is usually reluctant to write. Her handwriting is untidy and she finds the enterprise laborious preferring the immediate response of oral work. On this occasion, however, she quickly begins to write a poem from the point of view of the deserted house. The preceding discussion and drama have fed Chloë's apprehension of the house as a living, breathing entity. She is the only child in the class to produce a response in this format. Chloë uses *The Listener* as a model for her own writing, internalizing and incorporating features that are present in the original poem. Meek (1988: 3) writes:

> If we want to see what lessons have been learned from the texts children read we have to look for them in what they write. Of course they draw on the whole of their culture if we let them. We have to be alert to what comes from books as well as from life.

Clearly influenced by the impact of the poem's opening question her first lines read:

> Is there anyone there he demanded?
> As he stood alone at the door.

Like de la Mare, Chloë uses alliteration to ascribe qualities of a living organism to the house and provide contrast between silence and sound:

> Silence seeped through my ghostly corridors.

Chloë transfers literary language from her reading to her writing, exemplifying the interrelationship of the two modes as described in Perera's (1984) analysis. Writing matures as children become more competent readers (p. 266):

> Whether we think in terms of grammatical constructions that are required for thematic variety, end-focus, an impersonal style, and so forth, or the structural components that characterize different types of discourse, it is clear that these forms cannot be acquired by listening to spontaneous oral language, because they do not normally occur in speech.

Kieran is a confident writer who is usually able independently to generate ideas for his writing, but he often finishes his work quickly and rarely chooses to redraft his writing. Following the hot-seating lesson, in which he took on the role of the traveller, he chose to write a letter in role to the mysterious character who had failed to keep his promise:

> Dear Dick
> Last night I went to meet you at The Manor like we arranged. I knocked and I waited for ages but nobody answered. I was sure that somebody inside was listening and spying on me from behind the curtains. I looked all around the house but it looked deserted as

though no one had been near the place for ages. Ivy was growing over the door and the windows were covered in dust. Some birds flew out of the turret, I think something inside disturbed them but I saw nothing. There is something very strange about that place. I did not like the sound or feel of it.

Is everything still clear for tonight? I will not come unless you send word that it is safe.

Kieran had written in character and the letter conveyed some of the mystery of the original poem; he used an image quoted directly from the poem 'some birds flew out of the turret'. However, he did not include details of the elaborate and imaginative story that had emerged through the role play. In the subsequent lesson the teacher used a guided writing session to reflect on work in progress and to provide an opportunity for peer response and evaluation. Using scaffolding questions, the teacher encouraged Kieran to consider whether the omission of narrative detail was important (Graves 1983). After some thought, he decided that because the form he had chosen to write in was a letter addressed to a character who understood the context, there was no need to make the story explicit thus demonstrating his proficiency in explaining his goals and evaluating the extent to which they were achieved. The group discussed this and suggested that he could develop the story through a correspondence between the two characters. Kieran liked the idea and continued to work on the letters in independent writing sessions.

Furnished with opportunities and resources children respond in highly individual ways. Chloë was affected by the mood and atmosphere of *The Listeners,* while Kieran was stimulated by the enigmatic text and accompanying drama to construct an exciting story, which he went on to develop in the epistolary genre.

Summary

The three cameos exemplify key concepts and questions to take into account when we are preparing to teach writing.

Writing process and outcomes

It can be helpful to think about writing as both a process and an outcome. Historically, discussion has focused on whether teaching at one time or another has placed too much emphasis on the end product or the processes of writing. It is now generally accepted that writing should not be regarded as merely an artefact produced exclusively for display purposes. Neither should the process be the exclusive focus for teaching with the end product being considered irrelevant. As the examples in the cameos show, an artificial separation that fails to recognize outcome as part of the process is not constructive for teacher or children.

Writing is complex and involves many skills, which can be described as 'compositional' (meaning, structure, vocabulary choice) or 'transcriptional' (spelling, word processing, handwriting). This distinction may help us to focus on specific teaching objectives, which are detailed in the NLS Framework and organized under headings such as 'writing composition' and 'spelling strategies'. Certainly an aim in teaching writing is to achieve a balance in developing writing skills and these are best taught in a holistic way rather than in isolation.

In focusing on processes we can identify prewriting, writing and rewriting stages.

- Prewriting includes brainstorming for ideas, activating prior knowledge or writing a plan to aid organization and structure.
- Writing is the initial attempt to represent ideas by getting words onto the page. During this stage the writer's thoughts are often modified and refined.
- In the rewriting stages writers may redraft for meaning proof-read to check for errors in punctuation and spelling and work on the presentation of the final draft.

In *Making Progress in English*, Bearne (1998: 92–5) presents a useful guide outlining strategies that aid progression in the drafting process. However, it needs to be recognized that writing is a dynamic process and a writer does not necessarily progress neatly from one stage to the next. For instance, think about your own work; when writing an essay do you return to your original plan and amend it in the light of what you have discovered through the writing?

We need to consider carefully our own roles in the writing process:

- When and how to intervene requires thoughtful planning to ensure that we work with children at different stages of their writing.
- It is also important to provide time for reflection rather than moving too rapidly from one task to another.
- Children need space to evaluate their own writing, to identify what they have learnt and to set their own targets.
- Through reflective, social interaction with other young writers they are able to make explicit what they implicitly know; to refine and consolidate their learning.

Shared, guided and independent work

The cameos illustrate different types of writing activity, which the NLS terms 'shared', 'guided' and 'independent' (DfEE 1998). Together they provide the structures to promote children's writing development.

Demonstration and modelling are key elements of shared writing that allow children to observe the teacher composing, talking through solutions to problems and making thought processes explicit. For example, a shared writing lesson might incorporate how to structure a narrative or select appropriate strategies for spelling an unknown word.

In guided writing the teacher works closely with a group of children – scaffolding their learning by using, for example, content-free prompt questions (Graves 1983). Typically, a guided writing session might provide oral feedback on work in progress with the teacher modelling how to comment constructively on another writer's work. Essentially guided activity can be thought of as the bridge from dependence to independence.

Working independently children apply ideas from shared and guided writing. As the result of guided activity children might prepare a final draft for presentation or publication. They might write individually or collaboratively – for example, paired story writing at the computer. In fact children need opportunities to work both alone and with others. Sometimes collaboration can be most productive in the initiation stage; at other times response partners can help each other refine ideas making meaning. During independent time children should also have opportunities to play and experiment with written language in the knowledge that the outcomes will not be judged.

Purposes and audiences

The notion of purpose and audience, developed from the work of the National Writing Project of the 1980s, underpins the requirements of the NC and NLS. The term 'genre' is used to describe writing for a particular purpose exhibiting a unique pattern of organization and linguistic structures. At KS1, the curriculum requires that children write to:

- communicate with others;
- create imaginary worlds;
- explore experience;
- organize and explain information.

At KS2 the repertoire includes:

- narratives;
- play scripts;
- reports;
- explanations;
- opinions;
- instructions;
- reviews;
- commentaries

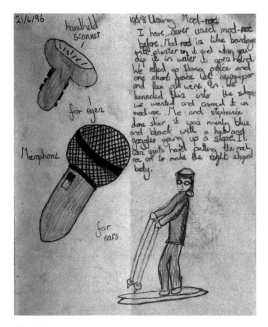

Guilding them to draw on previous experiences of writing, helps the children to make choices

Wray and Lewis (1997, 1998) advocate the use of 'writing frames' to scaffold children's writing but, significantly they stress that the ultimate aim is for the scaffolding to become internalized so that frames can be discarded. Furthermore, while frames are supportive for developing writers they need to be used judiciously not prescriptively. You will probably have noticed that interesting writing usually breaks with convention; a quick survey of contemporary cookery books will reveal that popular cookery writers often incorporate elements of narrative with standard features of procedural writing.

Asking children to study the linguistic features of text types and then employ this knowledge in writing for a repertoire of purposes is a sterile endeavour. Kress (1994) places genre in a social theory of language where social contexts are recognized as determining the recurring patterns of text, thus reminding us of the symbiotic connection between purpose and audience. When planning for writing we need to audit the audiences for whom children's work is provided. We should fully exploit opportunities within the school. For example, is work presented to children in other classes? Role play can extend the range of audiences that naturally occur in school but also consider using the wider community as a genuine audience for children's work (a curriculum requirement at KS2). For instance, a focus on persuasive writing might involve children in writing letters to a local newspaper, or a local history project might produce a display for the library.

Responding to children's writing

We need to consider when and how we respond to children's writing. It is rarely helpful for an initial response to be made after a final draft has been completed as this will not feed into development of the writing. We want to provide supportive feedback to enable young writers to reflect on their learning rather than making judgemental statements that emphasize the need for correction. When teaching writing it soon becomes evident that strategies for response require as much forethought as planning the stimulus for writing or content of a lesson.

The following prompts help to focus on planning to respond:

What is the purpose of the response?
- to help the writer initiate ideas?
- to provide an audience for the writing?
- to help the writer reflect on their learning?
- to build self-esteem?

When will I respond?
- in the prewriting stage; to help the writer clarify their initial ideas?
- in the writing stage; to check that the writing is progressing?
- at the rewriting stage; to encourage reflection and help the writer identify what has been learned?

How will I respond?
- oral feedback or written feedback?
- to individuals, groups or the whole class?

Often it is most appropriate to give immediate, oral, feedback. The *plenary* of a literacy lesson can be used to provide constructive criticism and encouragement, and to enable children to explain what they have learned in order to clarify their thinking. When is written feedback most appropriate?

Who will respond?
- the teacher?
- guided writing group or the class?
- a wider audience?
- peer response partners?

Consideration needs to be given to what needs to be put in place to ensure that children can respond constructively to each other's work. To what aspects of writing can they most productively respond? Does anything need to remain in the teacher's domain?

In supporting the developing writer the teacher's role extends beyond providing the stimulus for writing, teaching discrete word, sentence and text level objectives or assessing the outcome. Good teachers of writing are involved in the processes, are enthusiastic about the written word, open-minded and committed readers and writers themselves.

References and further reading

Bearne, E. (1998) *Making Progress in English*. London: Routledge.
Cambourne, B. (1988) *The Whole Story: Natural Learning and the Acquisition of Literacy in the Classroom*. Auckland: Ashton Scholastic.
Chambers, A. (1993) *Tell Me: Children, Reading and Talk*. Stroud: Thimble Press.
Crook, C. (1996) *Computers and the Collaborative Experience of Learning*. London: Routledge.
Daiute, C. (1992) A case study on collaborative writing, in J. Hartley (ed.) *Technology and Writing. Readings in the Psychology of Written Communication*. London: Jessica Kingsley.
DfEE (1998) *National Literacy Strategy: Framework of Objectives*. London: HMSO.
DfEE (1999) *The National Curriculum: English*. London: HMSO.
Evans, J. (ed.) (2000) *The Writing Classroom*. London: David Fulton.
Graves, D. (1983) *Writing: Teachers and Children at Work*. London: Heinemann.
Hartley, J. (ed.) (1992) *Technology and Writing: Readings in the Psychology of Written Communication*. London: Jessica Kingsley.
Kress, G. (1994) *Learning to Write*, 2nd edn. London: Routledge.
Mackey, M. (1994) The new basis: learning to read in a multi-media world, *English in Education*, 28(1): 9–19.
Meek, M. (1988) *How Texts Teach What Readers Learn*. Stroud: Thimble Press.
Mercer, N. (1995) *The Guided Construction of Knowledge: Talk Between Teachers and Learners in the Classroom*. Clevedon: Multilingual Matters.
Perera, K. (1984) *Children's Writing and Reading: Analysing Classroom Language*. Oxford: Blackwell.
Raison, G. (1997) *First Steps: Writing Developmental Continuum*. Melbourne: Rigby Heinemann.
Riley, J. and Reedy, D. (1999) *Writing for Different Purposes*. London: Paul Chapman.
Sharples, M. (1985) *Cognition, Computers and Creative Writing*. Chichester: Ellis Horwood.
Smith, J. and Elley, W. (1998) *How Children Learn to Write*. London: Paul Chapman.
Wilson, A. (1999) *Language Knowledge for Primary Teachers. A Guide to Textual, Grammatical and Lexical Study*. London: David Fulton.
Wray, D. and Lewis, M. (1997) *Extending Literacy*. London: Routledge.
Wray, D. and Lewis, M. (1998) *Writing Across The Curriculum: Frames to Support Learning*. Reading: University of Reading.
Wray, D. and Lewis, M. (undated) *Writing Frames*. Reading: University of Reading.

11

All the children want to do is get on with it! ICT in primary education

Nick Easingwood

Cameo 1

Alison is a student teacher embarking on her final school experience with a Year 3 class. A confident and capable user of Information and Communications Technology (ICT), she wants to use ICT to support her teaching during the course of the practice. However, the school does not seem to be appropriately resourced for it: she has access to only one computer in the corner of the classroom and, as the use of ICT to support teaching is a requirement, she immediately worries that she will not be able to deliver ICT. She is concerned that the literacy and numeracy hours take up nearly half of the teaching time in the school day, and with 30 children in the class, will she be able to ensure that every child has a turn using the computer to achieve something that is worthwhile?

Cameo 2

Alan is a newly qualified teacher who has just joined the staff of a large primary school. He has access to a brand new ICT suite for one hour a week with enough computers for one between two children. He has never taught in an ICT suite before and he worries that he will not be able to cope with 15 computers potentially all going wrong at once!

Having identified the ICT resources that are available to him, he then has to complete his planning. He needs to look at the long-term planning for his year group, which will indicate what curriculum content will be taught over the course of the whole year. Then he needs to produce the medium-term plans to identify what he is going to teach over the course of that all important first term. However, he discovers a difficulty – what does he actually need to plan and to assess? The very existence of an ICT document in the National Curriculum for England appears to give ICT the status of a subject in its own right, but the document itself clearly indicates that ICT should be used to support subjects, especially the core English, mathematics and science. Does he plan for the ICT or the subject?

Cameo 3

Claire is teaching her Year 4 class in the ICT suite. They are working in pairs on a LOGO task, where the children have been asked to produce a repeating pattern using procedures. Emma and Dipesh are drawing a flower – it has a stem, and the repeating pattern has produced a complex geometric shape for the flower at the top. Claire stops to listen to the discussion. The children like the idea of the repeating pattern, but they are not quite satisfied with the finished graphic:

E: I don't think that we turned the turtle far enough . . .
D: We turned it 140 degrees.
E: How far should we turn it?
D: (Placing his hand on the screen in the direction of the turtle)
  Another 20 degrees, I think . . .
E: I'm not sure. That will make 170 degrees.
D: No it won't, it'll be 160 degrees.
E: So what will it look like?
D: Let's try it and see!
  Emma types in the command. The turtle produces a much more pleasing result.
E: That's ace!

Claire is delighted. She can see that real learning has taken place, and not only was the outcome good but the process by which they got the product was excellent. The children have done exactly what Papert (1993) said they should – they have produced a procedure, produced an excellent turtle graphic and they have debugged it, through discussion and experimentation. This needs to be assessed and recorded for future reference. But what does she assess? Although she planned for assessment in her planning, she is not exactly sure what to assess. Does she assess the result (the flower)? Does she assess the process (the discussion)? Or does she assess the ICT skills that the children use (the typing and the pointing and clicking)?

Introduction

Alison, Alan and Claire should be pleased: they have the essential ingredients for teaching ICT – in fact teaching altogether – great enthusiasm and a willingness to learn. The very fact that they want to use ICT in their teaching is sufficient. They have understood what ICT can bring to learning and teaching and they are willing to use and incorporate it into their everyday teaching.

Exactly what is Information and Communication Technology (ICT)? Although a term that is now appearing in the wider world, it largely remains a title that is confined to the world of education. The inclusion of the 'C' for Communication, rather than the traditional 'IT' emphasizes the more interactive nature of modern technology and the importance of this to education in particular. Users are not confined to being passive recipients of information displayed on the screen but are using the computer as a tool to learning or to make informed choices. The use of email illustrates this perfectly, although other interactive tools might involve the use of word processing, desktop publishing or using a spreadsheet, or to subsequently enhance and aid personal learning. These applications can be embellished by the regular and integrated use of appropriate ICT resources such as digital cameras – both still and video, scanners, programmable toys such as floor turtles and interactive whiteboards. This is in addition to the basic technology such as tape recorders, analogue video cameras and recorders. ICT is not only about computers; in fact, it really has very little to do with computers! It represents a way of thinking, how all of the above elements can be employed to enhance the teaching and learning experience in a way that otherwise would not be possible.

Quite apart from the fact that children are highly motivated when using ICT, computers are very good at handling large amounts of a wide range of data very quickly, such as text, numbers, tables, graphics, images or sound, either individually or in any combinations. The automatic functions of the hardware and the software enable the user to spend less time on the menial tasks such as constructing graphs or tables and more time on the higher order thinking skills such as the analysis and interpretation of data. This chapter will identify how we can harness this power and use it to enhance the quality of the teaching and learning experience in a manner that will ensure that we understand and can apply ICT in our teaching.

We all know that the 'traditional' skills are very important and need to be taught and reinforced regularly. But this does not have to be every time that a child needs to produce a graph, table or passage of text. If we have decided that the focus of the task is on producing graphs, then we will get them to draw them by hand, thus ensuring that an understanding of how a graph is constructed is learned. But if the focus is on the interrogation and interpretation of data then this is where the power of the computer comes into its own. The computer has the facility to sort, filter and order information instantly. The teacher's role is to plan, prepare and deliver activities, which ensure that each child uses these functions to analyse the information and interpret what it presents on the screen before developing it for further use. Alison, Alan and Claire know this, so they will be effective teachers and the children in their care will have rich learning experiences.

The power and potential of ICT

All teachers in England have to follow the National Curriculum (Department for Education and Employment 2000). The document for ICT emphasizes an approach supporting teaching and learning in all curriculum areas rather than the teaching of IT key skills *per se*. The three students in the cameos have read the NC document and appreciate the approach suggested. In fact, they are delighted to see that all of the other curriculum documents actively demand the use of ICT, but are perplexed as to why this is not present in the document for Physical Education. With the opportunities for digital photography, both still and video, as well as the use of spreadsheets and databases for health-related fitness work, there is plenty of scope to enhance PE teaching through the use of ICT.

As far as the document for ICT in the primary phase is concerned, terms that have for many years been associated with good practice in primary education are frequently used. The main headings for KS1 and KS2 are 'Finding things out'; 'Developing ideas and making things happen'; 'Exchanging and sharing information' and 'Reviewing, modifying and evaluating work as it progresses'. This is reinforced by the frequent use of words and phrases such as 'gather, enter and store, retrieve information, try things out and explore' (at KS1) and 'prepare information, select, classifying, checking, interpreting, organising, reorganising, create, test, improve and refine, answer "what if . . . ?" questions, to investigate and evaluate' (KS2).

How can ICT do all of this? As teachers we are concerned with information, both its transmission and its development. If there is one thing that computers are good at, it is dealing with information! All information in any form on a computer is provisional in that it has only a semi-permanence. For example, a piece of written text can be changed as part of the drafting or redrafting process, either through editing or the addition of images, clipart, word-art or borders (see further ideas in the previous chapter). It can be constantly redrafted leaving no trace of the

When a computer is used the text (and pictures) can easily and quickly be amended to meet the varying needs of a range of audiences

many changes that it may have gone through, or it may be saved at every step under a new file name to illustrate the evolution of a piece of work. This will be particularly helpful to Claire when she comes to assess the children's work, as she now has a clear record of how the work has evolved. What is more she can look at the 'raw' work – unfettered by 'correct' spellings, grammar or images. All of this can be done quickly and a neat, tidy, 'professional' response will result. There is no correction fluid or rubbing out and no tired hands from having to keep rewriting what is essentially the same piece of text. As all teachers know, there is nothing worse than a handwritten draft with crossings out and corrections all over it! When a computer is used the text can be easily and quickly amended to meet the varying needs of a range of audiences. An example of this power might involve the précis of a passage of text to highlight key points, perhaps taking a 500-word piece to 250, then 100 and finally 50 words while preserving the essential meaning of the piece.

It is this interactivity on the part of the pupil that is of crucial importance. The child must interact continually, using the computer as a tool to assist learning, as Ager (1998) suggests, by being in control of the computer, not the computer in control of the child. To allow the child to become a passive recipient of information thrown at them by an electronic machine not only demeans the child, but it demeans the computer too, and all its powerful opportunities for imaginative and creative work.

The use of the computer is not just about using software to produce original matter – it can be used to amend, refine and develop existing work. It can also act as a gateway to other opportunities that new technologies have to offer, including the use of specialist or generic CD-ROMs, the Internet and email. Alison, Alan and Claire regularly use it for these purposes themselves, and they have made the conceptual link from their personal to professional use. They know that what is offered to them can also be offered to the children in their respective classes. They can find material from remote locations possibly on the other side of the world, from sites specially designed for children or from 'real' sites such as museums or art galleries. As they use the Internet and email to keep in touch with friends, so children's writing can be shared and/or collaboratively developed by posting it on the Internet and inviting reaction, or by emailing it to partner schools in other towns or countries. Modern foreign languages, or geographical work involving distant environments can also be enhanced in this way, perhaps by writing and illustrating with attached images that have been scanned or produced with a digital camera. Class work could be enhanced by getting up-to-date news, sport or weather information, or preparatory work for a class trip could be covered by visiting a museum web site. This might involve taking a virtual tour to discover the kind of things that will be seen, or by finding out such mundane minutiae as costs, opening times and whether there is a shop. Like all good teachers, Alison, Alan and Claire know that this could not and should not replace the experience of a real, focused and first-hand visit, but can certainly ensure that the maximum is gained from the day by careful forward planning. Expert questions could then be posed and emailed to individuals either at the museum to be visited or elsewhere as part of a topic or a programme of study. And all for the cost of a local telephone call!

The computer is also a very useful tool for modelling the real world through the use of simulation software. This is particularly useful where the real thing would be too impractical on the grounds of health and safety, expense or time. The growing of a plant or tree could be simulated, through the speeding up of the process, or conversely, the flapping of a bird's wings could be illustrated by slowing the process. When using a spreadsheet, the variables can be altered at will and new outcomes modelled, through asking open-ended questions of the 'What if . . . ?' variety.

When should teachers use ICT?

Accessing the power and potential of the computer is not just a matter of putting children in front of a computer screen and letting them get on with it, hoping that something magical will result from exposure to the technology. As with any other aspect of the curriculum, the effective use and incorporation of ICT demands careful consideration of key aspects on the part of the teacher. This includes planning, preparation and, above all, the application and promotion of a clear underlying philosophy. The successful use of the computer in the primary classroom is critically and entirely dependent on the teacher, as long as sufficient and appropriate hardware and software resources are to hand.

We must never overlook the fact that a modern computer, for all its sophistication, is after all purely an electronic machine that has no inherent intelligence of its own. Everything that it does it is told to do by a user accessing the functions on a program that, in turn, enables the computer to perform the required function. Therefore, it can be clearly seen that effective teaching and learning with ICT is utterly dependent on teacher involvement at all stages of the process. This will begin with the planning of the lesson, the preparation of materials for the lesson, the delivery of the lesson, supporting pupil-centred tasks during the course of the lesson, assessing the outcomes of the lesson and evaluating the lesson (see also Chapters 6 and 12). The greater the level of input at every step of the way from the teacher, the more effective the teaching incorporating the use of ICT will be and therefore the more effective the learning.

Alison, Alan and Claire know that this is a challenge but it is one they relish. They appreciate that whenever ICT is to be used it should be used constructively, not just because it is their class's turn in the ICT suite. As Alison has only one computer in the classroom she knows that she has to be organized to use it to its maximum potential. Like all teachers, she needs to be clear, when and when not to use ICT. As Circular 4/98 states (Department for Education and Employment 1998) the computer should be used 'because it is the most effective way to achieve teaching and learning objectives' and, should not be used for 'simple or routine tasks which would be better achieved by other means'. This makes good sense, both economically and educationally. As Alison is only too well aware, there is little point in using a computer that costs several hundred pounds to complete tasks that could just have easily been achieved with ten pence worth of plastic counters, especially if this is being covered in an ICT suite that may only be accessible on the timetable for one hour a week. The computer is a powerful piece of equipment that can bring a great deal to teaching and learning when it delivers power and interactivity to the curriculum that would not otherwise be available or accessible.

Planning and assessing with ICT

When planning to use ICT there are several key points that we need to consider. ICT must be appropriately present in planning, even in schools that have limited resources. Alison, Alan and Claire also know that the existence of ICT as an NC document means that there is a legal require-ment for them to teach it and consequently there is an entitlement for all pupils to have access to it.

Like all of us who teach, Alan needs to follow his school's scheme of work and consequently his medium-term plans will need to be directly written from this. The scheme of work is a very important document, as it details exactly what should be taught to each class/year group in a school during the course of the year. It ensures that there is continuity and progression and that every year the work develops and builds on that covered in the previous year. It also ensures that there are no gaps or repetitions, that is there are no instances of different teachers leaving certain topics out or covering the same material twice. The children should receive a balanced education in each curriculum area that is comprehensive yet logical. Dependent on the success of this approach is the fact that all teachers in a school have to follow this documentation – if anybody does not then the system breaks down.

Alan is particularly fortunate as his school, along with many others, is tackling the need for planning through using the QCA scheme of work for ICT. Originally published in July 1998 and revised in February 2000, this document is laid out in year groups, each of which has a number of units that tackle a particular aspect of ICT. Although the units tend to take a more prescriptive ICT key skills approach than the corresponding NC document, they also incorporate a more cross-curricular, computer-as-a-tool approach. Although non-compulsory, the units provide many good ideas in a logical structure where continuity and progression is assured. In Alan's school, the Year 6 children follow the Year 4 units as the lack of access to ICT resources prior to the provision of the ICT suite means that the children will not have had the range of background experiences necessary to be able to successfully tackle work at Yr 6 level yet. However, the Head and ICT Co-ordinator have introduced the scheme fully at Year 1, thus ensuring that within six years the scheme will be successfully implemented across the school as a whole.

Access to ICT in the primary curriculum

Alison's main concern is the issue of access. Although she only has one computer in her classroom, she does have the advantage of being able to incorporate ICT into the everyday curriculum easily and at any opportun-ity. If she had access to an ICT suite she would have access to more computers but she would not have the same flexibility as far as integra-tion into the curriculum is concerned, as access would be restricted to the timetable. Whatever our access to ICT, we need to be clear about how it is being used and that both the organization and the planning

reflect this. Alison knows that in order to ensure that the legal requirements for ICT are being met, she must ensure that planning for ICT
must be present, even where access to ICT resources is limited. She needs
also to consider in particular those children with special educational
needs for whom computer access is vital (see Chapter 14 regarding equal
opportunities).

We all often have the same problem in deciding exactly what is the
nature and role of ICT. We have already seen that the NC for ICT pro-
mulgates the view that it is very much a tool and a resource to learning,
and the vernacular of the document supports this. However, the very
existence of this statutory document ensures that it has the status of a
subject within its own right, which in itself implies that it has to be
taught separately. As Crompton and Mann (1996) have highlighted, the
very inclusion of the word 'technology' can infer that this is the main
focus of the use of the activity; this historically was caused by IT being
part of the original Design and Technology National Curriculum document in 1989. This can lead to confusion at both the planning and
assessment stages – what exactly is being planned and assessed? Is it the
subject or the ICT?

The NC, Circular 4/98 and the Identification of Training Needs document make it clear to us that we have to use ICT to support subject
teaching, especially the core subjects of English, mathematics and science.
This is of fundamental importance for, if the requirements of the NC
document for ICT are to be achieved, then clearly a curricular approach
is required. As teachers we cannot refine, analyse or interpret *without* a
subject context.

Besides, there is more to the debate than this. Technology enhances
everyday lives. Although at the primary phase it is not directly relevant
for us to be talking in terms of society needing computer-literate people
as far as the job market is concerned, it is true that the world in which
children live and teachers work is largely dependent on technology. All
members of society, be it for work or pleasure, will benefit by choosing
and using an appropriate technology or application to fulfil a need. At
the primary phase, it is important that we develop in children the higher
order approaches that will ensure they have the necessary knowledge,
understanding and skills that will enable them to make those informed
choices. Along with the rest of us, Alison, Alan and Claire need to teach
children how to learn (see Chapter 5). This does not only apply to ICT:
it applies to the whole curriculum. We need to teach the children how
to research, find, select, classify, interpret and analyse across a range of
subject contexts. ICT can help this through the power, speed and capacity that it brings. Here then lies the key for our three teachers; their
enthusiasm and philosophical approach needs to be geared towards these
ends.

Planning the lesson

When we plan a lesson where ICT is to be used, we need to consider several key points, educational, organizational and managerial:

- the ICT must be relevant to the teaching and learning objectives for that particular lesson, so if it is a data handling lesson, the objectives are directly related to this, drawn from the appropriate data handling attainment targets in the National Curriculum;
- the ICT should be overtly and obviously present in all planning, but should not dominate it. ICT is the vehicle that we will be using to meet the aims and objectives, but will not be the main focus of the lesson. Therefore, we need to put subject objectives first, ICT objectives second;
- the content that we plan and prepare should be appropriate to the capabilities of the children in the class: the subject content needs to be appropriately differentiated, and so does the ICT content. The lesson will be wasted if the program cannot be properly accessed because the children do not have sufficient mouse or keyboard skills, or because they cannot read what is on the screen;
- the ways in which we use ICT – what opportunities are we making available for collaborative learning? As we saw in Claire's class at the beginning of this chapter, the opportunities for discussion and shared effort are very important for extending children's learning;
- which key questions are to be asked to stimulate learning? If we use, sharply focused questions that are sufficiently open to allow the children to think about not only their answer but also the reasons underlying it, we will be extending children's thinking and thus their learning as well. We will also be providing the opportunity to provide positive feedback as the children work, thus raising their self-esteem and reinforcing their learning;
- deciding against which criteria assessments are being made to ensure that true progress has been made. These must be planned for at the planning stage. This was the problem that was particularly troubling Claire. Both she and Alan need to remember that ICT is supporting the teaching of the subject. Therefore, assessments need to be made against the criteria of the subject, but this must be considered at the planning stage. It is not appropriate to plan a lesson and then decide to blithely 'do some assessment'. If this happens it runs the risk of not addressing the key teaching and learning points as described in the lesson plan (see more detailed information in Chapters 3 and 12).

And all of this in one lesson! Once we have considered all of the above points, holistically and coherently, we have the basis of a successful lesson.

The classroom organization and management of ICT

Teaching with ICT is not difficult but it is different, as we have to think not only about organizing and managing the subject content but also the ICT component. The presence of ICT means that it is at least one more thing to think about. One of the most common models of teaching, especially where a new idea or concept is being introduced, is where a skill is demonstrated and the children acquire and then reinforce this skill. The children will need to be arranged in such a way that they can see the screen, possibly through the use of a large monitor, data projector or an interactive whiteboard. It will be in our best interests to move them away from computers or desks so that their attention is completely focused on the computer and what is being demonstrated and discussed. This by necessity needs to be short and limited to an explanation of the key points and ideas. It is much more effective to learn by doing rather than watching, especially where a computer is concerned! All the children want to do is to get started!

We then need to consider how learning is going to be organized. Once the key ideas and concepts have been introduced to the class, the work must begin! This may involve work at the computer such as a piece of work using a graphics package, or it might involve some work away from the computer – perhaps collecting data to enter into a computer for subsequent interrogation or analysis. We have already seen that it is preferable to employ a collaborative learning approach and given that a typical primary school may have an insufficient number of computers to enable each child to use a machine, this may well be forced on us anyway. Besides there are several advantages to this: the children have a critical friend to help them with their work, to help with the development and the refining of ideas, the classification and analysis of data and the use of the hardware and software. Single-user working is not really appropriate for younger children, as they need the social interaction that this approach brings. Working in pairs allows for pupil interaction, discussion and shared activity, yet enables the teacher to ensure that input and effort is equally balanced. Pairs can be arranged according to ability or gender, and should be changed frequently.

Health and safety

Whenever we teach, we have always to consider Health and Safety issues, and this is especially so with ICT. For example, there will need to be desk space around the computer for workbooks and other resources that the children may be using in order to complete their tasks. A computer trolley or space can become cluttered very quickly, and this in turn raises a host of associated issues. The mouse needs to be freely accessible, positioned to the correct hand and without obstructions, so that it can be easily and comfortably moved, and where possible wrist supports should be used. The monitor should be positioned so that light does not glare onto the screen and chairs should be adjusted so that eye levels are parallel to the screen to avoid eyestrain or neck problems. This is always a particular challenge as some children in primary schools are as young as 4 years old, whereas the computers that they use are designed for adults. When this is coupled with the need to position it so that it is integrated with other classroom activities and other resources to encourage research and/or collaborative learning, as well as ensuring that the teacher can easily monitor the children's work on the computer, it poses many organizational problems that are not easy to solve. Additionally there should not be any trailing electrical cables, and all electrical equipment should be regularly checked. If you can achieve all of that then you really have arrived as a teacher! (Chris Curran gives further guidance on these issues in Chapter 17).

In the classroom

As Alison has already discovered, organizing one computer in the classroom brings its own problems. Quite apart from the fact that there *is* only one, which means that the children will have to take turns to use it, the use of it will probably have to be fitted in around a range of other activities that are going on, as well as a host of other considerations. However, Alison knows that it is better to allow the children to spend a good deal of time on one task of value rather than many short tasks which serve no purpose other than to allow her to say that every child has had a turn today.

So how does she teach when she only has access to one computer in the classroom? A good way to begin is to gather the children around the screen and then briefly highlight the main features of the program that is to be used, which should take no more than about ten minutes. Then will come the transition, where the class will begin their tasks, which may or may not be connected to using ICT. Indeed, there could be several unrelated group activities beginning at this point. While this is happening, Alison should concentrate on getting the bulk of the class – perhaps 30 or more children – working on their tasks. As this may involve walking to trays, getting pencil cases, books, then going elsewhere in the room to get other resources, she should be concerned with the monitoring and management of this phase of the session. After all, it is these first few minutes that set the tone for the remainder of the lesson, and she needs to be on top of this. Therefore, she will not want to be distracted by two children struggling to come to terms with the computer. The use of a CA where one is available, as described in Chapter 6, can support this kind of situation.

One other effective way is to choose two children who are very confident and competent in the use of the computer. One child sits at the keyboard and uses this and the mouse, the other is on hand to provide the collaborative input. This may involve providing additional ideas about the user's work or help with technical features of the program. When the first child has finished and has printed or saved their work, the second child moves over to use the mouse and a third child, also ICT capable, arrives to fulfil the role of adviser. This scenario is acted until four or five children have all had the opportunity to work on the computer. This is crucial in allowing Alison time to settle the remainder of the class without being distracted by technical problems or questions. Having to deal with two children during the crucial transitional stage is not a very efficient use of her time.

This is not to say that she should start with the most able and work her way through to the least able child; this clearly would be unacceptable in terms of equal opportunities (Chapter 14) and would not allow for genuine social interaction with all members of the class. However, by having the first three pairs include the more able children does provide Alison with several invaluable opportunities:

- children who are confident in the use of ICT can manage themselves and will not be afraid to experiment: they will explore the different functions of a new piece of software and will not be so teacher dependent;
- when Alison does finally get to the point where interaction occurs, it is less likely to be a technical interaction in the sense that she is explaining how to use the program, but will have more quality in its nature, being able to pose questions such as 'What are you doing?', 'Why have you done this?', 'What happens if...?' These important open-ended questions, which extend children's learning as it is happening, become the central focus in the activity;
- very quickly there becomes a pool of technical knowledge within the class about the software being used, thus taking a great burden from Alison, as the children will often be able to troubleshoot their own problems. The fact that they may know more about the program than her does not matter, as she knows more about teaching and learning! After all, she cannot know the contents of every book in the school library, or how her car works, so why should she know how the computer works, as long as it does what she and the children want it to do?
- this approach raises pupils' self-esteem, and for this reason the 'elite' group should be changed frequently.

In the ICT suite

Since the 1990s, many schools have installed ICT suites and consequently different issues arise which will directly affect the organization and management of the lesson. This is particularly evident to Alan as he is used to teaching in a classroom where the desks may be laid out in groups, but now he has to teach in a different environment with different considerations for planning.

He notices that, at least at first, the computer appears to 'take charge'. He has to be careful that the aims and objectives of the lesson do not become altered from being subject-based to being too 'techie'. The children are restricted to where they can sit by the positioning of the computers, which limits flexibility. Desks are fixed and the children will be facing the computer screen rather than the teacher. They will have to be actively encouraged to turn physically to watch and listen to the demonstration. Alan also needs to consider technical issues such as who turns the computers on and when, who changes ink cartridges and manages and logs them into the network, and who troubleshoots problems. If the class gets only one hour a week in this facility, the last thing the teacher wants is to lose valuable time because the children cannot log on to the network or the file server is not working, or because the previous group has not left the room in a condition in which an immediate start to the lesson can be made. Ensuring maximum 'hands-on' time is a priority, so any preparatory teaching should be done prior to the start of the lesson in the normal classroom. It might even be possible to demonstrate a particular piece of software on the classroom computer if it is the same type as those that are in the ICT suite.

We can of course see several possible permutations to these two basic models. Some schools have computers on trolleys, which are wheeled into one room for an ICT lesson. Due to their mobility these can then be moved into individual classrooms to follow-up and develop ideas taught in the whole class lesson. The ideal compromise is to use laptops as these are not only a more suitable size for younger children to use, but can also be easily moved for secure storage, can be organized for whole-class teaching and learning situations, can be used individually for small group tasks, or can be taken out of the classroom environment for work elsewhere in the school or even for field trips. If the school should be fortunate enough to have a wireless local area network (LAN), the computers can be 'connected' to a network for access to the Internet, email or shared printing without the need for cumbersome wiring. In fact, often the greatest cost in networking computers is in the wiring of an ICT suite or a whole school.

Assessment

The main purpose of assessment is to ascertain whether the objectives of the lesson have been achieved and whether the children have learned what the teacher intended them to learn. Generally speaking, we as teachers will use formative assessment when we use ICT. This indicates what the children have learned during the course of the lesson, the next steps to be taken and may signal any potential problems that might need 'catch-up' activities. It is possible that if we use an Integrated Learning package – that is where a child is following a highly structured teaching scheme on the computer – that diagnostic and possibly, summative assessment will be used. Diagnostic assessment will attempt to diagnose why a child may have a specific problem, and summative assessment will measure learning (see Chapter 12 for further details).

As teachers we need to be clear exactly what it is that needs to be assessed. This should be in terms of the learning that is taking place, rather than the use of the ICT or in particular, the ICT key skills. If efficient planning has taken place, this will occur as a matter of course. If planning is for the development of subject-specific skills, then that is what should be assessed. It should be noted that if poor ICT key skills are hampering the activity, such as slow or inaccurate typing skills preventing an accurate completion of the task, then this is appropriate to mention in an assessment. This should not, though, be to the detriment of the main focus of the activity. Once we have determined the nature and purpose of the assessment, we need to consider the form that the assessment will take. In the light of our cameos, one most likely type of assessment where ICT is used will be by task. As with other curriculum areas, teacher observation (see Chapter 3) and possibly teacher questioning will dominate. Assuming that the computer is being used as a tool for learning, and that collaborative learning is taking place, key aspects of the pupil activity will also be a feature.

This will include assessing whether problem-solving techniques are being used, which may or may not directly include the use of ICT. A final cameo is a useful way of demonstrating this.

Cameo 4

Alison decides to complete a traffic survey. In order to do this, the lesson needs to evolve in the following way:

- Alison will discuss with the children how they will collect and record their data. They decide that the best way will be to use a simple tally chart using lines in groups of five every time they see a particular type of vehicle. In order to make it a fair survey, they will not have any preconceived ideas as to which field;

- accompanied by an adult, the children will go to a location where they can see a road in complete safety and watch and record the different types of traffic passing by;
- the children will return to the classroom and look at the raw data. They will discuss how to go about synthesizing information so that it can be entered into the computer in a form that is easy to interrogate, interpret, graph and chart;
- the discussion will be crucial here, as this will illustrate their understanding. Again, the importance of Alison's role is raised, as the posing of appropriate focused open-ended questions will assess the children's understanding of the key concepts and ideas that were taught as part of the lesson or series of lessons;
- she might also consider other issues such as whether the children are on task, and for how long. She needs to ascertain whether each child has a fair and equal part in the activity and that there is a balance of effort between collection, input, interpretation and analysis.

She can assess at several stages of the process:

- how the children discuss to decide which means of data collection will be used, or how the children analyse their raw data;
- how they synthesize the information for entry into the computer's database and how they interrogate the data;
- the quality of the discussion – she will ask focused, open-ended questions and use this information to determine whether there has been genuine understanding and, therefore, whether learning has taken place.

It is necessary for Alison to record the outcomes of her assessments. Record keeping is essential as it provides both evidence and a means of tracking the learning of an individual child. We have already seen that ICT can provide the catalyst for a wide range of assessment evidence and that, in turn, can be particularly useful for continuously tracking a pupil's progress and development, as well as for annual reporting to parents and for open evenings.

There are several effective means of recording pupil progress and achievement open to her. The main ones are:

- a tick sheet, either as a whole class or group list, which, although quick, lacks essential detail as it simply indicates whether a child has performed a simple task or used a particular application, it might be more sophisticated in that it is ticked against a standard or attainment target. Although very useful for a quick check of what a child has or has not completed, it lacks depth and analysis;

- a series of detailed comments and statements, but this can take much time and effort and although detailed, it is not easy to extrapolate the key information quickly or easily;
- a compromise between the two, where the teacher combines record keeping with assessment. The very presence of a short statement in a box against the child's name gives a sufficient level of depth while also making it clear what has and has not been achieved and completed;
- the child's comments can be added to the assessment. At FS and KS1 the child might state whether he or she enjoyed the activity or not, or at KS2 children might evaluate their work by stating what they would do if they had to complete the task again in order to improve it. It is also possible to set targets together that are achievable and on a realistic timescale.

Let's celebrate!

The final but no less important and natural extension to assessment and record keeping is the 'celebration' of children's work, which is an important part of the production of a piece of work and integral to its processes. Assuming that the child has put in an appropriate amount of effort and that the results are up to the standard of which that child is capable, then it can be shown to others during feedback sessions such as assemblies. Displays are also very important – the message on the classroom wall says a great deal not only about the children, but also the teacher and the school itself. Attractive displays of work around the classroom as well as in shared areas around the school gives a wide range of positive messages. It overtly praises the children's work, making a bold statement of the value of that child not only as a worker but also as a person. It also demonstrates the ethos not only of the class but also of the school, in that ICT is an important part of the life of the school and what it is trying to achieve (see Gill Robinson's comments in Chapter 8). When used in all areas of school life, such as newsletters and labels for walls, trays and so on, it gives an overall and co-ordinated impact that children's efforts matter both in ICT and other aspects of the curriculum.

Conclusion

So that's all there is to it! Congratulations! You can teach using ICT!

This chapter set out to provide some insights into the contribution that ICT can make to teaching and learning in the broadest sense. Although clearly a tool to learning, ICT offers so much more than that. Not only does it help children to think, it can also change the way that they think. The need to compose and arrange different elements, perhaps text, sound icons and graphics on a page, perhaps hyper-linked to other pages or parts of text, rather than in the more traditional linear way, requires a way of thinking that has not always been part of the primary school curriculum. The ability to make a floor or screen turtle draw a shape by moving a certain number of turtle steps, or turn through a certain number of degrees, or the need to synthesize information ready for data analysis, offers genuine opportunities for the kind of higher-order intellectual development that was largely inaccessible to previous generations of primary aged children.

In the light of reading this chapter, here are a few key questions you might want to ask yourself:

- How is ICT in its broadest form relevant to the lives of the children in your care both outside and inside school?
- How can you use hyper-linked text to change the way that the children think about and use the structure of texts?
- How much should you intervene when a group of children are working collaboratively to make the floor turtle move? How do you know when to lead the questioning and when to let them work it out for themselves?
- How can you encourage children to synthesize data to a form that the computer can handle, and then how do you get the children to draw meaningful and appropriate conclusions from what they have discovered?

These are not the kind of questions that should end the creative process with children. They should form the beginning.

References and further reading

Ager, R. (1998) *Information and Communications Technology in Primary Schools: Children or Computers in Control?* London: David Fulton.

Cook, D. and Finlayson, H. (2000) *Interactive Children: Communicative Teaching.* Buckingham: Open University Press.

Crompton, R. and Mann, P. (1996) *IT Across the Primary Curriculum.* London: Cassell.

Department for Education and Employment (1997) *Connecting the Learning Society,* National Grid for Learning, Government Consultation Paper. London: DfEE.

Department for Education and Employment (1998) *High Status: High Standards,* Circular Number 4/98. London: HMSO.

Department for Education and Employment (2000) *The National Curriculum for England.* London: HMSO.

Department for Education and Employment/Qualifications and Curriculum Authority (1998) *Information Technology: A Scheme of Work for Key Stages 1 and 2,* London: HMSO.

Papert, S. (1993) *Mindstorms: Children, Computers and Powerful Ideas* (2nd edn). Hemel Hempstead: Harvester/Wheatsheaf.

12

Keeping track: assessing, monitoring and recording children's progress and achievement

Morag Hunter-Carsch

Cameo 1

Note made by a student teacher after observing and assisting with teaching a Year 5 class: 'How can I possibly manage to keep track of all that is going on in the classroom? It's tough enough being expected to plan for all the subjects in the curriculum and all the children including the ones with special needs but, on top of that, to have to keep records is what really concerns me. Where can I get help with sorting out how to do it all?'

Cameo 2

Note made by a student after attending a primary school staff meeting: 'The teachers were talking about the school's policy for testing children throughout the year. Whole-class screening of the children is to be carried out to find out who should be followed up with individual testing. They worked in year groups and they brought along records of test results and portfolios of children's work. There seems to be a computer-based record for everyone to use. What does it all mean? It looks very daunting – I wonder if I'll be expected to do all of this during my teaching practice?'

Cameo 3

Notes made by a student after an early experience in an infant school: 'There was the usual cluster of parents coming into the playground and entering the nursery at "home time". One mother with a toddler moved determinedly through the crowd and right up to the teacher and asked her, "Mrs W, Can I have a word with you

It's really about the older one, Alan, – he's in Year 4 now – it's him I'm concerned about, but I just wanted to talk to you, particularly, and about the two little ones as well. You know how Alan was so slow with his reading, do you think it might be dyslexia? Do you think David and the little one might have it too?" I was very curious about how Mrs W would answer this. I don't know much about the details of how to recognize reading problems, let alone "dyslexia" – and just how to deal with a parent's questions. It was very impressive how Mrs W was so calm and organized and found just the right way of reassuring the parent – especially when she shared her records and her notes about David and she could remember the older child and talk about the details of his early literacy problems.'

Introduction

Keeping track of children's learning by observing, making assessments and recording their progress and needs constitutes a vital component of the primary teacher's work. In the current climate of concern about 'quality' and 'standards' in education, there are models of assessment continually being developed (see Gipps 1994). Beginner teachers need to get to grips with developments in assessment and recording pupils' progress as soon as possible both for accountability purposes and, principally, in order to *use assessment to support teaching and learning* (Qualifications and Curriculum Authority 1999). This involves many skills and processes and these are diagrammatically presented in Figure 12.1, which is adapted from the 'Curriculum in Action' Project.

It should be noted from the outset that there is no single ideal way for teachers or children to assess and keep track of activities and learning in the classroom. The important issue, Gipps (1994) advises, is 'fitness for purpose'. This chapter aims to introduce you to concepts, terminology and procedures for assessing and recording for a range of purposes. All three of the cameos reflect interest and concern in sorting out priorities and getting to grips with assessment, record keeping and communicating with parents and colleagues about children's progress and problems. The chapter begins, therefore, with discussion prompted by these three situations and builds on, and extends, some of Nick Easingwood's comments towards the end of the previous chapter. Observation as an issue has already been covered fairly extensively by Linda Hargreaves in Chapter 3.

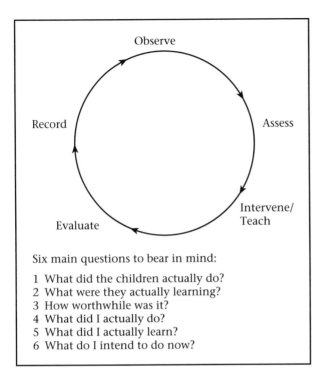

Six main questions to bear in mind:

1 What did the children actually do?
2 What were they actually learning?
3 How worthwhile was it?
4 What did I actually do?
5 What did I actually learn?
6 What do I intend to do now?

Figure 12.1 University of Leicester Curriculum in Action diagram and questions.

Priorities and issues

Cameo 1 reflects a quite normal response to the daunting recognition of the range of skills that teachers are required to develop beyond simply 'managing' children. For the beginning teacher 'testing' and teaching might appear to be quite separate areas of responsibility and consequently 'testing' might seem to be an extra burden. With increasing experience it becomes easier to understand how assessment relates to teaching and learning and particularly how teachers' and children's records can provide information that helps the teacher to plan in order to match the work as closely as possible to the children's needs: the essence of good teaching as shown by Janet Moyles in Chapter 6. However, it takes time to acquire expertise in assessment and record keeping, as indeed in all other aspects of teaching! It is helpful to be aware of a range of models and to have opportunities to explore different forms of assessing and recording children's progress and problems.

It would also be easier to develop greater understanding in this field if there was less conceptual confusion in some media reports on testing

Teachers are advised to employ a range of procedures for assessing and keeping track

and standards and relentless media interest in 'standards' and the issue of 'accountability'. It is not uncommon to hear or read angry comments about alleged falling standards in literacy and conclusions that 'half our children are failing'. Such reports may be based on popular misconceptions, for example, the assumption that all children of a certain chronological age should be achieving at the same measured 'reading age'. A less dramatic but equally erroneous idea would be to report positively that 'half our children are succeeding beyond the average reading age for their chronological age'! What is required is greater clarity about the purposes and meaning of different forms of describing children's achievements. This is particularly important in the light of National Curriculum developments since the Report from the Task Group on Assessment and Testing (Department of Education and Science 1988). Teachers have been advised to employ a range of procedures for assessing and keeping track of progress, not least the developments of Records of Achievement (RoA) and the involvement of *children* in keeping track of their own achievement and planning for priorities in their own learning.[1]

As Cameo 2 reveals, you need not feel alone in dealing with these issues since the policies at national and local education authority level are increasingly supported by guidelines that are being implemented by collaborative teams of teachers in individual schools. Their work includes the development of cohesive policy statements and workable, informative practices for their schools, some of which I describe later, to ensure continuity and progression throughout the curriculum for all children, including bi- and multilingual children and those with special education needs (see also Jenny Lansdell's comments in Chapter 15).

Cameo 3 shows how teachers may be consulted by parents about matters that may require fairly specialized knowledge about diagnostic assessment and they will need to consider how best to respond to parents' concerns. This does not mean just a familiarity with detailed records of individual children's achievements but knowing who to consult (for example, the special educational needs co-ordinator (SENCO)). In this case, the teacher responded in regard to identifying children with specific learning difficulties, including dyslexia – the term used to highlight a condition in which children find it difficult to deal with letters and words in the effective and efficient way that most of us do.[2]

Questions about literacy and reading difficulties are among the most frequently shared areas of parental interest and concern. In recognition of the centrality of literacy for independent learning in and beyond the school curriculum, the illustrations in this chapter are mainly of literacy or reading records though they equally apply to keeping track in other areas of the curriculum and for homework.

Questions and concepts

This section addresses some fundamental questions, provides reasons for making assessments and keeping track and considers some basic concepts and procedures. Our task as teachers, through addressing our own competences as described by Neil Kitson in Chapter 4 and reflecting on our own practices as outlined by Siân Adams in Chapter 13, will be to monitor, evaluate and plan requisite 'action' to lead gradually to a greater understanding of these issues.

Why assess?

There are several purposes for assessing children's progress. They include:

- to investigate the progress of the individual child;
- to provide a profile of the child's achievements across the curriculum;
- to investigate the range of children's attainments in the class as a whole;
- to plan the teaching programme;
- to evaluate the teaching programme;
- to monitor standards.

For whom are we assessing?

Some of your records of assessments may also be directly useful to the children themselves (for example, transfer between schools, traveller children) and for:

- yourself as teacher;
- colleagues, including, for example, nursery nurses, classroom assistants, subject co-ordinators, SENCOs;
- the headteacher;
- parents, guardians;
- school governors and managers.

Results of formal assessments may be of interest also to the wider community in the context of regional and national standards and international comparisons.

What is 'assessment'?

All teachers require skills for evaluating their own and the children's activities and outcomes. These skills include:

1 *Evaluation* – the measurement of learning in terms of competence, or the capacity of the child to achieve objectives. Evaluation implies some degree of judgement.
2 *Assessment* – a more limited form of evaluation. The assessment process is ongoing and should involve the learners. It forms a part of teaching and learning, informing future teaching and learning provision. It reflects the whole curriculum. There are different theoretical models of the process. The 'psychometric model' implies some form of measurement that is related to the performance of a particular group (norm-referenced assessment) or of a particular task (criterion-referenced assessment). The psychometric approach to assessment emphasizes *quantitative* descriptions or precise responses to selected criteria rather than *qualitative* descriptions of performance, the latter is much more likely to be used with younger children in the context of observation (see Linda Hargreaves examples in Chapter 3).
3 *Norm-referenced assessment* – this involves using tests of ability, achievement or attainment in which the individual child's achievements can be compared to a 'standardized sample' of children on whom the test was trialled. This yields a description of the child's achievements in 'norm-referenced' terms (that is, compared to another group of a similar age). This makes possible the comparison of standards across different groups as long as the same measurement instruments are used and administered, scored and interpreted accurately.
4 *Criterion-referenced assessment* – this involves the use of specific criteria (for example, the child can say the letters of the alphabet in order)

against which the child's attainment can be matched. This is probably the most commonly used assessment in primary classrooms.

5 *Levels of assessment* – these include:
   - screening or survey level, which, at its broadest, helps teachers to find out about the range of a class of children's attainments in the particular aspect being assessed;
   - individual or profile level, which involves describing performance at a given date across a range of areas (for example curriculum subjects, skills or aptitudes). This level of exploration may prompt a teacher to go on to study more keenly particular aspects of the children's learning abilities or difficulties at the next level;
   - intensive or case-study level, which involves collecting results of assessments over time. Work at this level is likely to include both structured observations and diagnostic tests (detailed in Chapter 3).

6 *Types of assessment* – these may broadly be described as threefold:
   (i) *formative* assessment, which is the ongoing process of keeping track of how well the children are progressing over a period of time;
   (ii) *summative* assessment, which involves presenting a summary picture at the end of a given time;
   (iii) *ipsative* assessment, which is developmentally related.

7 *Assessment in the NC* – the programmes of study within the National Curriculum are intended to guide the planning, teaching and day-to-day assessment of 5- to 11-year-olds' activities. Standard assessment tasks and tests have been designed to assist teachers in making summative assessments and attainment reports at the end of key stages (see, for example, QCA/00/624 on the website: www.qca.gov.uk). Teachers use 'level descriptions' in making judgements on an individual child's achievement (Schools Curriculum and Assessment Authority 1994, see also Exemplifications of Standards QCA/01/89 on the website above). A teacher's own assessments of children's performance are reported alongside the test results.[3]

When these indicate that the child has largely achieved attainment targets at one level in an aspect, the teacher tests the children using tests selected from the catalogue of national test units to see if a child can achieve further.[4]

8 *Assessing children with English as an additional language (EAL)* – The NC requires that children should be assessed in the language of instruction and consideration given in administering and interpreting their performance on assessment tasks to the possible impact of their first language. A lively example involves the 'over-literal' interpretations of instructions in a mathematics task requiring the children to 'draw round half of the children' resulting in drawings 'through' half of each child rather than half of a group of children!

The Leicestershire LEA in conjunction with the Bilingual Working Party (1991) has produced helpful descriptors of language levels to assist teachers in exploring possible gaps between children's social language, which might seem to be fluent, and their understanding of 'technical English' as applied to a range of school tasks.

9 *Assessing children aged 3–5 years* – There is increasing awareness of the importance of baseline assessment on entry to school and in relation to setting targets for working towards the achievement of ELGs (Department for Education and Employment 2000). The majority of forms of assessment described in this chapter can be used with young children. However, it must be remembered that only 5-year-olds and above are included in the NC assessment procedures: younger children's experiences are much broader as outlined by Nansi Ellis in the first chapter.

What is involved in record keeping?

Record keeping is a routine and essential part of teaching. Making records about professional work such as daily activity plans and children's responses to a range of tasks, forms the basis for decision making about what to monitor, which kinds of behaviours to observe more closely and, for example, what aspects of the interaction process of learning and teaching to select for further analysis.

Refining professional competence in keeping track should lead to self-evaluation, making informed choices about priorities for teaching and for further professional development and is included in the kind of self-reflection activities described by Neil Kitson in Chapter 4.

It is vital to keep records up-to-date – it is simply not possible to recall pertinent specific observations until, for example, the end of the day, week or term before making a note of them. It is also necessary to avoid trying to make notes of too many things. The challenge is to discern what records are essential and practicable and to maintain them, even if they are not ideal in every way. With practice it is possible to evolve an improved system for your own use. Teachers' records may differ in design according to their intended purposes (see Clift 1981; Fisher 1991). QCA (1999) advises that records should:

- be fit for the purpose they serve and help teachers, senior managers and parents (or others with parental responsibility) track the progress pupils make;
- arise from routine processes of teaching, learning and assessing;
- be manageable, concise and accurate.

Records can loosely be clustered into three main types – *'baseline' records, continuous records* and *summary records* – which correspond with the sequence of tasks likely to face the teacher throughout the school year. These will be explained later and examples given.

Portfolios and records of achievement

Some schools retain *School Portfolios* or *Class Portfolios*. These consist of a collection of examples of work which demonstrate the standard of consistency between groups of teachers. *The Individual Portfolio* consists of an annotated collection of work by an individual child, put together by the teacher in order to demonstrate the attainment for a particular child.

The Record of Achievement (RoA) is child-centred (with samples of work selected by the child) and provides examples of achievement. In primary schools this may cover many curricular subject areas as well as personal, social, health and moral education. This is a common kind of record in FS settings. Schools generally provide handbooks for teachers regarding matters of administration and management of the curriculum and assessment, which may include guidelines on principles of Records of Achievement. One such example, shown in Figure 12.2, serves as a useful guide. Schools may provide their own style of records for different aspects of the curriculum to assist the child. Figures 12.3 to 12.6 provide

---

The Record of Achievement should:
- be a positive record of the achievements and experiences gained during the period of a child's education;
- embrace the wider interests of the student and not be confined to achievements and experience within formal education;
- be drawn up through a process of discussion between a student, teacher and others over a period of time;
- be drawn up in a way which respects the student's right to privacy;
- be available to all children;
- be the property of the child to whom the record refers;
- facilitate the continuity of learning and transfer between stages of education and between education and adult life, from years 1–10 and beyond;
- be a catalyst for improving the teaching and learning within the school and fully integrated into the curriculum structure;
- encourage active learning styles through an emphasis upon the process of learning;
- encourage children to take greater responsibility for their learning by reviewing achievements and experience in negotiation with their teachers.

(from Eyres Monsell Primary School, Leicester)

Figure 12.2 Example of a statement of principles about RoA.

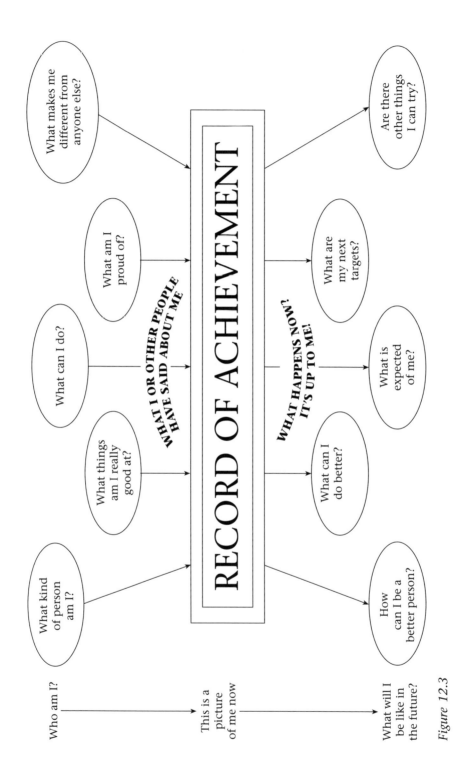

Figure 12.3

Early Years

Name _____

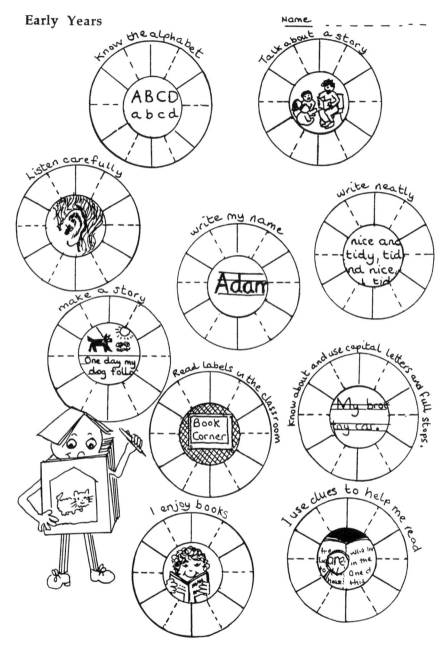

Figure 12.4

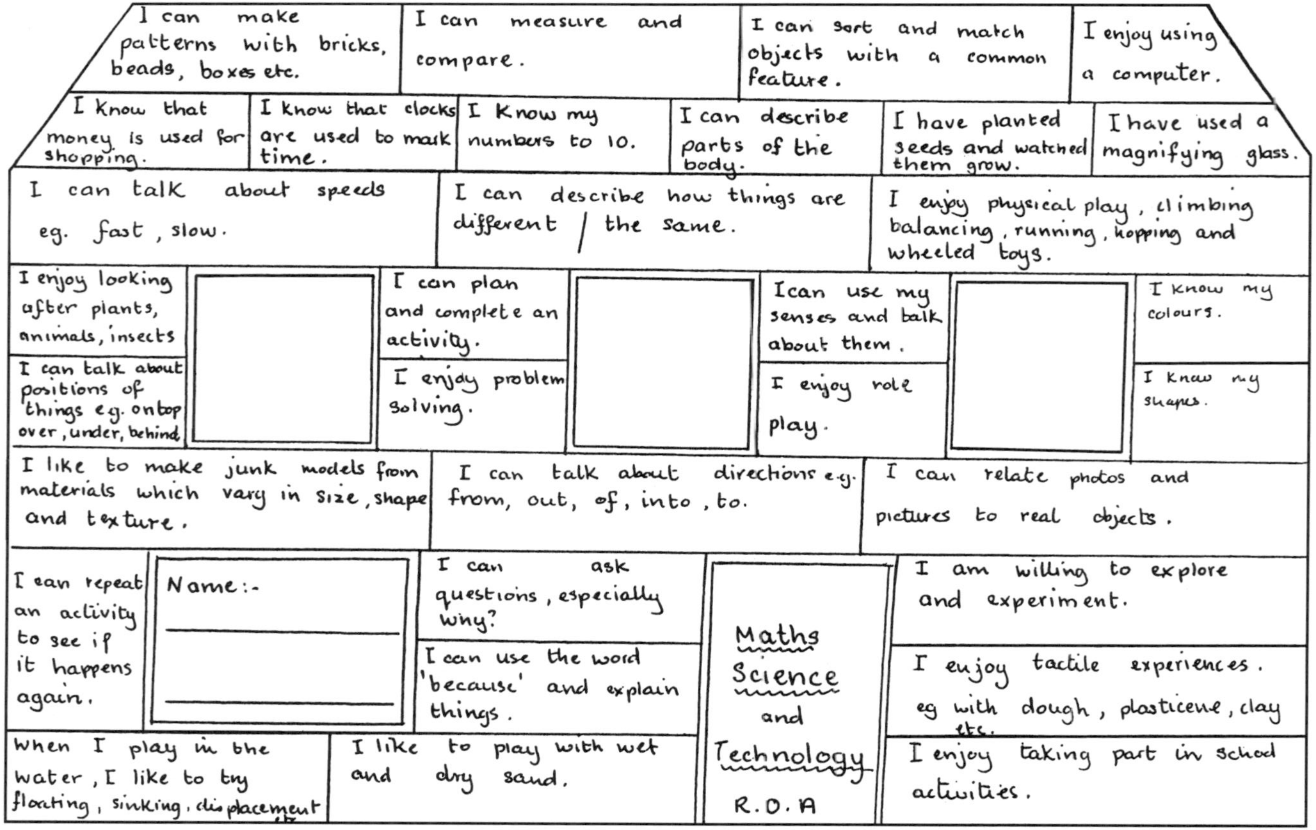

I can make patterns with bricks, beads, boxes etc.

I can measure and compare.

I can sort and match objects with a common feature.

I enjoy using a computer.

I know that money is used for shopping.

I know that clocks are used to mark time.

I know my numbers to 10.

I can describe parts of the body.

I have planted seeds and watched them grow.

I have used a magnifying glass.

I can talk about speeds eg. fast, slow.

I can describe how things are different / the same.

I enjoy physical play, climbing, balancing, running, hopping and wheeled toys.

I enjoy looking after plants, animals, insects

I can plan and complete an activity.

I can use my senses and talk about them.

I know my colours.

I can talk about positions of things eg. on top, over, under, behind.

I enjoy problem solving.

I enjoy role play.

I know my shapes.

I like to make junk models from materials which vary in size, shape and texture.

I can talk about directions e.g. from, out, of, into, to.

I can relate photos and pictures to real objects.

I am willing to explore and experiment.

I can repeat an activity to see if it happens again.

Name:-

I can ask questions, especially why?

Maths
Science
and
Technology
R.O.A

I enjoy tactile experiences. eg with dough, plasticene, clay etc.

When I play in the water, I like to try floating, sinking, displacement

I like to play with wet and dry sand.

I can use the word 'because' and explain things.

I enjoy taking part in school activities.

Figure 12.5

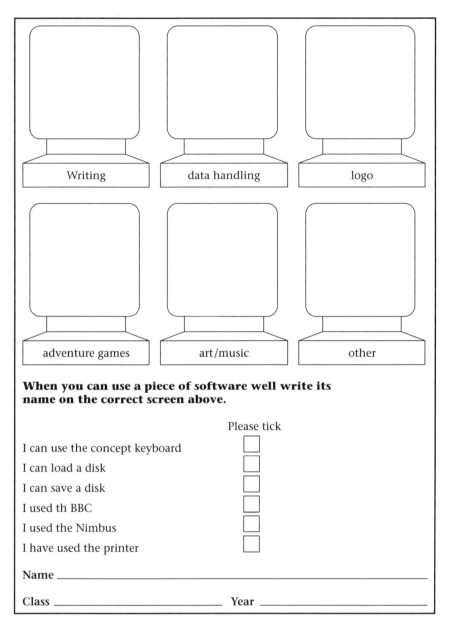

Writing	data handling	logo
adventure games	art/music	other

When you can use a piece of software well write its name on the correct screen above.

Please tick

I can use the concept keyboard ☐

I can load a disk ☐

I can save a disk ☐

I used th BBC ☐

I used the Nimbus ☐

I have used the printer ☐

Name _____

Class _____ **Year** _____

Figure 12.6 Example of a computer RoA.

a selection of record formats for children to use by colouring in as they acquire the relevant competences or complete them.

As can be seen, the format of records can vary considerably from school to school and this flexibility is both interesting and desirable – if only to keep teacher motivation! Teachers frequently use class *lists* (alphabetical or other orders of children's names) for the purposes of drawing up *matrices* to note, for example, tasks for children to complete or comments on their performance (see Figures 3.2 and 3.7 in Chapter 3).

Other lists, perhaps those for 'emergent reading', might be presented in the form of *tick lists,* sometimes with spaces for noting dates. The boxes for ticks or colouring are sometimes coded to allow for a range of additional messages to be quickly noted. The use of simple headed *columns* for entering comments is well illustrated in Manchester's Early Literacy Project (Manchester City Council Education Department 1988) (Figure 12.7).

How and when to assess and record

How, when and exactly what to record depends on the purpose of the assessment or record. Together with the detailed documentation to assist teachers with formal assessment of the NC, the following aspects aim to provide a framework and to develop points made above.

A framework for keeping track

We first need to be clear about the requirements in law within the NC and, just a word of warning, parents/guardians have a right to see any written records about their child. In order to establish our own knowledge base we need to:

1 Consult the NC framework and study the requirements for children's learning and assessment across the full curriculum;
2 Consult the LEA guidelines and teacher colleagues about ways in which these guidelines extend understanding of the national requirements and relate particularly to the locality;
3 Consult the School Policy Statement and teacher colleagues about the practical planning and implementation of the school's policies;
4 Decide on the particular purpose(s) of assessments or records;
5 Select or design the assessment procedure or record you require. Decide on the purpose(s) of the particular record;
6 Try it out, evaluate it and adapt as appropriate.

As teachers, we need gradually to establish our own ways of using (and where relevant, devising) records for the range of purposes mentioned previously. The most immediate ones will be:

Date	Book	Comments	Initials
			Teacher
8 Oct	The Two Snowmen	Liked this book, needed a little help	gCB.
10 Oct	The Hill + the Rock →	this will need more help but the class enjoyed the story greatly.	
			Parent
		READ IT ALL BUT STRUGGLED WITH ALOT OF THE NEW WORDS.	££ Teacher
12 Oct.	Peace at Last. (it's a hot favourite) ←	A lovely book, that holds the child's interest from beginning to end.	gCB.
13 Oct	The little monster.	Rather tired tonight. James started to read the left hand-side of the pages, but reverted to the right hand side after a drink.	gCB.
14 Oct.	Hairy Bear (I think he's having a rest cure). Glad he was at your house!	No problems tonight, James still finds this book amusing and told me he's going to have a midnight feast!	
15 Oct	The pirates ☺	James interested in the story especially their adventure in the tree house. ↓ James read this to me really well.	
16 Oct	Hungry mouse.		
19 Oct	To Town	must be having a rest. Book-partner easy	gCB.
20 Oct	The Rat. What a surprise.	Only like you or I reading "Woman's Own"! Read upto P.10: enjoying the story so far. Read some more to Mrs. Cryan.	
21 "	Little Monkey.	at low ebb tonight. Full of a cold. Hence not much reading done	
23 Oct	Boys + Girls	He's asked for it again. Read at his Mamma's	

Figure 12.7 Parent comment card

1 *Day-to-day records* – projective plans for organizing, managing and teaching class, groups and individuals which:
   - mainly relate to teaching activities (self/teaching assistants/visitors/ parents and other helpers);
   - mainly relate to individual children's progress;
   - can be records made by children about their work;
   - can include samples of children's work.

   Other records which are likely to be used include:
2 *Summary records* – these can be weekly/monthly/termly plans and reviews for all subjects and/or topics to include:
   - teacher's plan;
   - class achievement/attainment test results;
   - transition records (across phases, for example Early Years or Infants to Juniors or Upper Primary) for individual children;
   - transfer records (between schools when child moves).
3 *Diagnostic records*, including case studies (for example of 'gifted' children, children with English as an additional language, travelling children or children with special educational needs), involve:
   - screening/identifying special needs (see DfE 1994; DfEE 2000);
   - noting plans for individual educational programmes or relevant support strategies based on assessment.
4 *Welfare records*, which indicate liaison with outside agencies.
5 *Reports to parents*, which relate the child's achievements to previously stated (and noted) plans and expectations based on previous assessments (or home–school liaison in the case of children just starting school). It is preferable that parents are regarded as partners with teachers at all levels of their child's education, and that their knowledge is taken into account, as well as the child's views, particularly at the case-study level of assessment. This is particularly so where 'on-entry' assessments are made of children just beginning the process of schooling (see Wolfendale 1993).

Each of these five types of records relates to different forms of practice. The first two are more fully explored below and reference sources are provided for further information about all five kinds of records in the chapter notes.

Day-to-day records – the teacher's log

In addition to recording attendance, you will generally keep notes of daily plans on which to make comments on significant events. One of the purposes of informal daily records can be to remind you to adjust the timetable or the content of particular work sessions in the light of 'happenings'. A simple three-column layout for a 'day record' is shown

Time	Plan Curriculum subjects/ Activities (class/group/ind) Organization/resources needed	Record Were plans carried out? What changes were needed? Comments? Reminders?

Figure 12.8 A simple day-to-day record

in Figure 12.8. Such daily notes may form part of a 'teacher's log' or 'journal', which could also include spaces for dated entries about significant events in children's or your own learning and assist you to relate day-to-day plans to medium-term plans.

Informal continuous assessment
Advice on routine, informal assessment is provided in the Teacher's Guidebooks for most published 'schemes' across the range of subject areas. Increasingly there are examples of record formats for use *by children* in groups, pairs or individually. Very useful examples of such records are to be found within the Oxford Reading Tree Scheme as part of the Fact Finders Resources (1994).

With early years children, informal recording is the most usual means by which to identify children's activities. This may be as simple as merely noting what the child actually *does* within the choices available (see Figure 3.3 in Chapter 3) but will also be related to *how* children approached activities, who else was involved, how long they persisted, language competence and the presence of adults (see Moyles 1989). These will nearly always be related to specific observations from which assessment will be made (see Drummond 1993) and are linked to the FS guidance and the Baseline Assessment Scheme in operation.

Observation records may be made for assessment of particular activities or tasks. These may be for routine purposes of checking understanding at the beginning or end of a unit of activities. Such records may be made by teachers, assistants or children. In recording direct observations of children, objectivity in data collection and interpretation will need to be studied (see Chapter 3). Take-home tasks may also include records for

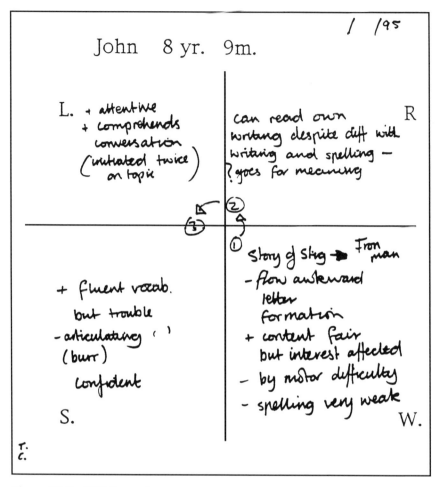

Figure 12.9 TIC Record

children or parents, for example where comments are sought from parents on their observation of children's reading at home. Some schools have homework books or cards.

When making speedy notes while talking with an individual child in the course of moving round the class as children work, the Teacher Interaction with Child (TIC) Record format, shown in Figure 12.9, has proved to be helpful as it relates to the immediate interaction and provides an instant check on the child's capabilities. It consists simply of drawing two intersecting lines in which to organize notes. Such notes take only a little time (2 minutes) to make while talking with the child and up to four children might be 'visited' during a single day. Thus, by using a class list, a rota can be established to remind the teacher to 'check' and have an encouraging word with every child in the class over a period of a week or two prior to starting the rota again. The notes can be added to logs, 'mark books' or portfolios. Such notes are particularly helpful in discussions with mentors or parents as you will have a ready vignette to bring to mind.

'Mark books' (and 'remark books'), or cumulative lists of comments about children's progress, may be kept by teachers in a different location from their day-to-day logs or journals. Such 'mark books', or Optical Mark Reader (OMR) computer records, record class and individual outcomes of periodic assessments throughout the school year. The results should yield information about the range or spread of attainment levels and developmental levels within the class as a whole. Mark books may also include information about individual children's profiles across the curriculum. A useful framework for individual assessment in reading is that provided by the Individual Assessment Record of the *Reading 2000 Storytime* materials (1993), reproduced in Figure 12.10.[5]

Summary records

At the end of each period of transition, such as moving from nursery to reception, reception to KS1, KS1 to KS2 and KS2 to KS3 (and secondary school) summary records will be required. These may be drawn on for reports to be communicated to parents and for passing on to the next teacher. There may be some aspects of *confidentiality* to be considered and undoubtedly there will be areas relating to curriculum continuity and progression that require to be 'connected' for efficient planning for the next stage.[6]

For summary records, as for informal, ongoing records, it is important that the information they contain can be readily related to plans for further learning. They should point towards likely requirements for support for learning and provision of further access to the curriculum through independent learning and collaborative learning. A record system that involves the children in setting their own goals through dialogue with peers and teachers and recording their attainment of these goals, is likely to be both enjoyable and effective in guiding children towards valuing learning, developing self-esteem and confidence in continuing to set goals and to keep track of their achievements.

Individual Assessment Record : School _Netherlee_	
Name _Hannah_	Age (D of B) _6yrs 2mths_
Class _P1_	Date _June '96_

Strengths	Comments
Hannah came to school already very interested in and enthusiastic about books. Within 2 months she could read very well. Her oral reading is fluent, expressive and meaningful. Reading silently she is capable of reading and understanding "novels" as well as picture stories. She is skilled in understanding characters' behaviour & feelings. When using follow up material from her class reading book she can readily find information needed to give an appropriate answer.	Hannah is a very able pupil in every area of the curriculum. Her reading skills are well in advance of her peer group and I have come across no reading material which she has been unable to read although she may not be able to understand some areas outwith her experience.
Developmental Needs	Support Strategy
Hannah needs to be given reading materials which will extend and consolidate her skills and encourage her enthusiasm for reading to develop even further.	Each week Hannah spent two twenty minute periods with a learning support teacher, working with other able children, in order that she could develop her full potential.
Outcomes	Future Targets (Next Steps)
Hannah was able to print out her own stories on the computer.	Increased experience of a variety of texts to improve and develop her comprehension and reference skills further.

Teacher _Isabel J. Eden_ Date _June '94._

Parent _____ Date _____

Reading 2000 Storytime, Teacher's Guide 2

Figure 12.10

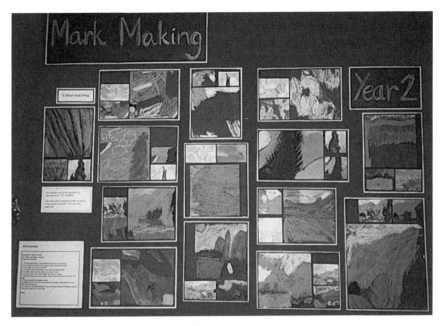

Teachers should use attractive and efficient modes of recording individual children's progress and competence

Conclusion

Knowledge and skill in assessment and record-keeping procedures are very much a part of 'real teaching'. It might seem daunting at first but remember, all student teachers have already demonstrated some of the necessary competences. For example, you have managed to organize your own note-making for planning, learning, reviewing and coping effectively with many practical events in your own life including successful completion of several examination courses.

This chapter has emphasized that, through use of appropriate assessment procedures and attractive and efficient modes of record keeping shared with children, we as teachers will be contributing in a directly and strongly motivating way to individual children's increasing self-confidence, competence and control as learners.

Acknowledgements

Thanks are due to the following people for their generous assistance and permission to include examples of records: Anne Baker and Knighton Fields Primary School, Leicester for Figures 12.6; Maureen Hardy and Saroj Seth for information about the Leicester Bilingual Project, Mr A. James, Headteacher, Levens Primary School for Figure 12.3; Manchester Education Authority for Figure 12.7; Mrs H. McLullich, the staff of Netherlee Primary School, Glasgow and Oliver and Boyd for Figure 12.10; Mr P. Ranson, Headteacher, Mrs J. Putick and the staff of Eyres Monsell Primary School, Leicester for Figures 12.2, 12.4 and 12.5; and, finally, Mr M. Roebuck, Mrs C. Hutchinson and Mr E. Spencer, HMI, for information from SOED; Chris Brady and Sharon Walker.

Notes

1 See also the NC; RoA National Steering Committee (RANSC) Report (1989) and the trend towards greater use of 'formative profiling' and goal setting through discussions between children and teachers.
2 With reference to specific learning difficulties (SpLD) and perhaps spurred on by the media through, for example, the National Literacy Campaign and the Dyslexia Campaign, several professional associations as well as LEAs and schools are involved in developing resources to assist teachers and children in this aspect of their work. Sources for further information include: the DfEE (1994) Code of Practice in identifying and assessing children with special educational needs; National Literacy Campaign including the '99 by '99 Campaign; British Dyslexia Association; UK Reading Association; The Schools Library Association Library Power Campaign (1995); Language and Reading Centre, Reading University.
3 In Scotland, the National Guidelines: English Language 5–14 (SOED 1991) provide descriptions of attainment targets that are set out in five levels of increasing demand (A–E). In *Assessment 5–14* Scottish teachers are required to 'report on children's learning and attainment across the whole curriculum, using their professional judgement and the evidence available to them from their own continuous assessment throughout the year' (SOED 1991: 1). They are provided with helpful guidelines including also *Reporting 5–14: Promoting Partnership* (SOED 1992).
4 Further information is contained in an HMI 5–14 publication *A Practical Guide for Teachers in Primary and Secondary Schools* (SOED 1994). The Scottish Examination Board 5–14 Assessment Unit provides a catalogue of national test units from which teachers may select reading, writing and mathematics units. See the QCA web site www.qca.org.uk/see, for example, QCA 99/382; QCA/01/89 and QCA/00/624.
5 Further information about reading tests and literacy assessment may be found, for example, in Wray and Medwell (1991), Pumfrey (1985, 1991). For further diagnostic information on literacy development see Kemp (1989) and Clay (1993a). For information regarding assessment in other areas of the primary curriculum and of children's development, abilities and difficulties in learning, see Blenkin and Kelly (1992) (who include discussions on bilingualism and assessment) and Harding and Beech (1991). Further information on the practicalities of ongoing record keeping can be found in *Primary Language Record Handbook* (Barrs *et al.* 1990).
6 If you are particularly concerned with young children in the FS, Bartholomew and Bruce (1993a) offer very useful guidance on making assessments and keeping appropriate records.

References and further reading

Bartholomew, L. and Bruce, T. (1993) *Getting to Know You: A Guide to Record-Keeping in Early Childhood Education and Care*. Sevenoaks: Hodder and Stoughton.

Barrs, M. and Johnson, G. (1993) *Recording Keeping in the Primary School*. London: Hodder and Stoughton.

Barrs, M., Ellis, S., Hester, H. and Thomas, A. (1990a) *The Primary Language Record Handbook*. London: ILEA/CLPE.

Barrs, M., Ellis, S., Hester, H. and Thomas, A. (1990b) *Patterns of Learning*. London: ILEA/CLPE.

Blenkin, G.M. and Kelly, A.V. (1992) *Assessment in Early Childhood Education*. London: Paul Chapman.

Clay, M.M. (1993a) *An Observation Survey of Early Literacy Achievement*. Auckland: Heinemann.

Clay, M.M. (1993b) *Reading Recovery: A Guidebook for Teachers in Training*. Auckland: Heinemann.

Clift, P. (1981) *Record Keeping in the Primary School*. London: Schools Council/Macmillan.

Department for Education and Employment (1994) *Code of Practice on the Identification and Assessment of Special Educational Need*. London: DfEE Central Office of Information.

Department for Education and Employment (2000) *SEN Code of Practice on the Identification and Assessment of Pupils with Special Educational Needs; SEN Thresholds: Good Practice Guidance on Identification and Provision for Pupils with Special Educational Needs*. London: DfEE.

Department for Education (1994) *Assessing 7–11-year-olds in 1995*. Circular 21/94. London: HMSO.

Department of Education and Science (1988) *National Curriculum Task Group on Assessment and Testing: A Report. (The TGAT Report)*. London: DES.

Drummond, M-J. (1993) *Assessing Children's Learning*. London: David Fulton.

Fisher, R. (1991) *Recording Achievement in Primary Schools*. Oxford: Blackwell.

Gipps, C. (1994) *Beyond Testing: Towards a Theory of Educational Assessment*. Lewes: Falmer Press.

Harding, L. and Beech, J.R. (1991) *Educational Assessment of the Primary School Child*. Windsor: NFER/Nelson.

Kemp, M. (1989) *Watching Children Read and Write: Observational Records for Children with Special Needs*. South Melbourne, Australia: Thomas Nelson.

Leicestershire Local Educational Authority in conjunction with the Bilingual Working Party (1991) *Assessing Bilingual Pupils at Key Stage 1 and Key Stage 2. Advice for Primary Schools*. Leicester: LCC.

Manchester City Council Education Department (1988) *Manchester's Early Literacy Project: A Framework for Assessment*. Manchester: MCC.

Mitchell, C. and Koshy, V. (1993) *Effective Teacher Assessment*. London: Hodder and Stoughton.

Moyles, J.R. (1989) *Just Playing? The Role and Status of Play in Early Childhood Education*. Milton Keynes: Open University Press.

National Curriculum Targets Class Record KS1 (1990) Blackburn: Educational Services Ltd.

Oxford Reading Tree Fact Finders Teacher's Guide 1 (1994) Oxford: Oxford University Press.

Pumfrey, P. (1985) *Reading Tests and Assessment Techniques* (2nd edn). Sevenoaks: Hodder and Stoughton in association with the UK Reading Association.

Pumfrey, P. (1991) *Improving Reading in the Junior School: Challenges and Responses*. London: Cassells.

Qualifications and Curriculum Authority (1999) *Keeping Track: Effective ways of recording pupil achievement to help raise standards*. London: HMSO.

Qualifications and Curriculum Authority/DfEE (2000) *Curriculum Guidance for the Foundation Stage*. London: HMSO.

Records of Achievement National Steering Committee (RANSC) (1989) *Records of Achievement: Report of the Records of Achievement National Steering Committee*. London: DES/WO.

Reading 2000 Storytime Teacher's Guide (1993) Harlow: Oliver and Boyd.

Schools Curriculum and Assessment Authority (1994) *The Review of the National Curriculum: A Report on the 1994 Consultation*. London: SCAA.

Scottish Office Education Department (1991) *Assessment 5–14*. Edinburgh: HMSO.

Scottish Office Education Department (1992) *Reporting 5–14: Promoting Partnership*. Edinburgh: HMSO.

Scottish Office Education Department (1994) *A Practical Guide for Teachers in Primary and Secondary Schools*. Edinburgh: HMSO.

Scottish Office Education Department (1995) *Taking a Close Look at English Language*. Curriculum Assessment in Scotland 5–14. Edinburgh: HMSO.

Wolfendale, S. (1993) *All About Me*. Nottingham: NES.

Wray, D. and Medwell, J. (1991) *Literacy and Language in the Primary Years*. London: Routledge.

Part 3

Responsibilities, roles and relationships

13

Putting the bananas to bed!

Becoming a reflective primary

teacher

Siân Adams

Cameo 1

The teacher has carefully transformed the home area into a grocer's shop. The day's topic has a mathematical focus: the children are to go to the shop and engage in role play with the intention of using mathematical language previously modelled by the teacher. During the session, a child selects a bunch of bananas, wraps them in a tablecloth, and gently puts them to bed. The child speaks quietly to the bananas, before choosing a story and reading to them. When the teacher notices what the 4-year-old is doing, the book and cloth are removed and the child encouraged to 'go shopping'.

Cameo 2

Ian has a Year 4 class with 24 children and is in his second year of teaching in a very small village school. He has been told by a peer appraiser that his 'teaching is excellent, class management is very good and the children are always attentive and well behaved'. Ian now wonders how to promote his own professional development – his very busy colleagues are supportive and encouraging, yet Ian observes 'I can't be that good already!'

Cameo 3

An adviser was recently invited into a nursery class to see 'all the lovely work we are doing'. The children are all aged 3 years and have been in the school since it opened – barely seven weeks. The adviser arrived in time to observe a small-group activity. Five children were with each of the adults and a remaining group of five were seated

around a circular table, playing with some 3 D coloured plastic
shapes, sliding them around the table. After observing the children
the adviser asked the children 'Would you like to tell me what you
are doing?' 'Colours, we're doing colours . . . yeah . . . and shapes . . .
blue, square, red . . .' The purpose of the activity was not clear to
the visitor, so she also asked 'So, when you've done your colours,
what then? What do you do? What happens when you've done your
colours?' One child responded 'Well, we just sit here and be bored'.

Introduction

This chapter explores the ways in which practitioners may develop a
reflective approach to practice. Many questions are raised, which can
guide the beginning teacher to make considered response to episodes
that frequently occur in the classroom. The two cameos – the first from
KS1 and the second from KS2 – provide opportunities for examining
ways in which reflective practice can support the professional development of teachers. Literature suggests there are many different levels and
stages that occur during the development of a reflective approach to
practice (Goodman 1991; Bain *et al.* 1999). Some of these stages are
explored during the discussion of the first cameo.

The episode of the child putting bananas to bed has been discussed by
many different groups of practitioners since the late 1990s. The range of
their responses reveal many levels of reflection, varying from an affective
response (emotionally oriented – ah!) to the child's unfulfilled wish to
engage in role-play, to considerations of the ethical and political issues
underpinning the practitioner's actions. During the discussion of cameo
1 the levels of reflective practice are identified. These levels are later used
to discuss the concerns expressed by Ian, the teacher in cameo 2. This
second cameo approaches reflective practice from a different perspective
through illustrating the ways in which beginning teachers might promote their own professional development. While exploring his own views
of teaching, Ian begins to confront some issues within his practice. Being
reflective also nourishes his sense of self-efficacy – a belief that teaching
can make a difference to learners – a very necessary element of development for the novice practitioner. Despite receiving many excellent reports
from colleagues and parents, Ian is struggling to apply to his own situation what he has learned about the reflective practitioner. His colleagues
are encouraging yet he finds that encouragement is not sufficient to
promote professional development. However, his comments do reveal
that he already has a developing awareness of the kind of teacher he
wants to be and is beginning to question whether being 'attentive and
well behaved' are necessarily adequate attributes of learners.

Certain skills and understandings are needed on the part of teachers in order to 'make sense' of children's responses

Before examining these two cameos in greater depth, the processes and purposes of reflective practice are discussed.

The processes of reflective practice

Reflective practice in defined in many ways, ranging from 'a way of being as a teacher' (Dewey 1933) to reflecting backwards, 'looking back and making sense of your practice' then using newly acquired insights to inform forward-looking reflection, in order 'to affect your future action' (Ghaye 1996). The first indicates an approach to practice – the attitude or disposition adopted by the practitioner – rather than a task that is fulfilled at a specific point in time. The second implies that certain skills and understandings are required in order to 'make sense' and impact future actions.

Reflective practice involves more than a gentle musing over past events, casually contemplating the events of the day. The process of making sense of practice is highly complex. There are many factors to be explored when attempting to understand why, in cameo 1, the child attempted to put bananas to bed or why, in cameo 2, Ian experienced a degree of dissatisfaction about his teaching. Before practitioners can 'make sense', they have to face the reality of their practice, through questioning, and confronting aspects of teaching and learning. So how can we ensure that the potentially destructive process of confrontation and facing up to the uncertainties and dissatisfaction of practice, can become a positive process contributing to continuing professional development?

First, it is important to understand the skills and processes within reflective practice. *Second*, as has been suggested (McIntyre 1993), reflective practice requires considerable time in order to:

- consider specific aspects of practice;
- step back from the immediacy and rawness of practice;
- deliberate;
- question;
- challenge;
- be challenged.

It also demands a repertoire of experiences and knowledge that are accumulated as practice matures. These experiences provide a bank of knowledge that is required in order to consider the variety of responses which might occur in any one situation. For instance, part of Ian's dilemma was that he knew enough to 'feel' dissatisfied with his lesson, yet did not have the experience or the knowledge to (a) interpret aspects of teaching and learning, or (b) to plan for change.

Third, practitioners require supported challenge. This might be provided by peer support, through colleagues, or for example, through developing curriculum knowledge or exploring more about theories of children's learning. *Fourth*, teaching is highly complex, so reflective practice benefits from a clearly defined framework that guides the practitioner through a process of facing specific aspects of practice. This might lead to confronting dilemmas, challenging and questioning actions and beliefs. Through time and with support, practitioners begin to reconstruct; to build on beliefs and to modify practice in a way that promotes confident, self-assured pedagogy.

The purposes of reflective practice

The processes listed above will contribute to developing an overall approach to practice – as Dewey (1933) suggested – a whole way of being. The result of promoting a spirit of enquiry will be to deepen pedagogical understanding, to comprehend the complexities and interrelationship of teaching and learning. In the two cameo examples above, through reflective enquiry, informed responses can be applied to the actions of the child and the practitioner (Lucas 1991; McIntyre 1993). In both examples, adopting a reflective approach will result in the practitioners' understanding more about the needs of the learners and consequently will be able to make informed, professional judgements about the actions of the teacher. Changes to, and development within, practice will result through building on newly acquired knowledge and understanding.

Cameo 1

The teacher in the reception class faces a dilemma when a child makes an unexpected response to the request to 'Go shopping'. Earlier, the teacher had transformed the play area into a well-resourced shop in order to provide opportunities for the children to incorporate shopping into their play. Plastic fruit and vegetables had been priced, shopping baskets provided, a small cash-register contained a variety of coins, and finally, notepads and pencils were placed in the shopping area for children to create shopping lists and issue receipts. The play was planned to support children's developing understanding of numeracy, 'the use of number in everyday situations' (FS guidance, DfEE/QCA 2000). However, instead of using the resources as the teacher had planned, one child carefully selected a bunch of bananas, cuddled it into a blanket, walked out of the 'shop' to the book corner, chose a story, then read her 'baby' a story. As she finished the story, she gently put the bananas to bed. Although working with another group of children the teacher noticed that the child was 'off task'. The adult's immediate response was to remove the bananas and suggest the child 'goes shopping'.

The banana cameo has been presented to many different groups of practitioners, during staff meetings, training days and in seminars. Discussions about the dilemma faced by the reception teacher have revealed many interesting aspects of reflective inquiry and the ways in which practice is informed and challenged by understanding teaching and learning. Some groups have responded to the emotional aspects within the cameo – others have explored the implications to teaching and curriculum policy. The responses illustrate the complex multi-layered aspects of teaching and are discussed under the following headings:

- emotional/affective response;
- pragmatic;
- philosophical;
- policy, ideological, curriculum issues;
- political, ethical or moral issues.

Emotional/affective response

The initial and most frequent responses have been affective – practitioners saying 'aaahh' 'how sweet' or 'how awful' before elaborating or offering any deeper comments. They have responded:

- to the emotion of the cameo – seeing a young child displaying an awareness of caring for an infant, behaving with sensitivity to a baby wanting to sleep or be cuddled and then gently placing the baby to bed;
- affectively to the notion of a child behaving with sensitivity but not within the framework of the teacher's learning intentions;
- to the polarity of sensitivities – a child apparently being sympathetic to the needs of a baby in stark relief to the apparent insensitive actions of an adult.

Interpretations and questions have also been based on the emotional needs of the child:

- Did the child have a young or new baby at home?
- Was the child exploring the intimacy of a new adult–child relationship within the family?
- Might the child be trying to come to terms with a new sibling, trying to understand her parents' responses of tenderness and affection to someone new?

These emotional responses by practitioners have been focused on the child and raise the further question:

- How significant is it that practitioners who uphold a 'child-centred curriculum' have made a child-centred response to this cameo?

Practitioners base their responses to this banana incident on their own pedagogical knowledge. This knowledge will include their understanding of how children learn and the ways in which that pedagogical knowledge informs their actions as teachers. Yet it is well documented that knowledge of teaching and learning is often buried under the sheer number of decisions that are made throughout the day – decisions about what to say to children, how to intervene, what resources to provide, how to respond to one question from a child, while also noting a child perhaps who is looking puzzled or inattentive, or, as in this case, putting bananas to bed. Under such relentless pressure, decisions often become intuitive; teachers often say such things as 'Well, I just do it . . . I don't have time to think about it'. The sheer 'busy-ness' of practice appears to prevent more explicit reasoning; decisions are made 'on the hoof' and practice moves forward, driven by further occasions where dilemmas are faced, decisions are made, responses made to the unexpected, spontaneous requests and behaviours of children. At the end of the day, many dilemmas are buried under the sheer weight of hosts of other spontaneous judgements. Unless practitioners have a system for recalling these actions and their accompanying decisions, their related values, beliefs and understanding remain embedded.

The process of scrutinizing the banana cameo has helped many practitioners articulate their own practice as they empathize with the immediate, complex dilemmas encountered by the reception teacher.

Pragmatic response

The second level or type of response has been made about the practical ways in which the curriculum was being provided. Questions have been asked such as why was the teacher trying to encourage children to use mathematical language in this way? Some practitioners have suggested that these days children have few opportunities to go shopping – parents frequently discourage children from going out on their own, credit cards are often used, so the exchange of cash for goods may be an inappropriate method of exchange for children's play. There are other more meaningful and relevant ways of encouraging children to use mathematical language in their play.

In what ways might the teacher have considered the child's interests? Maybe a more domestic setting could have been used, in which the 'bedtime story' might have encouraged the use of number in everyday situations. What systems were in place to ensure the teachers understood the child's starting point? Many ideas have been put forward during discussions at practical levels, considering the child's cognitive development suggesting that alternative resources in the learning environment might have encouraged the child to use mathematical language (see Roger Merry's comments on learning in Chapter 5).

Philosophical response

The third level of reflection explored the teacher's construct of play in which many practitioners have responded to this cameo by defining their own philosophy of learning. Consider the words, 'the teacher had organized' and 'told the children' to go shopping. This raises questions of ownership of play. Was the context of learning appropriate to the child's development and cultural context? Readers might like to consider:

• What is the teacher's construct of play?
• Who might have ownership of play?
• Is it possible for the child to make playful responses to a situation that has been planned and instructed by an adult?
• What is the role of play in learning?
• In what ways might playful learning be appropriate in this context?
• What role might the teacher adopt in support of children's learning? Does this cameo show us a little of the lost opportunities when

practitioners do not take the opportunity to observe children at play; had the teacher taken the time to observe the child's preparation for this domestic play?

- Did the teacher draw on other knowledge of the child?
- Did the teacher only see the child as a young mathematician – rather than also as a reader, a teller of stories, a carer, friend with a sense of empathy for a young baby?

These and other questions have been raised by many practitioners as a reflective response to the banana story. Cameos are often used in the development of reflective practice. In observing practice through stories or cameos, practitioners are distanced from the harshness of scrutinizing their own practice. Some practitioners began to explore the level and range of decisions made by the reception teacher during the course of the lesson. For example, her immediate response – to remind the child to 'go shopping' – was intuitive. But was it informed by an understanding of how children learn or was it informed by a commitment to fulfil curriculum demands?

Curriculum response

At a fourth level many practitioners explore curriculum issues and the appropriateness of the teacher's learning intentions. Were there lost opportunities here? Could the child have been applying some aspects of her developing literacy skills? Is it possible she has just begun to explore the wonders of engaging in a story and wished to enjoy the intimacy of sharing a story – maybe she has observed others reading, or maybe this is the first time she has experienced this for herself? Many have explored ways in which a mathematical lesson might also make provision for other aspects of a child's development (Moyles and Adams 2001).

Other groups of practitioners have deepened their pedagogical understanding by pursuing ways in which the curriculum can support the holistic development of the child.

Political, ethical or moral issues

Political ethical and moral issues have been raised, through questioning how the curriculum might support a child's entitlement to learn through play through asking what role does the practitioner have in discharging responsibility for the ways in which the curriculum is delivered? What responsibility does the practitioner have to assert pedagogical responsibility? Were there outside forces or pressures here on the teacher, providing a distorted view of the child's needs? Was the practitioner acting as arbiter, desperately trying to balance the needs of the child with the

Through developing a reflective approach during discussion, practitioners become more articulate, secure and able to justify practice

demands of the curriculum (Moyles and Adams 2000)? Some groups of practitioners have explored the political issues, pursuing an interest in promoting a child-centred approach to policy makers and government initiatives.

Reflection occurs at many levels

So, the pedagogue engages in reflection at many levels. There is no indication that one level is better than the other; the levels are not intended to be hierarchical. One response can inform the other. In exploring why the child put the bananas to bed, the practitioner might continue to examine the child's needs, exploring other activities that might have promoted the child's development or supported the learning intention. In exploring the political issues the practitioners may begin to acknowledge the conflict within early years and the impact of those tensions on practice (Wood 1999). While many have questioned why the practitioner apparently ignored the affective development of the child, many have also commented on how easy it is to be driven by curriculum expectations, allowing pressures to distort other values.

Through developing a reflective approach to practice it has been found that during many discussions, practitioners become more articulate, secure and able to justify practice in the face of challenge. The many questions reveal some of the processes and levels of reflection. The questions were applied initially to the banana cameo and later during discussions, to their own practices.

Reflection in Cameo 2

The principles of reflective practice can be applied to other settings. In the second cameo, Ian has just started his second year of teaching. From his training he knows that reflective practice is considered to be an effective way of promoting professional development. He is conscious that during a maths lesson, although all went according to his plan, somehow the lesson 'lacked excitement'. He comments 'I am sure one reason the children are well behaved is because the school is very formal, the classes small. The lessons do meet the learning objective but somehow it feels boring, safe and predictable.' He adds, 'If I was teaching in a more difficult area, or with a much larger class, I think the children would run rings around me'. Instinctively he feels that the lessons do not encourage engagement or independent thinking. However, without more experience he does not have the knowledge to be discerning, or the skills to determine more clearly how to build on his strengths, to create exciting, meaningful lessons. Similarly, in focusing on what might be 'wrong' in his lessons, he is at risk of overlooking very real and potential strengths in his role as a developing teacher. Consider the affective responses he has made.

Affective response

Ian's first response was positive and affective – 'I am feeling good about this because the children were well behaved'. He acknowledges that 'feeling good' is a positive way to begin, yet later adds that he had expected reflective practice to be relevant only in the context of things going wrong. Often in the busy-ness of practice, teachers turn to reflection in an urgent need to salvage professional respect from a potentially negative experience. In this instance, Ian records his awareness of a need, at this stage in his career, to nourish professional confidence and to build on strengths rather than focus on weaknesses. However, he finds he is unsure about how to respond to a lesson that lacked lustre rather than one that was heading for disaster.

The earlier discussion on reflective practice suggested that the process involves questioning and challenging, which may lead to confrontation. Ian has acknowledged or confronted his affective response to this situation – 'I am feeling good' – yet also senses a feeling of discomfort. This is a positive way to begin, for reflective practice involves confrontation – being prepared to face alternative ways of practising. We turn to the second level of reflective practice to explore ways in which Ian might develop practice further.

Pragmatic response

At this level he begins to examine the curriculum and relates his knowledge to theories of learning. He recalls that children learn best when engaged in practical authentic problems and able to relate to the context of the lessons. He can see that although the children completed the tasks he had set in his lessons, the problem-solving was far removed from any practical relevance to the pupils' experiences.

This level of reflection tends to be pragmatic, so Ian might consider the resources that were used – were there adequate materials; did the children have any choice or opportunities to make decisions? There was no provision in his plans (to use fractional notation such as $\frac{2}{3}$, $\frac{3}{4}$ and $\frac{7}{10}$) for children to engage in relevant problem solving. Through discussion, Ian considered whether he could have used the introduction to his lesson to relate this task to 'real-life', authentic problem solving. Could he have stopped the class during the main activity and shared ideas and strategies for discussing alternative ways of completing the task, encouraging more open-ended engagement in the lesson? He decides to change the next lesson and begins with a class discussion on the ways in which fractions might be used in everyday situations. Changing the learning intention into a more open-ended task might also have permitted the children to be more inventive during their deliberations.

It is difficult to adopt reflective practice without a range of relevant experiences on which to draw. Yet Ian is able to identify the issues that might be developed. He could also initiate discussion with his mentor and consider ways in which the lesson might have on the surface appeared to have been acceptable, yet confront the underpinning concerns that his practice was at odds with the emerging philosophy. He felt it was important to establish his own values and understanding, while also allowing himself to adopt a realistic and developmental approach to practice.

Evidence suggests that practitioners need time to promote a reflective approach to practice to work in a context in which professional discourse is encouraged, valued and promoted. Through asking specific questions of colleagues, it became possible for Ian to explore ways in which the teacher might make future lessons more exciting, motivating and relate his emerging philosophy to practice.

Through encouraging a culture of pedagogical discussion it was possible for Ian to maximize the experience and understanding of colleagues. Gradually, additional opportunities can be explored in which emerging issues and opportunities provide the basis for furthering good practice.

There is also evidence that practitioners do not have sufficient opportunities to talk about practice, with the result that values, beliefs and understanding often become embedded, resulting in teachers commenting that 'Well, you just do these things don't you?' Yet, it was a resistance to 'just doing things' that resulted in Ian stopping, questioning, challenging and confronting his own and the complacency of his colleagues. It was hoped that through discussion, he would deepen pedagogical knowledge, enriched by his recent experience together with the theoretical understanding gained from his studies.

Reflective practice enables teachers to make sense of daily occurrence, ensuring the surfacing of tacitly held beliefs. Yet Ian hoped that he would be able to define a pedagogical consciousness at this early stage. Early in this chapter Ian wondered if being attentive was automatically a sign that children were learning. There is evidence that children do learn how to be pupils and that reflective enquiry must take account of the children's construct of learning. Heaslip suggests that children are 'exceedingly good guests', which 'can so easily lead practitioners into believing that the programme on offer is suitable as children will most likely seem "happy enough"' (1994: 107). This is illustrated in the third, and final, brief cameo.

Reflection in Cameo 3

Within six weeks these children, all aged 3 years, had learned to be pupils. They had learned to sit still, to be well behaved and to adopt the posture of learners. They had determined the teacher's construct of learning and were behaving accordingly. It was only through observation and reflective enquiry that the deeper implications emerged.

Similarly, readers will remember that Ian felt a degree of disquiet about the children's apparent attentiveness. His construct of learning included the process of engagement; he wanted the children to be inspired and motivated through his teaching. He was beginning to define the theories that would underpin his practice. The comments he made provide evidence of moving from a focus of planning what to teach to deeper consideration of the ways in which children learn. A clear consideration of learning theories and deepening pedagogical understanding is beginning to inform his teaching style.

Berliner (1992) suggests that practitioner knowledge is partly based on experience and indicates that practitioner expertise is developed after applying that knowledge in familiar contexts. Berliner (1992: 245) states that pedagogical content knowledge develops through these processes of teaching, often from 'reflected-upon classroom experiences'. These experiences provide a repertoire of personalized knowledge that forms the basis of evidence for reflective practice. Ian's personal familiarity with the ways in which children respond in different situations has prompted a concern that the maths lesson did not offer adequate opportunities for their engagement in the lesson. Having confronted that perception, he is now in a position to consider, or reconstruct, alternative ways of planning for future learning. Through adopting a reflective approach to practice he is gaining deeper pedagogical understanding, promoting pedagogical development and change.

Conclusion

Reflective practice is a highly complex process. It involves thinking about practice at many different levels. It is possible that the practitioner's own values will determine how reflective enquiry is approached. The child-centred practitioner might begin with affective considerations of the child's responses. The manager might consider policy implications. However, these layers of critical enquiry are not intended to be hierarchical – one approach is not necessarily better than the other. The range of responses begin to address the dynamic nature of pedagogy and includes consideration of the child and adult as learners.

Through the process of becoming 'reflective practitioners', many teachers find they develop pedagogical awareness, an ability to understand many of the situations and dilemmas faced in the classroom. Engaging in reflective enquiry is a highly complex process. It may involve identifying positive aspects of teaching and using them to celebrate good practice and nourish self-confidence. However, it also involves confronting areas that might benefit from development. This process of confrontation requires support from colleagues and the school, time to reflect and opportunity to question practice, beliefs or understandings about teaching and learning. Through 'eavesdropping' on many responses to the banana cameo a range of possible reflective responses to one situation has been discovered. We have also explored ways in which Ian's practice might develop through providing appropriate conditions for maturing practice.

There are no right or wrong answers or responses to the cameos. Engaging in discussion about these and countless other scenarios that occur each day in schools, contributes to an emerging pedagogical awareness. Understanding more about our own actions, thoughts, values and beliefs and learning how to articulate them and expose them to scrutiny in a culture of support and professionalism, will lead to enriched understanding and changes in classroom and professional practices.

Confident, reflective pedagogues will result from supported, collaborative approaches to practice.

References and further reading

Bain, J., Ballantyne, R., Packer, J. and Mills, C. (1999) Using journal writing to enhance student teachers' reflectivity during field experience placements, *Teachers and Teaching: Theory and Practice*, 5(1): 51–74.

Berliner, D. (1992) Nature of expertise in teaching, in F. Oser, A. Dick and J. Patry (eds) *Effective and Responsible Teaching. The New Synthesis*. San Francisco, CA: Jossey-Bass Publishers.

Dewey, J. (1933) *How We Think: A Restatement of the Relation of Reflective Thinking to the Educative Process*. Chicago, IL: Henry Regenery Publishers.

DfEE/QCA (2000) *Curriculum Guidance for the Foundation Stage*. London: DfEE/QCA.

Ghaye, T. (1996) *An Introduction to Learning Through Critical Reflective Practice*. Newcastle-upon-Tyne: Pentaxion Press.

Goodman, J. (1991) Using a methods course to promote reflection and inquiry among preservice teachers, in R. Tabachnich and K. Zeichner (eds) *Issues and Practices in Inquiry-Oriented Teacher Education*. London: Falmer Press.

Heaslip, P. (1994) Making play work in the classroom, in J. Moyles (ed.) *The Excellence of Play*. Buckingham: Open University Press.

Lucas, P. (1991) Reflection, new practices, and the need for flexibility in supervising student teachers, *Journal of Further and Higher Education*, 15(2): 84–93.

McIntyre, D. (1993) Theory, theorising and reflection in initial teacher education, in J. Calderhead and P. Gates (eds) *Conceptualising Reflection in Teacher Development*. London: Falmer Press.

Moyles, J. and Adams, S. (2000) A tale of the unexpected: Practitioners' expectation and children's play, *Journal of In-Service Education*, 26(2): 349–69.

Moyles, J. and Adams, S. (2001) *StEPs: A Framework for Playful Teaching*. Buckingham: Open University Press.

Wood, E. (1999) The impact of the National Curriculum on play in reception classes, *Educational Research*, 41(1): 11–22.

14

Dialogue with difference: teaching for equality in primary schools

Alison Shilela

Cameo 1
A refugee child has recently joined Jane's Year 2 class. Jane is worried because although Malika has been in school for over a term and in Britain for over a year, she does not seem to be making progress. Jane has placed Malika with a small group of children, who have learning difficulties so that she can get more individual attention. Malika very rarely speaks in class and is reluctant to join in group activities. Jane has noticed that although Malika tends to be a loner, she is often involved in playground 'incidents'.

Cameo 2
Elise works in a small rural primary school. She is teaching the Second World War to her (predominantly white) Year 5 class. She is part of the Year 5 planning team. Elise feels that the resources and materials currently available in school convey a limited view of the war.

Cameo 3
Great Meadow Primary School has recently revised its policy for equal opportunities, including guidance for good practice. Tim is in the final term of his induction year and has been involved in the policy review. He feels strongly about issues of equality and has planned his teaching for the past term to ensure that his Year 6 class always works in mixed sex groupings. He has noticed however, that the academic performance of the five Muslim girls in his class has deteriorated since the introduction of the mixed grouping arrangements.

Introduction

This chapter explains why working for equality in education is fundamental to a successful learning environment for children. It explores
how good practice can be achieved, first by working within the framework of principles established by the Runnymede Trust and second, by
following procedures that enable us to fulfil the principles. The three-
point framework of principles makes it clear that our objectives for equality
are as follows:

1 To ensure high *quality* education for all;
2 To support the development of personal and cultural *identity*;
3 To prepare pupils and young people for participation in *society*.

As teachers, we have a good chance of implementing these principles
in the classroom if we adhere to the following three tenets of good
pedagogy:

1 Engage with the learner;
2 Engage with the curriculum;
3 Engage with the learning.

The three cameos at the beginning of the chapter are situations that
typically give rise to questions of equality in the classroom. Each cameo
is used in the section 'Procedures' to exemplify how the principles and
procedures outlined above may be put into practice. The chapter attempts
to demonstrate the causal relationship between teaching for equality
and effective learning so that beginning teachers may gain a practical
understanding of their role in enabling all children to achieve within the
education system. The chapter begins by outlining principles for equality and moves on to give an appraisal of the national picture, exploring
some external influences on attitudes, before finally addressing more
specific issues of equality facing all teachers in today's classrooms and
schools.

The principles

Equality in education is about rights, power and responsibility. Every
child has the *right* to achieve his or her potential. As teachers we all have
the *power and the responsibility* to make this happen. Equality in education is more than believing that all children have a right to achieve their
potential: it is the *practice* of ensuring that it happens! Our role as teachers
is, therefore, not simply to offer all learners the same chances, but to
breathe life into those opportunities.

Our understanding of the factors contributing to equality and inequality has been refined during the 1990s. Equality in education no longer means treating everyone in the same way. If differences are ignored, inequality results. On the other hand, if difference is the only factor taken into account, prejudice results.

Equality in education means engaging with difference, but ensuring that equal respect is given to all, in order for learners to achieve their own (different) potential (see also Jenny Lansdell's chapter on children with special educational needs).

Our role as teachers

The vision expressed by the government in the White Paper *Excellence in Schools* was to create: 'a society which is dynamic and productive, offering opportunity and fairness to all' (DfEE 1998: 9). This set the national agenda for schools, placing the responsibility of equality in education firmly on the shoulders of the educational professionals.

It can be assumed that the role of the individual teacher is primarily that of enabling pupils to learn to achieve their potential as fully as possible in order that they may make informed decisions for themselves and, later on, for their communities. Teaching children is about developing tomorrow's leaders and creating a 'better' world. Schools then, become the embodiment of this idea. Society should expect its schools to be catalysts for social change and work proactively to achieve that end. The idea that education should contribute to social justice is like an unspoken 'pedagogic oath'. This commitment forms the backbone of all education, lending purpose and structure to the work in schools. Teaching for equality is a conscious moral decision.

Teachers do make a difference – by design and not by chance.

Why is equality still on the agenda?

The reason we need to clarify our understanding and approach to equality is simple. Research evidence shows that particular groups of children are not benefiting as well as others from the education system in Britain. The Ofsted report *Raising the Attainment of Minority Ethnic Pupils: School and LEA Responses* (1999) shows that African-Caribbean boys, Pakistani, Bangladeshi and traveller pupils are not achieving the same academic success as their peers. This is despite the fact that no one group of learners is less capable of success than another, as Gillborn and Mirza (2000) demonstrate in recent research findings.

Equality in education means engaging with difference but ensuring that equal respect is given to all

The pattern of groups achieving success within the system has changed significantly in recent years: it is common knowledge that girls as a whole are now outstripping boys at GCSE. Although girls are achieving well generally, differences in achievement can be seen between different groups of girls, with Indian girls achieving most highly and girls from African-Caribbean, Pakistani and Bangladeshi origins achieving less well. The same research shows pupils from Indian backgrounds achieving as well as and sometimes outstripping their white peers at GCSE level and Bangladeshi children progressing at a faster rate than any other group of children monitored by ethnicity. African-Caribbean children achieve well at KS1, but, as a group, benefit the least of all six groups monitored at GCSE level (Gillborn and Mirza 2000). This pattern is reflected in exclusion figures. African-Caribbean pupils are four times more likely to be excluded from school than their peers from other ethnic groups (Gillborn and Gipps 1996).

Changes in the profile of attainment suggest that reforms to the education system have been effective for the academic success of some groups of learners, but have not met the needs of others. While we do not expect every child to achieve the same results, we DO expect *every* child to achieve to their potential. If the needs of all children were met, the group of lower achievers would come from a range of socio-economic backgrounds and ethnic groups.

Evidence of academic attainment is drawn from the results of national testing, which is just one measure of how different groups of young people are faring in the educational system. However, there is also debate as to whether the systems of assessment are reliable, adequate and fair. This is especially the case for baseline assessment. Academic attainment, while important, is only one aspect of school life. Other aspects of life need to be measured to get a fuller picture of the total experience of 'underachieving' children in school. Children continue to be bullied in school on account of differences attributed to ethnicity, language, religion, 'culture', sexuality or ability. While underachievement continues to be manifested by specific groups of children, identifiable by a shared experience, e.g. black, refugee, it is clear that inequalities exist within the education system.

The inequalities manifested in school are a reflection of deeper, broader social inequalities.

Attitudes

The media

We are all influenced by collective social values and where better to see these expressed than on television. This is an especially powerful medium to convey messages about what is acceptable and desirable. Advertisements are particularly influential. By using aggressive male voice-overs to advertise 'Action Man' and associating this toy with violence and destruction, boys are given a very clear message about their role as boys. 'Barbie' advertisements tell little girls about their accepted role: fashion, caring and an extraordinary physique are the accepted aspirations portrayed on television for girls. Over the past few years there has been an increase in the diversity of representation of different ethnic groups on television in general, but children's television (for example, after school, Saturday mornings) continues to perpetuate the traditional gender stereotypes. Subtle messages are also conveyed about people who are *not* represented: omission is an insidious form of exclusion. By omitting certain groups of people (people with disabilities, for example), the message received is that these people do not feature in our 'normal' daily lives.

Parents

Teachers often express frustration at the attitudes of parents, who may not support the school's stance on certain issues, for example, dealing

We are all influenced by collective social values

with conflict. This 'us and them' notion signifies a need for schools and families to work more closely together. (As Nansi Ellis suggests in Chapter 1, this happens more often at FS than during later years of schooling.) Parents are powerful allies in the quest for equality. After all, they are the first and most powerful influence on primary aged children.

Staff members

It may be that the attitudes expressed by other members of staff conflict with the messages you are trying to convey with regard to equality, for example a colleague may express a negative opinion about traveller children in the staffroom at break-time. While this would be disappointing we cannot expect to change others' attitudes overnight as Klein (1993: 129) suggests: 'Attitudes are extremely difficult to change . . . children only pass through the school once, and can't be put on ice to await the slow process of teachers' attitude to change.'

The emphasis here is to improve the practice in schools. By improving teaching and learning *behaviours* in school, attitudes towards equality will necessarily improve because the benefits of the practice will be evident. For example, before the seat belt laws were enforced, many people believed that wearing a seat belt in a car was unnecessary and didn't affect them. Since the reduction in deaths in road traffic accidents has been proven to be linked to the wearing of seat belts, not many people would deny the sense of the legislation. Teaching for equality, therefore, has to be a planned, explicit and measurable process, rooted in the daily behaviour of teachers.

Internal influences and expectations

Becoming a teacher does not give us immunity from our own socialization. Although it is essential to recognize the bias and stereotypes manifested by others, it is even more important to be able to recognize and decode our own attitudes and behaviours in terms of our upbringing as these deep-seated influences can significantly affect:

- our expectations of pupils;
- the ways in which we teach.

The Government acknowledges the need for high expectations for all pupils in its White Paper, *Excellence in Schools* (DfEE 1998: 25): 'One of the most powerful underlying reasons for low performance in our schools has been low expectations which have allowed poor quality teaching to continue unchallenged.' The Paper makes it clear that beginner teachers are expected to set 'high expectations for all pupils notwithstanding individual differences, including gender, and cultural and linguistic back-grounds' (DfEE 1998: 14).

We should question our own expectations with regard to the children in our care. For example, do we expect girls to behave in a particular way? And if so, do the girls fulfil these expectations? Do we perpetuate certain patterns of behaviour and attainment through our teaching style? If so, how does this reinforcement impact on the girls' overall perception of their own ability? Our attitudes to children impact directly on their success.

Difference

As teachers we are expected to take account of differences when planning lessons, especially as beginners, by:
'identifying pupils who:

- have special educational needs, including specific learning difficulties;
- are very able;
- are not yet fluent in English;

and knowing where to get help in order to give positive and targeted support' (DfEE 1998: 12).

The term 'difference' is used extensively in terms of equality. But what does it mean? Which 'differences' count? If we perceive differences as finite, homogeneous and static we cannot respond to the complexities of our learners. The teacher's response to the ever-changing profile of difference is the key to promoting or preventing equality in the class-room. Difference is dynamic, therefore our response to differences needs to be dynamic. Engaging with difference means recognizing that a 'one size fits all' approach to teaching may not meet the needs of all pupils. The following documented trends confirm this view:

1 *Gender*: boys are underachieving compared to girls;
2 *Ethnicity*: proportionally largest group of underachievers are black and Pakistani;
3 *Language*: pupils with EAL achieve less well within compulsory schooling;
4 *Religion*: Muslim children achieve less well than Sikh children;
5 *Ability*: (SEN) children with behaviour needs are more likely to experience internal or external exclusion during their school career;
6 *Social class*: research suggests that socio-economic background probably does impact on children's learning, with children from less financially secure backgrounds achieving less well (Gillborn and Mirza 2000);
7 *Sexuality*: at the time of writing, little research is available to ascertain the impact of sexuality on pupil achievement, but we do know that the experience of living with same-sex parents or an awareness that a child's developing sexuality differs from that promoted as the norm (i.e. heterosexuality) can impact on the psychological and physical well-being of pupils if only because such an experience can be considered to be unusual and possibly unacceptable in the eyes of the majority.

It is unlikely that any of these factors would contribute to underachievement in isolation of other factors, which may or may not be listed above. It is also important to note that the range of differences *within* groups are greater than the differences *between* groups. For example, the range of ability within a class of 29 girls will be far greater than the differences of ability between a class of 29 boys and girls in a similar socio-economic setting.

Legislation

The law provides a scaffold for equality in education. However, at the time of writing legislation with regard to equality is disparate, for example, The Race Relations Act (1976 and 2000), the Sex Discrimination Act (1975 and 1999), the Disability Discrimination Act (1995). The effect of this is that issues of equality are perceived to be the sole domain of discrete groups of people (i.e. those who suffer inequalities). The reality is that the elements in question do not exist in isolation: they are inter-active and interdependent. Everyone has a sex, an ethnicity, a language and a culture. Equality affects everyone and the basic principles of equality apply to all. The recent report from the Commission for the

Future of Multi-ethnic Britain (Runnymede Trust 1993, 2000) includes a recommendation for the establishment of one Equality Act. This would enshrine the fundamental principles of equality while maintaining procedures to address particular needs separately within the Act.

Article 14 of the Human Rights Act (1998) states:

> The enjoyments of the rights and freedoms set forth in this convention shall be secured without discrimination on any ground such as sex, race, colour, language, religion, political or other opinion, national or social origin, association with a national minority, property, birth or other status.

Such legislation makes the principle of equality a more global responsibility and, within state schools, this is reflected to some extent in Section One (The School Curriculum and the National Curriculum: Values, Aims and Purposes), more specifically in Section Three (General Teaching Requirements: Inclusion) as well as through the aims of the framework for personal, social and health education and citizenship:

> They [pupils] learn to understand and respect our common humanity, diversity and differences so that they can go on to form the effective, fulfilling relationships that are an essential part of life and learning.
>
> (DfEE 1999: 136)

However, while educational policy exists to protect some groups of people there still remains some legislation, which promotes institutionalized inequality. Section 28 of the Local Government Act (1988) makes it unlawful for LEAs to:

- intentionally promote homosexuality or publish material with the intention of promoting homosexuality;
- promote the teaching in any maintained school of the acceptability of homosexuality as a pretended family relationship.

This legislation counters the basic principles of an 'inclusive curriculum' and the government policy expressed by the TTA: 'that all pupils, irrespective of ethnicity, language background, culture, gender, ability, social background, sexuality, or religion should receive the highest quality education' (TTA 2000: 15). While such legislation exists, the education system will not meet the needs of all groups of pupils and the reality of many children's lives will continue to be denigrated and marginalized.

The practice of equality

The pre-requisite for teaching for equality lies in what can be described as 'the possible dream' (Freire 1998: 241) That is, *the belief that equality in education is possible and achievable.* How often do we hear teachers sigh in desperation, 'Yes, in an ideal world . . .' Such a response conveys a feeling of powerlessness and an abnegation of responsibility. Let us return to the unspoken 'pedagogic oath'. By engaging with the commitment to equality expressed in the NC 'to ensure that all pupils have the chance to succeed, whatever their individual needs and the potential barriers to their learning may be' (DfEE 1999: 3) the commitment to equality becomes unequivocal. There is no question of *not* working proactively to achieve it. However, good practice does not happen simply because we believe in the principles. Planning for equality has to be a deliberate act.

The Runnymede Trust's objectives for equality in education underpin all good teaching and help us to plan for equality. The principles (quality, identity and society) can be mapped against teaching and learning styles, government requirements and educational outcomes showing how crucial they are to good educational practice.

Quality

In order to provide a high-quality educational experience for our pupils, we must apportion appropriate importance to the learning process as well as the outcomes of learning. In practice this means ensuring that progress, as well as attainment, is acknowledged. In the case of Malika in Cameo 1, much of the quality of her educational experience will be attributed to developing learning skills and confidence within her new situation. Cameo 2 shows how teaching and learning can become impoverished if the curriculum is offered from a narrow perspective. Elise could improve the quality of teaching and learning by expanding the knowledge base to be taught (see the 'Procedures for equality' section below). In Cameo 3, however, providing a 'high-quality' educational experience, will mean that Tim needs to question his own interpretation of equality. Single sex grouping may, in fact, help him to provide a high-quality education *in some instances*. Tim should ensure that his grouping arrangements mean that all the pupils have the opportunity to work with all other pupils at some point, but his grouping arrangements should be planned with learning objectives for each individual in mind. Ensuring a high-quality education means working towards the statement of values expressed in the NC Handbook and using the learning context to develop the key skills (DfEE 2000: 20). Achieving quality means fulfilling the standards set by the DfEE for beginning teachers, fostering an enthusiasm for learning in pupils together with the confidence and skills to challenge and ask questions. High-quality teaching and learning means:

- employing a variety of approaches to learning;
- teaching for breadth and depth;

- differentiating to meet the needs of individual learners;
- integrating diversity into curriculum content and delivery as well as using assessment to inform future planning.

Teachers who have high expectations of *all* their pupils are more likely to achieve good results, and even more so if they hold high expectations for themselves. Pupils who see teachers as role models for learning, will themselves be challenged and motivated, become confident to make informed decisions and willing participants in whole-class endeavours.

Identity

It is a truism to say that we all perform well if we feel valued. The principle for equality that asks teachers to support personal and cultural identity is fundamental to enabling pupils to achieve their potential. This element of teaching demands that teachers know their pupils well enough to know how to support their identity. Stereotypes should be recognized and challenged. Pupils need to be encouraged to develop skills of self-criticism, while teachers need to develop a sense of self-esteem and self-worth in all pupils. This is often achieved through activities such as circle time and collaborative or 'trust games' during PE. Opportunities for self-expression and self-directed learning can be integrated into the school day through learning activities across all curriculum areas. (Further information about supporting identity is explored in the section 'Engaging with the learner'.)

Children who are confident to act independently are more likely to take responsibility for themselves, express themselves with confidence and show initiative. Typically, children who feel valued at school have the self-awareness that enables them to respect the needs of others within the learning environment. This sense of self within a larger community is an essential precursor to achieving the final principle of preparing pupils and young people for participation in society.

Society

Preparing pupils for participation in society means fostering a sense of interdependence. Teachers are in a prime position to do this through their teaching methodology. Take the case of Tim in cameo 3: the Muslim girls will need to learn how to interact with other people in the class, not just their friends. This does not mean that it is wrong to place them with their friends, but Tim should be using his grouping methods strategically, ensuring that each child has the opportunity to interact with the others. Collaborative learning activities and problem solving are effective methods of ensuring that this takes place (see also Chapter 7). Discussion and debate encourage pupils to develop concepts of fairness and turn-taking. An ability to negotiate and participate in decision making is a skill, which teachers can nurture from the Foundation Stage upwards. Pupils should be confident to manage and initiate change, rather than see change or difference as a threat. By encouraging open dialogue, through the curriculum and teaching methodologies, teachers can set the fundamentals for pupils to participate in society with confidence and empathy. In addition, teachers who involve parents in the education of their children convey an important message about the role of school within the wider community.

Procedures for equality

An effective teacher engages with the learners, the curriculum and the learning. It is not sufficient to engage with the knowledge to be transmitted alone. How often do we hear students bemoan their teachers? 'Oh yes, she knows her stuff, but she can't teach' and by the same token, it is inadequate simply to engage with the pupils with insufficient enthusiasm or knowledge of the subject to be taught or how children learn. Our challenge as teachers is to ensure that we know our pupils sufficiently well to be able to offer a relevant and challenging curriculum to them in ways that meet their learning needs. This means getting to know their families and backgrounds as well as their dispositions and attitudes to learning and their knowledge base.

Valuing and exploring difference, both explicitly through the curriculum content and implicitly through teaching methodology is fundamental to achieving equality. We have seen, therefore, that engaging with equality in education lies in the dialogue between teachers' commitment to social justice and their practice in creating this reality in the classroom.

Engaging with the learner

The first step in planning for equality is to start with the pupils' life experiences. What do the children bring with them? How will you support the development of their personal and social identity? Consider cameo 1 in the light of this tenet.

Malika has been in the country for over a year, in Jane's class for over a term and does not appear to be making progress. There are many issues to take into account in this situation. Jane needs to find out as much as possible about Malika's *life experiences* to understand how she may have been affected by them. Jane should find out what Malika's personal situation is now – is she living with her parents or carers? What conditions is she living in? Does she have anyone to speak to in her first language? Jane could introduce the topic of migration into the curriculum (through history, geography, RE or PSHE) to show that Malika's experience is valued. Although the experience of a refugee may not be familiar to other pupils, many children will empathize with the idea of moving to a different town for a whole variety of reasons. These could be explored.

A useful strategy to adopt for any new arrivals is to allocate a 'special friend' to the newcomer. This friend would be responsible for 'looking after' the new child in particular ways (introducing her to the games of the playground, helping with work in the class, explaining routines, etc.) for a limited amount of time. When children are traumatized it is absolutely essential to gain their trust before any learning can take place. What makes Malika feel safe? Sudden noises can upset children who have come from war-torn areas and automatic responses to particular behaviours can be deeply ingrained. I have experienced children hiding under the desks every time they heard an aeroplane fly overhead, so terrified were they that a bomb would follow.

Jane should be investigating the allegations of violence in the playground, monitoring the response of the other children to Malika. She could include activities in the curriculum which build trust and self-esteem as well as activities that enable pupils to deal with conflict. While it is important for Jane to understand Malika's background, it is also important not to dwell solely on these issues especially as potential problems. Children should not be made into icons of difference: they also have a right to be ordinary! The emphasis of Jane's strategy to include Malika in the learning experience of the class should be centred around how she and the other children are making it possible for Malika to be a valued and participating member of the class.

Malika is probably quiet in class because she speaks another *language.* As a developing bilingual learner Malika would benefit greatly from being placed with articulate children during activities that involve discussion. It is also important to remember that, when learning a second language, children normally understand more than they are able to express. Children learning English as an additional language may remain silent for up to a year, but this does not mean that they are not absorbing English language patterns and new concepts. Jane should find out as much as possible about Malika's first language, is it written from right to left or left to right? How advanced is Malika in her first language development? How is she able to continue the development of her first language? Jane can show that other languages are valued in the classroom in very small ways, for example, taking the register in the morning, children could be asked to reply in any language that is not their first. Displays and dual textbooks are obvious ways of showing how other languages are valued. Using other languages in our teaching gives formal recognition to the value of bilingualism. There are a number of strategies for doing this, one successful way is to read a story to the children and replace two or three words, which are repeated in the story, by the translation of those words into a different language. Tell the children that this is what you will be doing. The sense of the story will not be diminished and children have learned words in another language by the end of the story. This simple approach shows engagement with diversity of language. The message received by the children is that English is not the only language.

Language and *culture* are closely linked. Jane should find out as much as possible about Malika's cultural background. In some languages, for example, there is no word for 'please' or 'thank you', as respect is conveyed through tone and inflection. Direct translations from such languages can, therefore, appear rude to English-speaking people, who may then make assumptions about children with regard to behaviour. Other social mores may also be different, for example, it may be considered rude in some cultures to look an adult in the eyes, especially if the adult is in authority, so if this happens to us, we must not automatically assume the child in question is being evasive or challenging.

Many cultural mores are driven by *religious influences*. What religion does Malika follow? Can Jane cater for Malika's particular religious practices at school? If so how (with regard to diet, fasting, praying, assembly?) can Malika be supported? Jane should find out what the stance is for Malika with regard to music, dance and art for example. Are there particular dress codes for Malika that have not been recognized by the school, but which might make her feel more comfortable if she were explicitly allowed to wear them? Malika's apparent lack of progress may be due to the fact that she is used to a different *teaching style*. It may be that her previous educational experience favoured a different kind of relationship between teacher and pupils. Jane could monitor Malika's readiness to engage with her work according to the different styles of teaching she employs.

Engaging with the curriculum

The learning diet of primary school children needs to be varied and balanced as we saw in the Introduction. Diversity and equality of opportunity underpin the National Curriculum. Including issues of equality is not an optional extra but an essential ingredient of the daily diet. Planning a curriculum for equality means engaging with the content of the subject area to be covered, adapting or supplementing it where necessary, choosing resources that will promote equality and value diversity, and employing teaching methods that encourage learners to discuss, challenge, collaborate and initiate.

What about Elise in Cameo 2 in relation to promoting equality in the classroom? She is teaching the Second World War to her Year 5 (mainly white) class. It is extremely important for Elise to ensure that the messages she conveys through her approach to the curriculum do not reinforce the inaccurate belief that the Second World War was the exclusive domain of white English and white German people. To counterbalance this view, Elise decides to include activities and materials that teach about the contribution made to the Second World War by black and Asian people. She explores the concept and manifestations of racism through Nazism, which she then follows through during PSHE. This is an obvious way of engaging with issues of social justice and offers the children a broader, truer perspective on British history.

This approach to the topic allowed Elise to challenge the children's received knowledge about the war, foster empathy, and recognize and discuss inequality. The positive effects of engaging with the curriculum are not limited to the children's learning experiences.

The other Year 5 teacher admitted that she learned a lot more about the war this time round as Elise had prepared the materials and she felt that it had expanded and challenged her own perspectives of the Second World War in particular, and teaching history in general. If Elise had been teaching a multi-ethnic class, this approach would support the development of the children's social and cultural identity by acknowledging the role played by their grandparents and great grandparents in British history.

The curriculum is a basic body of knowledge to be taught and learned, but it should offer opportunities for children to explore different values, lifestyles and traditions, and reflect others' experiences and understanding of the world.

Engaging with the learning

The interaction between the teacher and pupils and between pupils and pupils should be a reflection of our educational values. We cannot expect children to respect others' opinions if there is no forum in learning activities to express and develop opinions or any respect for the children's opinions. The way in which we teach sets expectations of the culture we wish to foster. Engaging with the learning means interrogating our teaching/learning methodology and considering *how* the curriculum should be delivered to meet individual learning needs. Activities need to be challenging, but accessible. One of the skills of a good teacher is to make the curriculum accessible by presenting it in a variety of ways to meet a variety of learning approaches. For example, mental mathematics can present difficulties for pupils if they do not understand or cannot retain the language of the question. This may not necessarily mean that they do not understand the mathematical concept being tested.

Children should experience working with a variety of peer groups and learning approaches, including investigations and problem solving (see Chapter 7) and collaborative and individual opportunities. This enables learners to become familiar with change, to work as part of a team and to be confident enough to take the initiative or work alone. Using a variety of approaches fulfils some of what is encompassed in the third Runnymede Trust (Runnymede Trust 1993) objective 'Preparing pupils to participate in society'.

Cameo 3 raises questions about engaging with learning. Tim is committed to the notion of equality and has put into practice grouping arrangements that he feels meet with the principle of equality. Tim notices that the work of the Muslim girls has suffered and he knows it is because they will not interact with the boys. The girls are extremely shy and loath to make any contact with the boys at all. Tim thinks this is due to the girls' cultural background. He feels strongly that the girls should develop the confidence to interact with all members of the class. This case shows that 'one size' does not fit all. If the girls' performance is suffering as a result of Tim's grouping arrangements, he should review his grouping strategy. It might have been easier to split the Muslim girls and put them with other (non-Muslim) girls before expecting them to work with boys. Tim might structure his grouping so that all pupils have the opportunity to work with all other pupils during the course of the term, but he could also allow pupils to sit and work with their friends for specific subjects or at specific times. Although he might feel that the girls should be able to work with the boys, his role in achieving equality is to ensure that each child achieves maximum potential. In this case, single sex grouping may be an appropriate way to achieve the goal as part of a long-term strategy for equality.

It is often difficult to know whether we are succeeding or not. Working towards equality is a process, it cannot be achieved overnight, and sometimes there are nebulous areas. It is for these reasons that we need to be clear about how to recognize our successes.

Measuring success

Monitoring your own practice for equality in the classroom is a crucial aspect of your own development (as Siân Adams pointed out in the previous chapter and is also a key feature of Chapter 4). Here are some suggestions as to how we can monitor our own classroom practices to engage with equality issues:

- Curriculum: map objectives for equality (quality, identity, society) in curriculum plans;

- Methodology: map teaching/learning styles for equality in curriculum plans (collaborative activities, activities to promote empathy);
- Achievement: systems already in place include monitoring standard attainment tasks (SATs) results by gender and ethnicity. Keep records of progress as well as attainment, investigate different behaviours with different groupings and activities. Include elements of self-assessment for all children (see Morag Hunter-Carsch's comments in Chapter 12). Is any one group in your class achieving poorly? If so, why? Check your systems for monitoring *access to the curriculum* (as opposed to success and attainment within it);
- Policies and procedures: a whole-school approach to addressing racism, sexism and bullying should denote clear procedures that are followed by all;
- Resources: review resources regularly, plan access to resources to ensure that all pupils have opportunities to use them appropriately, monitor the use of resources and note any trends;
- Behaviour: ensure that any behavioural programme you are following is shared with parents and pupils;
- Staff training: share information and training with lunchtime supervisors, CAs and helpers and make sure you find time for regular discussion with colleagues;
- Parental links: monitor attendance at parents' evenings, school events, classroom activities and meetings. Do all parents feel involved?
- Liaison with other agencies: make sure you know who to contact from external agencies, should the need arise, for example, educational psychologists, EMAG (Ethnic Minority Achievement Grant) teachers, Traveller Education Teams, Learning Support Services, Child Protection Service;
- Physical environment: you may feel unable to change the following things, but how might you support changes to create a more equal environment for all, for example, wheelchair access, playground design, religious needs?
- Governors: make sure you know who is the named governor for equality of opportunity and make a note of feedback at governors' meetings;
- How do your systems of monitoring link to the whole-school systems? Is there an overlap? How do your results compare with the results of the school as a whole?

Conclusion

Teaching for equality is good practice: the difficulty is making it our good practice! It means believing that we have a role in achieving social justice and working proactively to make this a reality. By engaging with the unique differences of all of our pupils, we can tailor the curriculum and learning activities to challenge inequality and foster equality in the classroom. This is both the duty and the gift of the teacher.

Questions for further consideration

1 How do you engage with difference in the classroom?
2 Write a list of classroom practices you use or intend to use that promote personal and cultural identity.
3 When applying for a post in a new school, what evidence would you look for to show that the school takes equality in education seriously?
4 A new child starts your class. Her name is Kulvinder. You discover that the secretary calls her 'Karen' because she finds the name Kulvinder difficult to pronounce. What might you do?
5 A boy in your class is constantly being bullied because he lives with same sex parents. What might you do?

References and further reading

DfEE (1998) *Teaching: High Status, High Standards*. Circular 4/98. London: DfEE.
DfEE (1999) *The National Curriculum Handbook for Primary Teachers in England*. London: QCA/DfEE.
DfEE (2000) *Removing the Barriers: Raising Achievement Levels for Minority Ethnic Pupils*. London: HMSO.
Freire, P. (1973) *Education: the Practice of Freedom*. New York: Writers and Readers Publishing Co-operative.
Freire, P. (1998) *Pedagogy of Hope*. New York: Continuum Publishing.
Gaine, C. and George, R. (1999) *Gender, 'Race' and Class in Schooling*. London: Falmer Press.
Gillborn, D. and Gipps, C. (1996) *Recent Research on the Achievements of Ethnic Minority Pupils*. London: HMSO.
Gillborn, D. and Mirza, S. (2000) *Educational Inequality Mapping Race, Class and Gender*. London: Ofsted.
Green, P. (1999) *Raise the Standard: A Practical Guide to Raising Ethnic Minority and Bilingual Pupils' Achievement*. Stoke-on-Trent: Trentham Books.
Klein, G. (1993) *Education Towards Race Equality*. London: Cassell.
Ofsted (1999) *Raising the Attainment of Minority Ethnic Pupils: School & LEA Responses*. London: Ofsted.
Osler, A. (2000) *Citizenship and Democracy in Schools*. Stoke-on-Trent: Trentham Books.
Runnymede Trust (1993) *Equality Assurance in Schools: Quality, Identity, Society*. Stoke-on-Trent: Trentham Books.
Runnymede Trust (2000) *The Report of the Commission on the Future of Multi-Ethnic Britain*. www.runnymedetrust.org.uk
TTA (2000) *Raising the Attainment of Minority Ethnic Pupils. Guidance and Resource Materials for Providers of Initial Teacher Training*. London: HMSO.

15

All children are special: but some are more special than others! Special educational needs in the primary school

Jenny Lansdell

Cameo 1

Catherine has just taken up her first teaching post. The children in her Year 2 class seem pleasant enough and, as yet, she has had no lessons that she would call a disaster. However, she is already worried about whether she will be able to keep the class running smoothly for the rest of the term. Every time she faces the class, a sea of faces looks back at her, but she is acutely aware that it is the individual behind each face that she needs to get to know. Each child has individual potential and represents a particular challenge. How on earth is she going to handle all these different needs and do her very best teaching the whole class?

Cameo 2

The literacy hour is in progress in a Year 5 mixed ability class. After sharing a persuasive text with the class, Emily focuses on connectives, asking the more able individuals to volunteer and identify examples in the text. The text is not large enough for all the children to see it clearly, so not all are able to contribute. The children are then each given the same worksheet to complete to consolidate their understanding of connectives.

Jason, Wayne, Lee and Chelsea are in Red group. They know, and all the other children know, that they are the 'less able' group, even though this is never articulated overtly. The other groups always finish before them and are often given more exciting things to do. Red group is seldom asked to show their work to others, or to have it displayed. They often have a CA who sits with them to make sure they behave. They work individually on tasks, but when they do work together they are not able to support or help each other, as they are all operating at about the same level and experience the same difficulties. They are very dependent on adult help when stuck, and spend a lot of time off task, giving up easily and not expecting to keep up with the rest of the class.

As she circulates, Emily tells off Wayne and Chelsea for not paying attention earlier before she explains the worksheet to Red group again. When they are left on their own to finish the task, none are able to read the worksheet unaided, and they simply guess the answers based on the few words that they can read. The lesson ends with them having learned little about connectives, and feeling that they have failed at a task which they should have been able to achieve. Emily, in turn, feels frustrated that these children have yet again not finished their work.

Cameo 3

Grant is attending his first staff meeting in his new post. The SENCO wants to discuss how best to support those children in the school who have special educational needs. Grant has a wide range of ability in his Year 3 class, which includes two children with writing difficulties and a child who does not seem to listen to him. There are also two children who seem exceptionally bright, and one Italian boy who has only just arrived and speaks very little English. If only he knew more about SEN and which children are eligible for additional support. He really hopes the staff meeting will help.

Introduction

Many teachers feel that they want help and advice about special educational needs, often support from others whom they see as more expert than themselves. However, this chapter will argue that it is in fact the daily class teacher who is best placed to understand the child's needs in the context of their learning environment, and best placed to be the most effective in meeting those needs. A visitor or specialist will only see a snapshot of what is happening in the classroom, which may not be representative of what normally occurs. It is all too easy for outsiders to come in and give advice about particular children on the basis of limited and possibly atypical evidence, when the teachers know the reality of the problems they are facing. Indeed, the presence of a visitor can change the dynamics of a class so that the children (and teacher) behave differently to normal. As teachers, we can sometimes feel that the judgements about children's capabilities and the advice offered by external services

How can school and curriculum targets be met for the whole class when every child within it has individual, and very often special, educational needs?

do not seem to go beyond our own, and may even contradict it. With a little further knowledge, understanding and confidence we can all become well placed to enable any child to become a full member of the class and learn successfully.

This chapter intends to go some way towards addressing Catherine's concerns in Cameo 1. How can school and curriculum targets be met for the whole class when every child within it has individual, and often special, educational needs? In Cameo 2, Emily unintentionally *created special educational needs for children*, which were not there to start with, especially for Red group. We need to be conscious of the fact that it is easy to create difficulties for our pupils through our planning, our use of resources and our own teaching. Before labelling children as 'possessing' learning difficulties, it is important to first make sure that we have done everything to minimize any problems they may encounter.

Classroom organization is critical to the success or failure of our intended learning outcomes (as we have seen in Chapter 6). In Cameo 2, we also see how different types of *grouping* can have dramatic and often unexpected effects on the performance of children with special needs. *Creating an ethos* through modelling and encouraging positive attitudes towards each other will raise the self-esteem of all children in the class (as Alison Shilela has indicated in the previous chapter).

In Cameo 3, Grant needed to know more about special educational needs and the individuals in his class before his first staff meeting. *Finding out about individual children* enables teachers to plan effectively for them, giving them tasks that will *build on their successes* and develop their confidence. In order to identify what help can be made available to the teacher and child when difficulties are experienced, the meaning of the term 'special educational need' will be explored. This will help Grant identify which children are classified as having special educational needs, and which are not. The characteristics of intermittent hearing loss, one of the most common difficulties encountered in the primary classroom, will be used as an example to illustrate some of the implications for teaching children with specific learning difficulties.

It is important to involve everybody, the parents/carers, and all the children and adults in the class, in implementing a policy for SEN. It is critical that the whole school is involved in the *inclusion* of children with SEN. Various forms of inclusion are considered in order to raise some of the issues currently being hotly debated as the legislation for children with special educational needs is yet again modified.

Creating special educational needs for children

Have a look again at Cameo 2. Try to identify any problems that Emily appears to have created for some of the children in her class. The following quote from a recent government document will probably help:

> It should be recognised that some difficulties in learning may be caused or exacerbated by the school's learning environment or adult child relationships. This means looking carefully at such matters as *classroom organisation, teaching materials, teaching style and differentiation* in order to decide how these can be developed so that the child is enabled to learn effectively.
>
> (DfEE 2000b: 27) (writer's italics)

As you will see, Emily had:

- only included the more able children in the whole-class shared session and she had grouped the pupils according to ability, which prevented them from helping each other (*classroom organization*);
- not enlarged the text sufficiently for all the children to be able to see it (*teaching materials*);
- reprimanded children inappropriately for a problem that she had created for them (*teaching style*);
- not *differentiated* the worksheet to match the range of ability within the class.

It is all too easy inadvertently to make tasks harder for children without being aware of the fact that it is the teaching itself, or the activity, which are the causes of the children's problems rather than anything intrinsically to do with the children themselves. Unless we can be sure that these types of problems do not exist, there will be little more that can be done to help our pupils achieve success. As the Government encourages, we need to carefully scrutinize our planning and organization to avoid such common pitfalls. We therefore need to:

- ensure that any resources we use are accessible to all children;
- be aware of how easy it is to create difficulties for children in our own planning and teaching;
- have expectations of each child that match their capabilities;
- avoid blaming the children for our own shortcomings;
- create a positive ethos that encourages all children.

These issues will be explored in more detail throughout this chapter.

Classroom organization, grouping and creating an ethos

Classroom organization and grouping

With the advent of the literacy and numeracy hours there has been more time spent on whole-class teaching for these two subjects. The principle is that pupils of all abilities can be taught together for a significant part of a lesson (Reynolds 1998). Whole-class teaching aims at the middle range of ability, and the teacher targets specific children with appropriate questions and challenges to keep them engaged in the lesson. This requires skilful teaching with a sound knowledge of each of the children's strengths and abilities (social and emotional as well as academic). Group work can then be differentiated to cater for the range of abilities.

Grouping children by ability as described in Cameo 2 is fairly typical in primary classrooms today. As a result of pressure from government for academic success, and concern for the progress of the most able children, teachers have used ability groups in order to teach the NC, literacy and numeracy. In many schools classes are divided into ability groups so that teachers can differentiate tasks relatively easily to meet the needs of the majority of children. In other schools children are 'set' for the core subjects, so that each teacher takes a particular ability group from across a year group. In both cases planning seeks to match the needs of children who fall within a particular range of ability, and the children then work independently on the common task set (Bennett and Dunne 1992).

Although grouping children by ability can make the teacher's job of planning and assessing easier, it can also create very real disadvantages for certain children. We saw in Cameo 2 how low the self-esteem of those in Red group was, as they sensed that less was expected of them than the others. Such children are not prepared to risk failure, and they are less able to concentrate and, therefore, to learn. Since the introduction of the National Curriculum they have also received less individual attention from their teachers (Croll 1996).

Children in the lowest ability groups do not get an opportunity to share their thinking with others who may be more motivated and task-oriented. They may have more difficulty in achieving work that they can be proud of, resulting in them being less motivated, and more likely to give up easily. Recent research also indicates that children in high ability groups are disadvantaged by ability grouping (Boaler *et al.* 2000).

In a mixed ability group, on the other hand, all participants can benefit. The more able can be encouraged to help the others (by taking the lead, or acting as scribe for the group). They will need to develop a deeper understanding themselves of what they explain or teach to others. The less able may well flourish once they can contribute their ideas to a responsive and varied group. In addition, the divide between those who can and those who cannot becomes less obvious, and all children are made to feel valued as important contributors to the work of the group. Giving children more, rather than less, opportunities to learn through teaching them the full curriculum in mixed ability groups is, therefore, the challenge.

Creating a positive ethos

This leads us on to the impact of other children's attitudes towards individual children and a couple more 'stories':

Example A
A child runs crying to the teacher: 'Miss, they've been calling me thick because I didn't know the answer again'. The teacher comforts her, saying 'Never mind, Rachel, they don't really mean it'. Then she continues with the lesson, sitting Rachel beside her.

Example B
It is the start of a science lesson exploring electricity. The teacher wants to reinforce the names of various pieces of equipment. She asks Verity, a child who is generally slow to respond and does not contribute to class discussions, to demonstrate how a crocodile clip works. The rest of the children watch intently, waiting patiently as Verity plucks up the courage to speak. When she has finished, the teacher praises her and thanks her for showing the class.

The teacher is most important in establishing a particular ethos within the classroom. It is all too easy to respond positively to Rachel at an individual level without taking the opportunity to reinforce particular social values and attitudes with all the children. In Example B, the teacher overtly includes a child with learning difficulties into a whole-class session, and has clear expectations of the rest of the children's behaviour towards her. Having a regular circle time is a very useful forum for encouraging discussion about tolerance and the acceptance of others. However, if an incident does occur (as in Example A), then it is important to respond to it rapidly (as Alison Shilela has indicated in the previous chapter). This will help those individuals directly involved to resolve their differences and will reinforce the children's positive attitudes to each other through class rules that encourage tolerance and inclusion. If it proves impossible to discuss immediately, then the class can be told that this will happen at the next opportunity.

Finding out about the children and building on their successes

Research has shown that those teachers who have high expectations engender greater achievement in children (Rosenthal and Jacobsen 1968). However, expectations need to be realistic. We cannot begin to have realistic expectations of a class of children until we know exactly what each child can do socially, emotionally, physically and cognitively. This involves gathering as much information as possible about all the children in the class. Initially the school records and information from previous class teachers and staff in the school can be scrutinized (Morag Hunter-Carsch discusses such records in Chapter 12). Where there are particular concerns or uncertainties about a child who has come from another school, it is worth contacting their previous school for more information. The child's records may well not arrive until after they themselves have become a fully-fledged member of the class!

As teachers, we all need to be aware of the fact that children may perform differently for different people, and that our own expectations about them will greatly influence their performance. Thus a child who was a real problem for one teacher may have no difficulties with another and, of course, the reverse is true. A fuller understanding of the whole child can be gained by contacting the parents/carers and developing a good relationship with them, setting up a dialogue with them on a regular basis.

Observation of the children while being taught by others is extremely helpful, as is observation of the children in the rest of the school (in assembly, at dinnertime and playtime, interacting with other adults and children). It is important to be as open-minded and positive as possible about each child and their capabilities, giving them a chance to prove you and others wrong about any concerns that there may be.

The Code of Practice (DfEE 1994) and draft Code of Practice for 2001 (DfEE 2000a) both define a child as having a special educational need (SEN) if he or she has a greater difficulty than the other children of their age and requires additional provision to be made. This does not in fact offer much help to class teachers, since what is 'normal' for children of a particular age will vary from school to school and from class to class. In addition, there may be many reasons why a child (or a number of children) may have a greater difficulty in learning than the others in the class. The Green Paper *Excellence for All Children* goes further, agreeing that the statutory definition of SEN above can be misleading and lead to unhelpful assumptions (DfEE 1997). Incredibly, it confirms that a child may be said to have SEN in one school, but not in another (DfEE 1997)!

It may be that the system, the school, or the teaching are creating learning difficulties for a child, or for children, that they may not experience in another situation (remember Emily in Cameo 2?).

One in the crowd

A child who has come from a different background to the majority may well experience a greater difficulty than the others in particular areas. On the other hand, placed in a school with peers who have had similar experiences, they would not have any specific problems. A child in one school may not stand out as different, while in another they might be the only one with a particular need.

Similarly, some schools are more able to cater for a variety of abilities, while others struggle with a wide range of ability and require more support from outside agencies. Research has shown that schools vary in their effectiveness in educating pupils even when they come from similar home backgrounds and have similar initial levels of achievement (Rutter *et al.* 1979; Mortimore *et al.* 1988).

A spectrum of need

It must also be remembered that children who are gifted or talented in particular areas are also classified as having special needs. They may be way ahead in one or more areas of their development, yet behind their peers in others – for example, children who are verbally very able may not be patient enough to be able to write their ideas down successfully (as Marilyn Foreman and Nikki Gamble show evidence of in Chapter 10). Children who have E2L do not have a special educational need, although they could be deemed SEN if they have an additional or related learning difficulty. Grant (in Cameo 3) would therefore not include his Italian boy in his list of children with special educational needs. As long as the child has acquired a first language successfully, there is no reason to assume that they will not learn a second language proficiently.

All children can be placed on a continuum of need, and those with SEN can be seen at either end of the spectrum – the gifted children at one end, and those with the most severe difficulties at the other. It has been estimated that at least 20 per cent of all children may have some form of SEN at some stage in their school careers (DES 1978). The vast majority of these will have their needs met by their school, with outside help if necessary. Only two per cent will require a Statement to be made. The Government (DfEE 1994) acknowledges that these figures are broad estimates and that the proportion varies significantly from geographical area to area. A recent survey (DfEE 2000b) found that in 1999, primary schools had 21 per cent of pupils with SEN, including those with Statements.

Hearing loss – an example

Information about a child's health is particularly important. For example, it may well be that in Cameo 3, Grant's child who does not seem to pay attention and tends to be noisy, in fact, has some form of hearing loss. The most common problem that children of primary age will experience is conductive hearing loss caused by otitis media with effusion, or 'glue ear'. This condition occurs when the middle-ear gets blocked with fluid that muffles the sounds that can be heard. In many cases this problem goes unidentified, as the hearing loss is often intermittent and may not be picked up when a hearing test is administered.

Estimates vary, but there may be as many as 20 per cent of children in primary schools who suffer from conductive hearing loss at any point in time (Webster and McConnell 1987). Glue ear has been found to be much more frequent in small children, where nearly 20 per cent of children in the age range 2–5 years are affected (cited in Knight and Swanwick 1999). Because glue ear is a fluctuating hearing loss, a child's hearing can vary and the condition is often difficult to pinpoint. Children can therefore be labelled as 'difficult' because they appear to hear 'when they want to' (selectively) (Knight and Swanwick 1999).

For teachers like Grant who are uncertain about a child's ability to attend and hear adequately, a very simple test can be tried: find as quiet a place and time as possible, and ask the child to give you something, speaking in a fairly quiet voice with your mouth masked from view. Do this at least three times with a variety of objects to see whether they have any difficulty in hearing you. Parents and other staff will be able to provide further information to back up or reject the possibility. If confirmed, a hearing test can be requested for the child, either at school or by the child's own doctor. There are various treatments available, ranging from the prescription of antibiotics and reduction of milk products in their diet, to the removal of adenoids and/or tonsils and the insertion of grommets in the eardrum. Alternatively, the condition may be left to resolve itself, since at around 8- to 9-years-of-age the child will grow out of it.

Some of the possible consequences of glue ear are:

- an over-sensitivity to loud sounds;
- poor speech discrimination in everyday situations;
- reduced attention span leading to bad behaviour or 'dreaminess' (Gregory and Knight 1998).

We can expect children who have had a hearing loss over a period of time to have other associated language difficulties: they may have difficulty in pronouncing certain sounds, their vocabulary may be limited, and their progress in reading and writing may be behind that of their peers. Knowing that a child has a particular difficulty can reduce teachers' own sense of frustration as they begin to understand the child's needs. It can also suggest a series of strategies for helping to reduce the difficulties for a child with hearing loss, for example:

- reducing noise levels by encouraging the child to work with one or two other children in a relatively quiet area for certain periods;
- ensuring that all adults know about optimum practices to enhance the hearing of speech, and the possible 'social withdrawal' effect;
- placing a child with hearing loss near to a wall where there will be less surrounding noise;
- ensuring the child faces the person who is speaking so that he or she can see the person's lips, and offering visual aids to confirm what is being heard (i.e. written or diagrammatic instructions to reinforce verbal instructions);
- ensuring that the speaker calls the child's name and waits until he or she can see the speaker's face before addressing the child;
- providing the child with appropriate work and workspace will also minimize the risks of bad behaviour and punishment for something that is beyond the child's control.

Gregory and Knight (1998) offer a range of other strategies, which is worth reading if you find yourself in the position of having children with this condition.

As well as finding out all we can about our pupils from others, we need to identify the range of ability within the classroom and assess each child's capabilities. Again, we need to focus on what each child *can* do rather than what he or she is struggling with. 'The assessment process should always be fourfold. It should focus on the child's learning characteristics, the learning environment that the school is providing for the child, the task and the teaching style' (DfEE 2000a: 27).

The activities planned for children will then build on their successes rather than reinforce their failures, thus developing their self-confidence and allowing them over time to respond to further challenge and begin to take risks. Lawrence (1978) demonstrates very powerfully how children's reading ability can be improved by raising their self-esteem. He shows how adults who befriend individual children in school and spend time simply talking with them can improve their ability to read. Identifying what a child can do with adult support, ably described by Vygotsky (1978; see also Chapter 5), points the way towards helping children to achieve success unaided. We must not underestimate the power that we as teachers have to raise children's self-esteem by offering them challenges at which they can succeed. Emily, for example, in cameo 2, could have given Red group a specific task that they were able to read, and could have asked them to report back in the plenary.

We need also to be aware of the fact that children do not respond in the same way in all situations. A child may be perfectly confident to speak to the rest of the class on the carpet, but may refuse when asked to do the same to a larger audience in the hall. For this reason it is important to keep notes of the contexts within which we assess children's social and communication skills.

Inclusion or not?

The principle of mixed ability teaching can be extrapolated to the much broader picture – the notion of inclusion, which has been vigorously promoted by government departments. The government's Green Paper (DfEE 1997) followed by the SEN and Disability Rights in Education Bill (2000) both advocate the inclusion of children with SEN, incorporating those with statements of SEN, in mainstream schools. The number of children with SEN who are in mainstream schools has been steadily increasing since the mid-1990s, rising to 60 per cent now being taught in mainstream schools as compared with 54 per cent in 1995 (Dean 2000). Arguments can be made for individual children to be placed either in special or mainstream schools depending on their particular circumstances and needs. There is no general rule that could possibly apply to all children, though the principle that mainstream should be the first option for children with SEN is perceived by many to be a positive step forward. The provision offered within the school is clearly critical to the success of the scheme.

There are three possible scenarios for inclusion:

1 the resources and expertise already available within the school are used to good effect to support children with SEN. The consultation document for the revision of the Code of Practice suggests that most pupils will make progress within an inclusive curriculum without any great difficulties if teachers use a wide range of strategies to meet whatever learning needs pupils may have (DfEE 2000a).
2 a possible scenario for inclusion occurs when there is a need to call on expertise that is external to the school (for example, learning support teachers, behavioural support, advisers).
3 resources will be needed that can only be accessed through a statement of SEN.

The overriding benefit for *all* children in an inclusive setting is that variety is seen as the norm, the acceptance and tolerance of difference is actively promoted, and all individuals are seen as part of the school community, which is thus enriched (see also Chapter 14).

The danger, which may arise as inclusion becomes more common, is that children will join schools which are not able to offer them appropriate provision. The most frequent cause of inadequate provision has been through a lack of resources being appropriately channelled, sometimes occurring as a result of a lack of understanding of children's particular needs. In these instances children can become alienated and demoralized, losing any fragile self-esteem that they might have had.

Whole-school support

The discussion so far has concentrated on what we can do to support all the children, each of whom has an individual need. It should not be forgotten, however, that this cannot be done successfully without the support and approval of the headteacher and governors. More than this, the best practice will take place in a school that has whole-school policies which embrace special educational needs. The most recent policy document on curriculum access confirms that this should form part of the school's SEN, pastoral and curriculum policies (NASEN 2000).

This will enable us to plan effectively within the whole school's scheme of work to meet the needs of those children at either end of the continuum. It will also help to ensure that resources (both material and human) are planned for and made available. Finally, it will encourage a positive attitude in all staff towards children experiencing special educational needs.

Schools should ensure staff have knowledge of and a willingness to use the widest possible range of strategies and teaching styles to enable all pupils to have access to the curriculum. All staff should be aware of their responsibility to address the range of SEN in their school, both in terms of content and delivery. There should be flexibility in approaches to teaching all aspects of the curriculum.

(NASEN 2000: 2)

Using other adults in the room/Learning support assistants

The presence of additional adults in the classroom on a regular basis can be an invaluable asset to any teacher. They can be used to support practical activities, or to work with individuals or small groups of children, giving the teacher the chance to teach the rest of the class more intensively. They may well be employed to work with a particular child or children as a special needs/learning support assistant. It is always as well to communicate with helpers on a regular basis before and after lessons. This ensures that they understand what the objectives are for the children as well as themselves. Sharing observations with them about the children, and developing joint assessment records can provide a richer account of children's capabilities (as they may respond differently to different adults). Perhaps keep a notebook, journal or daily diary in class in which to write down instructions for support staff (see also Chapter 6), and yours and their observations and findings. This will serve as an alternative if there is little immediate time available for discussion. It is worth noting, however, that the best use of classroom assistants is to give the teachers, themselves, more opportunity to teach (Moyles and Suschitzky 1997).

Parents/carers

Parents/carers are absolutely critical to the successful teaching of children with SEN. The draft Code of Practice (DfEE 2000a) confirms this view, adding that parents need to feel confident that schools actively involve them and take account of their wishes, feelings and unique perspectives on their children's development, particularly if a child has special needs.

In the first place, parents/carers know their child better than anyone else, and can tell us about specific characteristics that their child may have that could be relevant. Second, if we can agree with the parents/carers a child's learning targets, these can be reinforced at home as well as at school and are more likely to be effective. A child who is expected to behave in a particular way at home, and differently at school will not necessarily learn the code of behaviour that teachers might wish. (They are more likely to learn that they can behave in different ways in different environments, and become more adept at manipulating people in either!) Government legislation has increasingly strengthened the role of parents, giving them the power to influence the choice of school that their child will attend. As NASEN point out (2000: 2) 'Schools should view parents/carers as partners and involve them fully in discussions about access to the curriculum in its widest sense.'

It is far better to set up regular contact with parents/carers at the outset, rather than waiting until a problem arises. This will cause the parents/carers to become anxious and defensive, possibly identifying with their own past experiences as a pupil, when their parents were only called up to the school when there was something wrong. Establishing a relationship with parents/carers that is open and sharing is very rewarding, since any concerns on either side can be expressed in the knowledge that both parties are seeking to help overcome problems and have the child's best interests at heart.

It is a sad fact that despite the Code of Practice (DfEE 1994) urging the development of partnerships with parents, many schools have not necessarily established viable home–school links (Ofsted 1996). Too many parents still remain 'unreached and seemingly, unreachable' (Wolfendale 1997: 1–2) as the divide between them and the professionals shows little sign of reducing. Here, then, is the challenge: to realize, in the classroom, the government's commitment to partnership principles so that the parents are partners in the planning and delivery of services, rather than passive recipients of provision (Wolfendale 1997).

Conclusion

The key point of this chapter has been the matter of responding to the individual first and foremost. We as teachers are in the very best position to know how to meet the needs of particular children in the class. Supported by information from the parents, specialist information can tell us much about particular types of difficulty (for example, dyspraxia, Down's syndrome, hearing or visual impairment, autism, diabetes). It is clearly important to know about medical conditions, particularly those that might have implications for safety. This knowledge, however, can only guide us as we make our own judgements about how best to work with each individual. One child may well have developed strategies to overcome a difficulty, where another has not, and each will therefore require a very different teaching approach. Some of these differences have been discussed through the cameos presented – remember poor Emily!

The good practice that teachers demonstrate with children experiencing difficulties of one kind or another is good practice for all children. The key to effective practice is to be able to work out what a child's specific

Rising to the challenge of teaching all children is one of the reasons for joining the teaching profession

needs are at any one time, and to find ways of creating opportunities for them to succeed. This cycle of identification, assessment and provision, followed by reassessing provision through evaluating learning and teaching, is a model that applies to all teaching. The way we do this is likely to vary for every single child we teach, and will at times seem like a daunting prospect. However, as we learn through trial and error what works for each child, so we gradually become the experts.

Teaching, as we all know, can present a considerable challenge to the patience, ingenuity and determination of the teacher. Teaching children effectively across a wide spectrum of ability is an even greater challenge which is ever increasing as more and more children who are experiencing learning difficulties are included in mainstream schools. Rising to that challenge is one of the reasons for joining the teaching profession – it can be incredibly rewarding and exciting. The unpredictability of what is in store for us as teachers means that we are learners alongside our pupils – as the title of this book seeks to affirm. We can reduce the sense of anxiety and frustration that Catherine felt in cameo 1 by having the confidence to take control, to find out what a particular child can do and what works for them. There will be times when we are made to fall back on our own personal, sometimes unexplored, resources. We need to be aware of our own hidden strengths and to know where we can find additional information, advice and help.

Our role as teachers is to support every child, enabling each child, in turn, to gain the confidence to take risks and strive for their own success.

A few questions to set you thinking

Select a child from a class who gives you cause for concern as he or she is not progressing as you would hope.

1 Does the child have low self-esteem? How do you know?
2 Write down three examples of successes for her or him. Be specific about what they achieved and the context of that success.
3 What caused the child to succeed in these cases?
4 Write down three examples of difficulties he or she has. Again be specific about the problems and the context.
5 What caused the difficulty in each case?
6 Write down as many things as possible that you could do for the child:
   • to help raise self-esteem;
   • to help achieve more successes;
   • to prevent the difficulties experienced.

References and further reading

Bennett, N. and Dunne, M. (1992) *Managing Classroom Groups*. Hemel Hempstead: Simon and Schuster.
Boaler, J., Wiliam, D. and Brown, M. (2000) Students' experiences of ability grouping – disaffection, polarization and the construction of failure, *British Educational Research Journal*, 26(5): 631–49.
Croll, P. (ed.) (1996) *Teachers, Pupils and Primary Schooling: Continuity and Change*. London: Cassell.
Dean, C. (2000) Stress alert over more pupils with statements, *Times Educational Supplement*, 1 December: 9.
DES (1978) *Special Educational Needs (The Warnock Report)*. London: HMSO.
DfEE (1994) *Code of Practice on the Identification and Assessment of Special Educational Needs*. London: HMSO.
DfEE (1997) *Excellence for All Children, Meeting Special Educational Needs*. London: HMSO.
DfEE (2000a) *Draft SEN Code of Practice on the Identification and Assessment of Pupils with Special Educational Needs and SEN Thresholds*. London: HMSO.
DfEE (2000b) *Special Educational Needs 2000*. London: HMSO.
Gregory, S. and Knight, P. (1998) *Issues in Deaf Education*. London: David Fulton.
Knight, P. and Swanwick, R. (1999) *The Care and Education of a Deaf Child: a Book for Parents*. Clevedon: Multilingual Matters.
Lawrence, D. (1978) *Counselling Students with Reading Difficulties*. London: Good Reading.
Mortimore, P., Lewis, D., Sammons, P., Stoll, L. and Ecot, R. (1988) *School Matters*. London: Open Books.
Moyles, J. and Suschitzky, W. (1997) *Jills of All Trades: Classroom Assistants in Key Stage One Classrooms*. London: Association of Teachers and Lecturers.
NASEN (2000) *Policy Document on Curriculum Access*. Tamworth: NASEN.
Ofsted (1996) *The Implementation of the Code of Practice for Pupils with SEN*. London: HMSO.

Reynolds, D. (1998) Schooling for literacy: a review of research on teacher effectiveness and school effectiveness and its implications for contemporary educational policies, *Educational Review*, 50(2): 147–62.

Rosenthal, R. and Jacobsen, L. (1968) *Pygmalion in the Classroom: Teacher Expectations and Pupil Intellectual Development*. New York: Holt, Rhinehart & Winston.

Rutter, M., Maugham, B., Mortimore, P. and Ousten, J. (1979) *Fifteen Thousand Hours: Secondary Schools and Their Effects on Pupils*. London: Open Books.

Vygotsky, L. (1978) *Thought and Language*. Cambridge, MA: MIT Press.

Webster, A. and McConnell, C. (1987) *Children with Speech and Language Difficulties*. London: Cassell.

Wolfendale, S. (ed.) (1997) *Working With Parents of SEN Children After the Code of Practice*. Home and School: A Working Alliance. London: David Fulton.

16

It takes two to tango: working with experienced teachers

Wendy Suschitzky and Barbara Garner

Cameo 1

Initial visit by beginner teacher to teaching practice school:

Mentor: I've read the Teaching Experience Handbook and it all looks rather a lot of work for you and for me.

Beginner teacher: Yes I'm going to need to have so much information before I start.

Mentor: So it will be best if we start by just looking at the requirements for the first few days.

Cameo 2

Beginner teacher observing mentor teaching: Child A asks permission to go to the toilet and is allowed. A few minutes later, child B requests the same and is refused with the mentor referring to the class rules that all children should go to the toilet at playtime.

The beginner teacher's interpretation is that the mentor is inconsistent and that making class rules are a waste of time. The beginner teacher does not have the mentor's knowledge that Child A has frequently wet themselves in the past. Also when making the rules together, the class had agreed that anyone who is desperate could go to the toilet.

Introduction

There are now many models of teacher education, with the establishment of new routes into teaching and changes to existing courses. In all of these models, the training that is provided by schools is of paramount importance. Recognition has been given to the role of the classroom teacher as the trainer or 'mentor' of beginner teachers. The success of this is dependent on the establishment of a real partnership between trainer and trainee, where each side respects and understands the other. During an initial teacher-training course, a beginner teacher will be placed with an experienced teacher in whose classroom teaching experience will take place. A newly qualified teacher is now required to have an induction tutor, who has responsibility for induction into the art of teaching (DfEE 1999). This chapter will help you to benefit from school-based ITE and the induction period by examining aspects of the partnership with experienced teachers, who are responsible for your learning. The term 'mentor' will be used to describe both supervisors and induction tutors.

Let the dance begin!

The greater the understanding of the concept of mentoring and its implications for schools, the greater the effectiveness of the process. Being a good classroom teacher does not necessarily mean that one will be a good mentor (Jacques 1992; Harber 1993). The skills and knowledge required for teacher education are in many ways different from those considered valuable for the education of children. Mentoring makes new professional demands on the classroom teacher but can empower the mentor by giving recognition to the craft knowledge and practical wisdom of the classroom teacher (Wilkin 1992).

The terms 'mentor', 'mentoring', 'mentee' and 'protégé' have entered educational jargon. The word 'mentor' originates from Greek mythology, where Ulysses appointed Mentor, his trusted friend to care and guide his son, Telemachus, during his absence. Mentoring is sometimes likened to apprenticeship, where a master craftsman passes his skills to young recruits to the trade. However, in teacher education, a beginner teacher should also gain a high level of understanding of the purpose and place of those skills (Monaghan and Lunt 1992; Moyles *et al.* 1998). Learning how to teach must be valued as an intellectual discipline (Aldrich 1990). The tasks of learning to teach and of mentoring, therefore, are complex.

Both mentor and beginner teacher need to develop skills and strategies. For example, in Cameo 1, both need to breakdown the requirements for the teaching practice into manageable parts. Next it will be important to gather sufficient information to be effectively prepared for the first week. As Cameo 2 demonstrates, each classroom situation and the interactions found there are unique. In order to learn how to teach, one must understand the underlying reasons behind professional judgements. Superficial

In order to learn how to teach, one must understand the underlying reasons behind professional judgements

observation of performance does not provide this. Only by mentor and beginner teacher exploring together the meaning of a teaching episode can mentoring be effective.

In every school setting teachers will work alongside many people, so although for a beginner teacher the relationship with a mentor will be the most important one to establish, ways of working with other adults in the classroom will need to be examined.

There are, of course, some differences between the roles and responsibilities of HEI staff and that of the school-based trainers according to the requirements of each individual course. Establishing a constructive relationship between beginner teacher and mentor provides a framework for the mentoring process. But what type of relationship should be formed? Should the relationship be one of 'critical friend' or 'critical colleague'? There are differences between the relationship established between a student teacher and mentor and that of an NQT and induction tutor (Moyles *et al.* 1998). Bleach (1999) states that the framework of this latter relationship should develop and change during the induction year. If the mentor and beginner teacher are from different cultural, gender, age or social backgrounds then it is important to maintain objectivity to avoid stereotypical assumptions by either partner.

As cameo 1 shows, the first few meetings between beginner teacher and mentor are crucial. An agenda might include:

- reaching a shared understanding about the purpose of the teaching experience;
- sharing of expectations of each other's role;
- understanding of each other's priorities, i.e. classroom teacher's commitment to her class, beginner teacher's workload from college;
- sharing views on the process of adult learning and how this will be carried out, i.e. will a sink or swim approach be used or practice followed by evaluation;
- giving recognition to the beginner teacher's prior experience and skills;
- recognizing that beginner teachers will have individual values and theories about teaching;
- making an assessment of needs;
- setting realistic and achievable targets;
- agreeing the format of tutorials;
- recognizing the need to induct beginner teachers into the hidden culture of school, i.e. where to sit in the staffroom, how to address the headteacher.

Structures and strategies

Like all aspects of education, training in schools will vary according to the particular context, personalities, skills and experiences of the people involved (Calderhead and Shorrock 1997; Moyles *et al.* 1999). For this reason, it is imperative that beginner teachers know how to get the best out of the situation in which they are placed. It is their responsibility to be active in framing the training period (Simco 2000). It should be a partnership in which the professional development of both trainee and mentor will be enhanced.

The ideal mentor would be:

> An excellent, well-organized, experienced teacher, who is a perceptive observer and a good communicator, in a school that appreciates the education and training role and has a sound policy for its interpretation.

No mentor could be all of those things all of the time: most will have strengths and weaknesses in varying degrees in varying situations. You are most likely to measure your mentor's skills against your own needs whatever you perceive these to be. What you define as excellent/poor, or well organized/poorly organized will relate to *your* level of understanding of good primary practice and may not be the interpretation of others. Since you will wish to emulate what you perceive as successful practice and reject the opposite, it is only by continuous questioning of your assumptions that you will further your development (see Chapter 13).

You are likely to measure your mentor's skills against how you perceive your own needs

In order to achieve the best possible supported teaching experience, you need to clarify your own needs by giving *structure* to your thinking processes and to have *strategies* for meeting those needs. Remember that each of the highlighted mentor qualities above is a quality you wish to develop further yourself. Pause for a while and make some notes about how you will:

- clarify your own understandings of each aspect;
- identify what it is you want from your mentor;
- develop strategies for getting the best from the situation in which you find yourself.

Taking each of the main statements about the ideal mentor, we must first ask the following questions.

What is a 'perceptive observer'?

A perceptive observer notices strengths, weaknesses and needs, not from continual comparison with their own methods, but from the interaction between you and the children. They note in which circumstances you and the children relate well and the causes of this. They recognize the symptoms that arise from difficulties in establishing complex relationships. They are aware where there is a lack of understanding on either side so that needs can be clarified. This maintains a balance between your needs, those of the children and the relationship as a whole. Valuable observations are made, not only during lessons, but also from any interactions between you and the children, from how you and they deal with any number of situations and learning strategies.

Structure for considering the 'perceptive observer'
Unless the act of observing is approached systematically (as Linda Hargreaves suggests in Chapter 3), both you and your mentor are likely to be confronted with more information than is manageable. It is quite common to feel totally overwhelmed by the number of things that require attention and for mentors to assimilate so much that there is neither time for discussion nor useful depth of observation.

How can a systematic approach be developed between you and your mentor? As a beginner teacher, you have to know what it is you need help with and to make this the basis for observations. Together you need to choose a specific focus by using the QTS Standards (DfEE 1998) as a means of setting appropriate targets. But, you need to see it not only in the light of your own performance but also in the light of its effectiveness in creating learning.

Strategies for dealing with the mentor as 'perceptive observer'
Discuss the chosen focus with the mentor and decide on the particular focus for a day. This means that even if the mentor, for all manner of reasons, is unable to be in the classroom for any length of time, observations remain focused during even the briefest of opportunities. An experienced teacher can quickly see what is actually happening.

What is a 'good communicator' in relation to the teacher educator role?

A 'good communicator' is primarily looking to develop your learning and secondarily to share their greater experience and expertise with you. By questioning, they seek your understanding of a given situation. They share their positive observations of what was successful and ask why you think that was. They help you look at what was not successful in the same way, drawing on your understanding, rather than unloading theirs on to you. They encourage you to develop strategies of your own, sharing possible strategies of theirs. A good communicator only talks in response to your needs and if you are not recognizing them, no amount of good advice is going to be acted on by you. They will leave you with questions unanswered rather than answers for which there have been no questions formulated.

Structure for considering the 'good communicator'
The best possible structure for effective feedback, is to agree a time and place, ideally once a day, or at least once a week. A formal session takes the training role seriously: incidental feedback often only fulfils the supportive role that keeps things running smoothly.

1 *Know exactly what it is you want to know.* This should be directly related to the focus you have chosen. If you expect the entire lesson or day to be dissected then this is unhelpful and often results in clichés and unqualified statements. You will want to know – what went well and why; what can be improved on and any advice, strategies or information in respect of criticism.

2 *Ask the right questions.* It is important to recognize that misunderstandings will occur if you have not established that you and the mentor are referring to the same focus for your discussion. McAlpine *et al.* (1988) recommends that your questions concentrate on the positive events in the lesson, are framed to explore specific happenings, are open-ended and that you allow plenty of time for the mentor to respond.

3 *Make your questions very specific* as time for feedback will probably be limited. 'How did it go?' will probably result in 'Fine. You're doing very well', or 'Not too badly. I think you are going to have to be firmer, don't you?' The former is encouraging but does not further your learning and the latter leaves you wondering how.

If you are to benefit from your mentor's observations, this framework should help:

• With regard to . . ., what did I get right?
• What aspects of . . ., could I improve on?
• Can you give me any (advice/strategies/information) in respect of . . . ?

The discussion based on these three questions, however brief, is far more likely to make you feel positive, the task at hand manageable and the mentor more able to answer your needs. More importantly, theories underpinning practice will be reflected on. For example, in answer to your request for strategies, your mentor may advise that to ensure children do not finish too quickly and become potential nuisances, you should examine whether the material being used is appropriate and have extension tasks to hand.

Here are two other questions raised by beginner teachers in relation to communication:

I am constantly being criticized and given advice I haven't asked for! What shall I do?

Strategy: Even though the mentor means well, this can have an undermining or overwhelming effect. If you first show gratitude for the help then you can use the three questions suggested above, focusing on points raised that concern you and so make sense of the overload.

> My mentor gives me lots of written feedback but never seems prepared to discuss things with me face to face.

Strategy: Put your three questions in written form to the mentor to handle when time allows. Receiving a request for additional written responses may trigger your mentor to talk to you instead.

What is meant by a 'teacher who appreciates the education and training role'?

Mentors who appreciate their role in this way will give as much help and guidance as possible, passing on how they work, record, observe, plan and organize, providing forms, lists and information about children. They will support students' understanding of prescribed plans and also allow the student to take some ownership of interpretation and make use of their individual strengths. A partnership will be formed giving as much assistance as possible. Such a mentor will have the children at heart and place importance on their learning as well as yours. As previously stated, the root of effective mentoring is the establishment of the relationship between beginner teacher and mentor. This takes time and thought and other demands and pressures may prevent its easy fulfilment. You can do much to establish a good working relationship regardless of the difficulties, if you first acknowledge this. Then you can identify your needs in respect of the mentor's role.

Structure
You must have a clear perspective on what your mentor's role is if you are able to relate effectively to it and benefit fully from it. The relationship whereby this can happen, is built up through good communication, so the key words are:

- Communicate • Ask • Question • Share • Praise

The role is to teach you by providing a learning environment, to support you, to protect you in respect of your inexperience, to challenge you and to accept you as a developing professional. Each of these aspects is discussed in turn below.

Teach
Listen and be open to what your mentor is saying or doing. A learner is exploring beliefs and trying out possibilities. Learning has stopped if you think you know the answers.

> My mentor seems constantly to lecture me and tell me what to do. I don't feel as if I ever use my own ideas.

Strategy: You may ask if this is an effective way of creating learning for you (or children). You will have to try and focus your mentor by asking specific questions. You may disagree with what you are told but your views may come from inexperience. How does theory work in practice? Until you have tried your mentor's way and then your own, you have no evidence on which to base your judgements. Are you a realist moving towards the idealistic, or an idealist moving towards reality?

Support

In order to support you, your mentor must appreciate your needs, which you must communicate. Fear of appearing ignorant, vulnerable or incompetent might stop you doing so. Remember that your mentor may not be unhelpful but may be suffering from anxiety too. One of the complexities of the job is to know when to intervene, challenge, accept your levels of competency or leave you to find out for yourself.

> My mentor doesn't ever seem to really listen to me or understand what my needs are.

Strategy: There could be a variety of reasons for this, such as other pressures. If you ask your mentor 'Who should I ask about . . . ?' the required support may be proffered or another member of staff with expertise identified. If neither happens then go and find someone yourself to offer support.

Protect

This means that your mentor has to make judgements as to what you should be protected from at what stage in your learning. The mentor will also have the children's and school's welfare at heart in making some protective decisions. You may feel you are being underestimated. There is a very fine line between allowing errors that are valuable tools and stopping potentially damaging situations.

> My mentor tried to protect me from everything . . . or nothing!

Strategy: The more able you are to voice your inexperience/experience, uncertainties/certainties and doubts/confidence, the more able the mentor will be in taking appropriate action. For example, 'I am feeling much more confident with the class now. Shall I have Paul (behavioural difficulties) in my lesson tomorrow?' Or, 'As I'm having the whole class tomorrow, I feel inexperienced in handling Paul. Could he be excluded until I find my feet?'

Challenge

Your mentor has to recognize your potential, and your ability to take risks but so do you! How you react to pressure gives you the opportunity to know yourself better, where your limits lie and whether you view difficulties as problems or challenges. Remember, a problem cannot be overcome until you see it as a challenge.

My mentor just leaves me to sink or swim.

Strategy: If your mentor thinks that you have to deal alone with a wide range of situations or that your training institution will have prepared you for all eventualities, then they may see your practice as a test and not a learning experience. You should view this as an opportunity to benefit from the experience and from this build your own construct of what is valuable. If you are sinking, is it because you have not followed the structures recommended above? If you are swimming and so have been given little feedback during the last few weeks of practice, have you sought out your mentor to ensure further communication?

Acceptance

In order for your mentor to accept you, you must be someone who is prepared to respect the conformities of the school, and to seek to understand the individual expectations of your mentor. You will not easily be accepted if you are seen to be rejecting the status quo: it is a case of being professional. If you accept the reality of your situation then energy will not be wasted fighting it but, instead, used to enhance it or reach a happy compromise through understanding.

If the relationship established with your mentor is based on the clearly defined role given above, then it will provide the best possible training. However, you should recognize that 'the way we relate to others is affected by the way we relate to ourselves, and particularly how we perceive ourselves'. Also 'the way we perceive others has a strong effect on the way we relate to them' (Hall and Hall 1988). A good working relationship is a two-way process, half of which the beginner teacher is responsible for.

I don't think my mentor really likes me – it's very difficult having to work together.

Strategy: First, ask yourself and then your mentor whether you are behaving in an acceptable way. Then ask yourself whether you actually like your mentor. You could be projecting your negative feelings on to the mentor who is then sensitive to your resistance, which is an extremely common defence mechanism (Hall and Hall 1988). You need to concentrate on the professional role of the mentor, as outlined above, and not their weaknesses as perceived by you. Any anger you feel will come from negative rather than positive action on your part. Tensions arising between you and your mentor may build into mutual dislike for each other through a series of judgements and misunderstandings. It then becomes impossible for either of you to communicate effectively with the other as you both feel threatened. You need to take responsibility for your half of the relationship if you wish to resolve the uncomfortable situation and could start by asking the mentor if you are to blame and what can improve the situation. Try to appreciate what your mentor does for you and give positive feedback on their help. You will not overcome difficulties by pride or anger or by seeing yourself as guiltless and the mentor as guilty.

As schools evolve policies for teacher education, it is highly likely that many of the difficulties described above will cease. However, we must remember that teachers are individuals. How a beginner teacher relates to a mentor will reflect the quality of the relationships formed with children in the classroom. Any number of strategies may fail you if you are not working within a clear framework. It is from this framework that you can safely learn and move forward in your professional development.

Working relationships with other adults

In primary classrooms, you will find that teachers work alongside many adults with whom relationships need to be established. The role of these adults will vary greatly according to individual qualifications and the school's needs. These teams contribute to classroom effectiveness and raise standards. In particular, support staff are deployed working with children carrying out Literacy and Numeracy activities. This will include supporting children with SEN, working directly with groups and assisting the teacher with management (DfEE 1999). Before a main teaching experience you should request a list of people who will be present in the classroom and the times and frequency of the support. A typical list may include classroom assistants, language support teachers (monolingual and bilingual), special needs teachers and support workers, students (who may be teenagers on a community course from the local secondary school), parents, volunteers, governors and personnel from outside agencies. Interactions with such a wide range of people requires a high level of interpersonal skills from planning partnership teaching with language support staff to requesting practical help from busy classroom assistants.

Strategies

- Gather as much information as possible concerning the role of classroom supporters and their expectations of your role.
- Find out the procedures for briefing support staff.

- Provide explanations of what children should be learning from an activity and not just what the children should do.
- Ensure that children understand the adult's role and behave accordingly (Moyles 1992).
- Prepare lessons that include plans for the work of other adults and review these in lesson evaluations.
- Communication is important so that staff who work intermittently in the classroom can have relevant information concerning the teaching situation.
- Establish common policies of discipline, organization and assessment.
- Acknowledge that you and the support staff are working together to solve common problems.
- Build accountability to each team member (Balshaw 1999).
- Value the different perspective that other adults bring to the classroom especially culture, language and gender.
- Discover the talents and specialized knowledge of all support staff to improve classroom management and extend children's learning.
- Give specific tasks to parents and volunteers in order to make them feel useful.
- Maintain confidentiality at all times.

Working with the youngest children

Collaborative teaching in Foundation Stage settings requires careful consideration. Many nursery nurses believe that they are doing the same job as nursery teachers (Moyles and Suschitzky 1994) which can arouse feelings of frustration as pay and status are less than that of teachers. In recent years the roles of the two have become blurred in the name of equality with teachers sharing the 'chores' and nursery nurses teaching Numeracy and Literacy. It is in the areas of planning and assessment that a shared understanding is vital in order to enhance children's learning (Moyles and Suschitzky 1997). A young beginner teacher can easily feel threatened by an experienced nursery nurse. Information concerning the beginner teacher's course content and assessment procedures should be shared with nursery nurses.

Conclusion

Learning to teach is a demanding process but with skilled support you can succeed. If both mentor and beginner teacher appreciate the complexity of the task then the mentor can take satisfaction from witnessing the professional development of the beginner teacher. The new entrant to the profession can feel that they have gained access to the knowledge that experienced teachers use in their teaching and that they have received the best possible education and training from an experienced and thoughtful mentor to complement and support their college-based activities.

References and further reading

Aldrich, R. (1990) The evolution of teacher education, in N. Graves (ed.) *Initial Teacher Education*. London: Kogan Page.

Balshaw, M. (1999) *Help in the Classroom*. London: David Fulton.

Bleach, K. (1999) *The Induction and Mentoring of Newly Qualified Teachers*. London: David Fulton.

Calderhead, J. (1987) *Exploring Teachers' Thinking*. London: Cassell.

Calderhead, J. and Shorrock, S. (1997) *Understanding Teacher Education*. London: Falmer Press.

DfEE (1998) *Teaching: High Status, High Standards. Requirements for Courses of Initial Teacher Training*, Circular 4/98. London: DfEE.

DfEE (1999) *The Induction Period for Newly Qualified Teachers*, Circular 5/99. London: DfEE.

DfEE (1999) *The National Literacy Strategy. Additional Literacy Support*. London: DfEE.

Hall, E. and Hall, C. (1988) *Human Relations in Education*. London: Routledge.

Harber, C. (1993) Overseas students and democratic learning, *British Journal of In-Service Education*, 19(2): 72–6.

Jacques, K. (1992) Mentoring in initial teacher education, *Cambridge Journal of Education*, 22(3): 337–50.

McAlpine, A., Brown, S., Hagger, H. and McIntyre, D. (1988) *Student-Teachers Learning From Experienced Teachers*. Edinburgh: The Scottish Council For Research In Education.

Monaghan, J. and Lunt, N. (1992) Mentoring: Person, process, practice and problems, *British Journal of Educational Studies*, 4(3): 248–63.

Moyles, J. (1992) *Organizing for Learning in the Primary Classroom*. Buckingham: Open University Press.

Moyles, J. and Suschitzky, W. (1994) The comparative roles of nursery nurses and nursery teachers, *Educational Research*, 36(3): 247–58.

Moyles, J. and Suschitzky, W. (1997) *The Buck stops here. Nursery Teachers and Nursery Nurses working together*. University of Leicester report funded by The Esmee Fairburn Trust.

Moyles, J., Suschitzky, W. and Chapman, L. (1998) *Teaching Fledglings to Fly. Mentoring and Support Systems in Primary Schools*. London: Association of Teachers and Lecturers and Leicester University.

Moyles, J., Suschitzky, W. and Chapman, L. (1999) Mentoring in primary schools: Ethos, structures and workloads, *Journal of In-service Education*, 25(1): 161–72.

Simco, N. (2000) *Succeeding in the Induction Year*. Exeter: Learning Matters.

Wilkin, M. (1992) *Mentoring in Schools*. London: Kogan Page.

17

I don't want to worry you, but . . .!

Teachers and the law

Christopher Curran

Cameo 1

It had been one of 'those days'. In different physical education
(PE) lessons, two children had tripped and banged their heads. The
incidents were curiously similar. Both had been accidents caused by
untied shoelaces. Only the ages of the children differed: one was
5 years, the other 10 years.

Colin, the newly qualified Year 5 teacher of one of the injured
pupils, was very concerned, especially as he had to hurry his class
getting changed for PE as assembly had gone on far longer than
expected. Sandra, the highly experienced Year R teacher in whose
lesson the other accident had happened, was much more relaxed.
'Accidents happen' was her reaction.

Cameo 2

A group of five 8-year-olds is busily engaged on a design and
technology activity that is part of the school's scheme of work. They
are working on a small table situated next to the classroom sink. Their
work is being supervised by Pat, a teaching assistant who has done
this work before with the class. Ali, the experienced class teacher, has
trained the class in the safe use of a range of tools, including craft
knives. Ali was careful to ask Pat to remind the group of 'safe use'
before they began the activity.

The classroom is particularly busy that afternoon, with children
moving about from place to place to collect the materials that they
need for their various tasks. At the sink, one of the girls, Sara, has
difficulty with a tap. She gets sprayed with water and jumps back in

surprise, knocking into one of the craft group. As a result, Ranjit receives a deep cut that requires hospital treatment.

Cameo 3
Nadine is a wilful 10-year-old in Clare's class. Often, she leaves her place, wanders around the classroom and interferes with other children. Today Nadine has been particularly irritating and has tried Clare's patience, especially when Clare sees Nadine deliberately knock over the water pot and spoil another child's painting. Remaining outwardly calm, Clare tells Nadine to return to her seat. Nadine ignores her. Clare walks over to Nadine, takes her firmly, but not violently, by the hand and leads her back to her seat. Nadine is furious and struggles, calling out 'Take your hands off me. My mum says you can't touch me.'

   After school, Clare is chatting to Joan, the school's deputy head teacher, and describes the incident with Nadine. 'Don't worry about it, Clare. We can do what we want, short of actual violence or corporal punishment. We've got *"loco parentis"*' is Joan's response.

Cameo 4
Frank, a newly qualified teacher in his first term, is having a hard time with his Year 6 class. While many of the children will behave reasonably, there is a significant minority who seem to enjoy making his life a misery. They are expert at doing things behind Frank's back and adopting an air of injured innocence if challenged.

   Wisely, Frank seeks advice from his colleagues. Tom, a teacher of many years standing, advises him not to 'muck about. If you think the problems are coming from one group, keep them in after school. Don't worry about who actually did the thing, punish them all. That way you're sure to get the guilty one. Anyway, it will serve as a lesson to them all.'

Introduction

The aim of this chapter is to introduce you to those aspects of the law that underpin a teacher's daily activities. Rather than seeking to develop an expert level of knowledge, the intention is to promote a level of awareness and understanding sufficient to allow teachers to go about their professional duties with relaxed confidence. As such, nothing in this chapter should be construed as giving definitive advice on any particular incident – we can learn from all cases, but each one is unique, like the children and the teachers! Faced with any incident that seems to carry the possibility of legal liability, the cautious teacher will seek professional advice often, initially, through a professional association.

Despite the occasional headline in the press, the vast majority of teachers go through their entire careers without facing any form of challenge to the legality or professionalism of their conduct. Nevertheless, it is helpful, particularly to new teachers, to have some basic knowledge of *four areas* of the law that, together, form the main framework that supports and constrains daily actions. These are:

1 The duty of care.
2 Physical contact with pupils.
3 Punishment.
4 The teacher as an employee – the issue of personal liability.

Each of these is explored through the discussion of the cameos of classroom life.

The duty of care

We begin our consideration of this notion through an exploration of two minor accidents. Although their coincidence may seem somewhat unrealistic, these two incidents are, perhaps surprisingly, the sort of low-key event that can lead to allegations of negligence being made against a teacher. There is much that careful teachers can do to reduce the risk of such charges being made. The key is to have a secure understanding of the fundamental legal concept that underpins our professional responsibilities. It is the notion of the *duty of care.*

The duty of care is part of our framework of civil – as distinct from criminal – law. It applies to all of us in every aspect of our lives. In essence, the duty of care holds that we must take into consideration the *reasonably foreseeable consequences* of our actions (or choice not to act) on other people. Put another way, it means that we are not entitled to do as we please; we must consider the impact of our actions on others.

> You must take reasonable care to avoid any acts or omissions which you can reasonably foresee would be likely to injure your neighbour ... [who are those] ... persons who are so closely and directly affected by my act that I ought reasonably to have them in contemplation ...
>
> (Lord Aitkin in *Donoghue* v. *Stevenson* 1932, cited in Bridgman 1958)

If it can be shown that damage occurred as a result of a teacher's action or inaction to someone to whom a duty of care was owed, then the teacher would be found to have been *negligent.* (See the section on 'The teacher as an employee' for a brief discussion of the employer's associated legal liability.)

As teachers, we have a range of specific responsibilities that have been established by statute and by our contracts of employment. In addition to these, we have additional duties under common law, duties that stem from our being in the place of the parent (*in loco parentis*) while the child is in our care. The legal force of this view was first established by Mr Justice Cave in 1893 when he ruled that: 'The schoolmaster is bound to take such care of his boys as a careful father would' (Cave 1893). This established both the principle and the standard by which a teacher's actions would be judged – that of the 'careful father' [*sic*]. Thus, as a teacher, we must show a parent-like concern for the well-being, safety and development of all the pupils entrusted to us. This does not mean that we can be held to have been negligent if any of our pupils has an accident. For as Mr Justice McNair ruled in 1955: 'A balance must be struck between the meticulous supervision of children every moment of the day and the desirable object of encouraging sturdy independence as they grow up' (McNair 1954).

Let's return to cameo 1 to see how these two rulings might be applied to the two incidents.

Focus 1

There are three statements that can be made with confidence.

1 Both teachers, Sandra and Colin, had a duty of care towards the pupils in their charge.
2 Damage did occur.
3 Both events were accidental; there is no suggestion of malicious intent.

At first glance, the McNair ruling seems to support Sandra's more relaxed view of the events. After all, McNair seems to recognize that accidents do happen and that the occurrence of an accident is not sufficient in itself to establish that a teacher has been negligent. There is, however, a further question that must be asked. It is one that brings to bear on the incidents at the very heart of the duty of care; the question of to what extent was each event *reasonably foreseeable*? If the answer to this question is positive, then the case for negligence is established.

What, if any, are the salient differences between these two accidents? Both classes were engaged in a normal activity. Both were supervised by their teachers in a way that was consistent with established custom and practice. The events were identical in all details save one; the age of the pupils. Is this an important difference?

Again, McNair is influential through his notion of the desirability of the development of a 'sturdy independence'. Applied to this cameo, it means that it is reasonable for us, as teachers, to expect that our pupils will develop sufficient independence to be able to take responsibility for their own shoelaces. Once they have reached that stage of development, then such a shoelace incident is an accident; an allegation of negligence would be likely to fail. For Colin (Year 5 teacher) it seems reasonable to assume that these children would have reached that stage of 'sturdy independence' and so Colin ought to be in a secure position.

Sandra's situation is far less secure. It is common for young children to have difficulties with shoelaces. Sandra, as a teacher, would be expected by the court to know this and, therefore, to be in a position to foresee that accidents with shoelaces can occur. Her duty of care requires that she take all reasonable steps to prevent damage occurring. If, and only if, she can show that she had checked the footwear of all the children before starting the PE activity, then, and only then, would she have a credible – but not a secure – defence. If she cannot convince a court (should it come to that) that she had taken all reasonable measures, then the ruling may go against her. The court will consider the well-being of the children in her care to be Sandra's most important duty and so is unlikely to be swayed by Sandra's argument that she was busy, forgot on that day or that 'the Classroom Assistant who usually checks was away'!

Would Sandra's position have been less precarious had the accident occurred while the children were walking from their classroom into assembly? Probably so, since *Paris* v. *Stepney Borough Council* (1951, as cited in Owen 1997: 28) established the principle that the seriousness of the harm was a significant factor in determining negligence, even when the likelihood of mishap was slight. PE, being a more robust activity than walking to assembly, carries both a greater probability of mishap and the likelihood that any damage suffered would be greater. Thus, a fall on the way to assembly would be likely to be seen by the court as carrying the risk of only slight damage. This would reduce the court's expectations of 'all reasonable precautions'. However, in advance of the case being heard, there can be no certainty how the judge would rule on its merits.

Focus 2

A number of points of general relevance for us as teachers emerge from this discussion.

1 The well-being of the children in our care is our prime duty.
2 We are considered to have expert knowledge of children and so be able to foresee many of the difficulties they may encounter.
3 In assessing the foreseeable risk, we must use our knowledge of the actual children involved rather than rely on some notion of the typical child. We should think about: their age, physical, mental, social and motor development.

4 If there is a *reasonably foreseeable risk*, then we *must* take *all reasonable steps* to prevent damage occurring to any child.
5 The precautions taken should be proportionate to the seriousness of the potential damage.
6 The details of the specific situation are of great importance. We should consider: the nature of the activity and the demands its safe completion places on the children; the context in which the activity takes place; the physical setting – size, space, obstacles, location of resources, etc; the emotional setting – are they, for example, excited at the end of term or by the 'newness' or special nature of the activity?
7 What is acceptable in one situation may not be so in another.

Returning briefly to Colin and his class; Ian (an otherwise sturdily independent and intelligent 10-year-old), is known to have arthritis in his fingers and so has difficulties with fine motor control. He uses specially adapted writing tools. What if it were Ian who had tripped and fallen; what then is the legal position? Given this knowledge of Ian (see point 3 above), Colin should have taken steps to check that Ian's laces were secure; all the more so as the changing for PE had been rushed (see point 6 above). It was, in my view, reasonably foreseeable that Ian might have had difficulties in that situation. Colin's need to be able to fulfil his legal obligation when under pressure and to do so in a way that protected Ian's self-esteem serves to highlight the complexity of the demands that all teachers face during the routine of their professional lives.

The statements made in the first list above apply equally to Cameo 2 but the circumstances are very different. Let's explore this situation by responding to some questions.

Q1   Was the craft activity itself inherently dangerous and, hence, an 'unreasonable risk'?

The inclusion of the task in the school's scheme of work is a powerful argument that the task itself was a reasonable one for that class. Working in a way that is consistent with *general and approved practice* can be a powerful defence against a charge of negligence but is far from a certain defence.

There are two important qualifications to this principle. First, no amount of custom and practice can compensate for acting in a way that was self-evidently dangerous – the doctrine of *obvious folly*. Second, there is an expectation on all who act in a professional context that they should keep abreast of developments in their field. Many of the practices that were commonplace in the writer's early days as a science teacher are now expressly forbidden by Health and Safety regulations. Others, while not outlawed as such, would be very hard to defend such as the use of glass containers.

The McNair ruling would also suggest that it is reasonable that children should, at some stage, learn the safe use of sharp implements.

Q2   Had all reasonable precautions been taken?

Ali knew that this was not the first time these children had used knives. She had trained the children herself and so had grounds to believe that they were sufficiently competent to meet the demands of the task. If this were not the case, then her negligence would be obvious. Ali had taken steps, the use of a suitably experienced adult to give close supervision, to ensure the safety of the group. This argument gains force if such arrangements are the *general and approved practice* in that school. However, did Ali check that Pat actually reminded the children of the safety points? Let's assume that Ali did reassure herself that the reminders had been given. Is, then, Ali's position secure?

Ali may be vulnerable because of a location issue. She has allowed a potentially dangerous, although adequately supervised, activity to take place in the immediate vicinity of an area where a degree of disruption could be expected. While Ali could not be expected to have been able to foresee the specific difficulty that the child encountered with the tap, she should, as a *skilled person*, be aware that children and sinks do, on occasions, lead to unpredictable and spontaneous behaviour. Knowing this, Ali could have foreseen the possibility of interference with the craft table and the associated increased element of risk. She should have taken steps to prevent this. Relocating the craft activity would be one such step. Moreover, the potential seriousness of any mishap is relatively severe so greater care will be expected. Neither the fact that the classroom is too small nor that Ali had done this activity before without mishap would constitute a secure defence.

In Cameo 2, Ali was described as being an experienced teacher. Would her legal vulnerability be lessened had she been in the first days of her career? A ruling given in a medical negligence case in 1988 may seem surprising:

> it was stated that a young, inexperienced doctor is judged by the standards of a competent doctor even though, by definition, he is unable to attain that standard.
>
> (Owen 1997: 31)

The above cameos show that quite mundane and seemingly trivial occurrences – often simple oversights – could expose the teacher to a charge of negligence. But clearly, lest readers get very anxious at this point, this is not common! There is much that the teacher can do to limit this exposure. The key is to develop the behaviours of the *prudent* teacher (so far in this chapter called the cautious or careful teacher). A prudent teacher will:

Develop a culture of risk assessment both as part of your planning and as part of monitoring and supervising classroom activities

- have a secure knowledge of the school's policies and act in accordance with them;
- seek and act on guidance from more experienced members of staff when unsure;
- develop a culture of risk assessment both as part of planning (*write it down – much more convincing than a mere verbal assurance*) and as part of the monitoring and supervision of classroom activity;
- assess the risks of the particular situation; those particular children, that activity, that room layout, the location of resources, lines of sight and of movement, etc;
- adopt a 'safety first' culture rather than relying on 'good fortune'.

Successful suits for negligence against teachers are very rare but has some tendency to increase as our society becomes more litigious. Good leadership, appropriate and well-communicated policies and effective staff development all help. However, the person best placed to reduce the risks is you – the individual and prudent teacher.

The next section considers a question of concern to the new and the experienced teacher alike: under what circumstances, if any, is physical contact with pupils defensible in law?

Physical contact with pupils

The use of force

While it is now generally well-known that to strike or shake a child is an *assault*, there remains considerable uncertainty over less aggressive forms of deliberate contact with pupils as is shown by characters in the cameo 3. Let us begin our exploration of these issues by considering the common law notion of *trespass to the person.*

This notion, in essence, treats a person's physical being as if it were a piece of 'property' owned by that individual (yes, I know: the law is strange!). As such, no other person is entitled to assume any rights over that 'property'. Thus, and again in essence, all contact must be with the consent of the owner. Society can and does, as we shall see later, use legislation to grant an entitlement to trespass to certain post-holders under specified conditions. However, the principle remains intact; teachers have no *general* entitlement to make any form of physical contact with a pupil simply because it is their wish so to do. It's best to view the pupil's physical being as private property.

Trespass to the person has a number of aspects; that of *battery* is of particular relevance to this situation. *Battery* is defined as 'the intentional and direct application of *unlawful* force by one person to another' (Owen 1997: 75, writer's emphasis). *Assault* is 'an *attempt to offer* or to apply unlawful force to the person of another' (Keenan 1995: 391, writer's emphasis). Note that the use of an ill-considered phrase to a child could be sufficient to substantiate an action for assault if the court believed that the phrase, in the mind of the child, constituted a credible threat.

There can be no doubt that Clare's 'application of force' was deliberate but was it *unlawful?*

Focus 3

There exist a limited number of recognized defences against an action for trespass to the person. These include:

1 self-defence;
2 defence of property;
3 recognized authority – such as that given to teachers and teaching assistants under Section 550A of the 1996 Education Act (Department for Education and Employment 1998);
4 necessity.

In addition, the court will take into consideration whether or not the physical contact fell within the ill-defined boundaries of that which 'is considered acceptable in the ordinary conduct of daily life' (*Collins* v. *Willcock* 1984, as cited in Owen 1997: 76). Guidance given in paragraph 33 of Circular 10/98 suggests that teachers should exercise 'professional judgement' over a range of non-forceful contacts with children (see below for a fuller discussion of this point). Given the situation as described, Clare could not claim either of the first two defences listed above. As a teacher, does she have *recognized authority*?

In the past when corporal punishment was legitimate in schools, a teacher was considered to have been delegated the parents' entitlement to inflict moderate chastisement to pupils especially, some would say only, when the parents had specifically given their consent to this. Since the Education Acts of 1997 and 1998, any and all forms of corporal punishment are unlawful. However society in general, and the courts in particular, have recognized that the maintenance of proper discipline is an essential part of a teacher's responsibilities. Until recently, the boundaries of a teacher's recognized authority, including use of physical force, remained unclear.

This lack of clarity was recognized in the Elton Report (Department of Education and Science 1989), which called for teachers' disciplinary authority to be given a firm foundation in law. It took nearly ten years for this to be accomplished; see Section 4 of the 1997 Education Act. This provision had the effect of inserting a new Section (550A) into the pre-existing 1996 Education Act. Section 550A gave teachers the legal power to use 'such force as is reasonable in the circumstances'. (Note: For clarity, all subsequent references will be expressed in terms of the modified 1996 Education Act.) However, this power is limited in its scope. The Act went on to lay down specific circumstances in which this power might be used; that is, to prevent a pupil from:

- committing a criminal offence;
- causing personal injury to, or damage to the property of, any person (including the pupil himself);
- engaging in any behaviour prejudicial to the maintenance of good order and discipline at the school or among any of its pupils, whether the behaviour occurs during a teaching session or otherwise (1996 Education Act; 550 A s1).

The third provision would seem to cover Clare's situation.

There remains one final consideration: that of the extent of the force used. Clarification of this issue will have to await a ruling in court on an appropriate case. Until that time, all we can do is consider the underlying principle that has governed a range of rulings on issues relating to the use of force in a variety of contexts.

As seen above, the interpretation of *reasonable* force will be determined by the specifics of the situation. The underlying principle is that the degree of force used should be the minimal level that is both *necessary* and *sufficient* to meet the demands of the situation. Also, the force must be applied to an *appropriate* part of the body.

- *Necessary* means that there is no credible alternative, given the specifics of that circumstance. It does not permit the teacher to use force because to do so would be the more convenient option. It also demands that the force was used only to prevent harm; there must be no punitive element to the use of force. Most definitely, it does not justify the use of force in anger.
- *Sufficient* means that the extent of the force must be proportionate to the demands of the situation, e.g. to the scale and imminence of threat, the age, size and physical power of the child.

Undoubtedly, the amount of force used by Clare was *sufficient* to restore order and there was not any suggestion that she used excessive force. However, was the use of force *necessary*? Only a fuller knowledge of the events and its antecedents could answer this. It is to this point that a court would be likely to give considerable attention. Although lacking the force of law, the view expressed by Michael Bichard, the then Under-Secretary of State for Education, in Circular 10/98 would be influential on the court's thinking. Writing in a section headed 'Reasonable Force', he expressed the view that

> the use of force can be regarded as reasonable only if the circumstances of the particular incident warrant it ... Therefore physical force could not be justified to prevent a pupil from committing a trivial misdemeanour, or in a situation that clearly could be resolved without force.
>
> (DfEE 1998: 17)

To return to the two contrasting views expressed by Nadine's mother and by the deputy head teacher, both contained elements of legal sense. The mother's view of the privacy of the person has a foundation in law. Joan's view that teachers can, and perhaps should, use physical force was accurate but misleading in its failure to place any limitations on this use of force. Both gave highly misleading interpretations, relying, as they did, on their intuition rather than on a secure knowledge. Neither was a reliable guide.

The issue of non-forceful contact

One final comment on the views expressed by the characters in Cameo 3. Paragraph 33 of Circular 10/98 removes any doubt over the legitimacy,

Young children and children with special educational needs may need staff to provide physical prompts and help

as seen by the then government, of physical contact in certain other circumstances. The paragraph recognizes that:

> physical contact may be proper or necessary . . . in order to demonstrate exercises or techniques during PE lessons, sports coaching, or CDT, or if a member of staff has to give first aid. Young children and children with special educational needs may need staff to provide physical prompts or help. Touching may also be appropriate where a pupil is in distress and needs comforting. Teachers will use their own professional judgement when they feel a pupil needs this kind of support.

(DfEE 1998: 33)

Two cautionary notes should guide the interpretation of this paragraph. First, the court is not bound by any guidance issued in a Circular. Such advice should be seen as indicating governmental policy rather than being a definitive and binding statement of the law. Courts have disagreed with and over-ruled the views expressed by ministers. Second, paragraph 33 does not give an unrestricted entitlement – the doctrines of the 'privacy of the person' and of 'reasonable conduct' would still be central in the court's deliberations.

Paragraph 34 of the same Circular advises the exercise of particular caution in relation to a child's 'cultural background or because they have been abused'. It alerts us all to the need to develop 'a common approach where staff and pupils are of different sexes'. It concludes with a phrase that should guide our actions in all cases: 'staff should bear in mind that even innocent and well-intentioned physical contact can sometimes be misconstrued' (DfEE: 1998: 34).

After the event – what then?

Paragraphs 28–30 of Circular 10/98 recommend any teacher involved in any incident that included the application of physical force (as distinct from the type of 'ordinary' physical conduct covered by paragraph 33 of the Circular – see above) should make a:

> Detailed, contemporaneous written report . . . [of the incident.] . . . that should include:
> - the name(s) of the pupil(s) involved, and when and where the incident took place;
> - the names of any other staff or pupils who witnessed the incident;
> - the reason why force was necessary (e.g. to prevent injury to the pupil, another pupil or member of staff);
> - how the incident began and progressed, including details of the pupil's behaviour, what was said by each of the parties, the steps taken to defuse or calm the situation, the degree of force used, how that was applied, and for how long;
> - the pupil's response, and the outcome of the incident;
> - details of any injury suffered by the pupil, another pupil or a member of staff and of any damage to property.

It is further advised that the teacher: 'may find it helpful to seek advice from more senior colleagues or a representative of their professional association when compiling a report' (DfEE 1998: 28–30 abridged).

We now turn our attention to the issue of *detention*.

Punishment

In reading Cameo 4, the first question must be 'Should Frank act on Tom's advice?' Our attention is drawn immediately to the interplay between two frameworks that should inform and guide our conduct as teachers; the legal framework and that of sound professional practice. Tom's advice is, at best, highly uncertain in law. One basis for this view would be the generally recognized entitlement for teachers to act to maintain good order. However, this entitlement is not unlimited as we have seen above. A further support for this view can be found in The Children and Young Persons Act (1993): Section 1.7 of this act states that:

nothing in this section shall be construed as affecting the right of any parent, teacher or other person having the lawful control or charge of a child or young person to administer punishment to him.

This section is, however, addressing the issue of cruelty to children. It is not certain, therefore, that this section can necessarily be applied to normal events in the classroom.

A third aspect of trespass to the person is relevant in this scenario. This is the notion of *false imprisonment*. The legal notion of imprisonment is very broad. It encompasses any restriction of movement. Requiring a child to remain in school at the end of the school day is a restriction of that child's freedom of movement and hence was, until the 1997 Education Act, potentially a form of imprisonment. Section 5 of this Act gives express authority to schools to detain pupils at the end of the school day without the consent of the parents. As ever, this authority is not unlimited in the entitlement it confers. There are conditions that must have been fulfilled if its use by teachers is to be lawful. It is rarely likely to be used in primary schools, of course. Amongst the special factors to be considered are:

- The use of detention must have been incorporated into the school's disciplinary code;
- 24-hour notice of the intended detention must have been given;
- The impact of the detention on individuals must also take into consideration their age; the distance from home; and any special educational needs.

Above all, the use of a detention as a punishment is only lawful when 'the detention constitutes a proportionate punishment in the circumstances' (1997 Education Act, 550(B): see also Annexe C of Circular 10/99, DfEE 1999). A period of detention that is consistent with the school's established practice would, in all likelihood, be seen as a 'proportionate punishment' when applied to the actual miscreants. It is hard to see any argument that could justify its application to those whose misbehaviour had not been established. For this reason, Tom's advice should not be followed. The largely unwritten code of good professional practice also provides an argument for rejecting Tom's advice.

As teachers, we want our pupils to develop into people with the capacity of moral reasoning and with a sense of 'fairness' or 'justice' (as Alison Shilela has outlined in Chapter 14). We teach this best by creating within our classrooms an environment that is fair and is driven by reason. To act in the manner suggested by Tom would be contrary to this and would teach a very different set of values. The legal and professional considerations both argue against Tom. In other situations, the law might support (as distinct from require) a particular course of action. This does not mean that this course of action is the best line to take from the standpoint of good practice. Obviously, whenever a duty has been imposed on teachers by statute, then all teachers must fulfil that duty. In the absence of any such statutory obligation, the law will consider the extent to which our actions were *reasonable* rather than being *best practice.*

For reasons of clarity, in the sections above the potential vulnerability of the individual teacher in any possible legal action has been our only concern. As an employee, the teacher has some degree of protection in law. It is now time to explore the boundaries of that protection.

The teacher as an employee

In the discussion above, the individual teacher has been the focus of our attention. While it is undoubtedly the case that each of us can be sued as a result of our actions, in reality *this is not the norm in everyday teaching contexts.* The reason for this is very straightforward; the size of the compensation that could be obtained from a private individual is much less than that obtainable from the employer. As a result of this pragmatic reasoning, most legal actions are taken against the emplo*yer* rather than the emplo*yee*, although actions can be instituted against both parties.

The legal doctrine that supports such employer-focused actions is called the *doctrine of vicarious liability.* In essence, this doctrine holds the employer responsible in law for the consequences of the actions of the employees, although there are limitations to the protection given by this doctrine.

The 'prudent' teacher will not see this doctrine as providing an all-embracing protection but rather as a source of support. Teachers will recognize that they are unlikely to suffer personal liability when carrying out their professional duties in a manner that is both *reasonable* and in accordance with *general and approved practice.*

Conclusion

As teachers, we try to be 'prudent' all the time. In a way, our common sense about teaching, developed through professional experience and training, ensures a level of knowledge and a sense of responsibility. Not only are we likely to be concerned about the law and its effects on us, children, parents and communities, we are primary teachers mainly because we like and respect children and our actions are governed by a personal commitment to both the education and care of children. A knowledge of the law and our responsibilities is vital to all primary teachers, especially in relation to the areas outlined above, and teachers' unions and other professional bodies will support you should you encounter any difficulties. If in doubt about a course of action, ask!

Points for further consideration

1 To what extent do you follow the practices of 'the prudent teacher'? How does your planning and record keeping demonstrate this?
2 To what extent might the doctrine of 'vicarious liability' apply to an unpaid parent helper?
3 You are accompanying your class on an approved trip to a licensed outdoor activities centre. You feel that one of the planned activities is rather too ambitious for some of your class. The instructor in charge dismisses your concerns, asserting his greater experience. You remain concerned. If you allow the children to take part what are your responsibilities?

References and further reading

Bainham, A. (1998) *Children: The Modern Law*, 2nd edn. Bristol: Jordans.
Bridgman, G. (ed.) (1958) *The All England Law Reports*. Reprint edition. London: Butterworth.
Cave, Justice (1893) In Williams v Eady, 9TLR 637, 10 TLR41 CA: LCT.
Cazzi, J. and Hancox, N. (eds) (2000) *Butterworth's Education Law Manual*. London: Butterworths Tolley.
Department for Education and Employment (DfEE) (1998) *Section 550A of the Education Act 1996: The use of Force to Control or Restrain Pupils*. Circular 10/98. London: HMSO.
Department for Education and Employment (DfEE) (1999) *Social Inclusion: Pupil Support*. Circular 10/99. London: HMSO.
Department of Education and Science (1989) *Discipline in Schools: Report of the Committee of Inquiry chaired by Lord Elton*. London: HMSO.
Gilliat, J. (1999) *Teaching and the Law*. London: Kogan Page.
Hims, N., Robinson, J. and McGoldrick, D. (1994) *Education Law Reports*. Bristol: Jordans.
Keenan, D. (1995) *English Law*. London: Pitman Publishing.
McNair, Justice (1954) In Jeffrey v London County Council, 119 JP43: LCT243.
Owen, R. (1997) *Essential Tort*. London: Cavendish Publishing.

Concluding remarks

The road to Damascus: learning

from continuing experiences

Janet Moyles, beginner teachers

and tutors

One group of PGCE students asked to pass on their own messages to readers of this book, chose to make their offering in a 'Recipe for the perfect teacher', which is faithfully reproduced in Figure 18.1. This shows just the kind of warmth, humour and beliefs about primary teaching that characterizes the new teachers of today and is worth preserving in our teachers of tomorrow through a balanced and supportive teacher education programme. Moves towards even more school-based training are met with some scepticism in both training institutions and schools, for the priority task of primary school teachers is to teach *children*. The skills of classroom teacher and course tutor have many similarities but working with other adults is very different to working with children – as many class teachers learn when they take on a mentoring role.

Teacher educators have themselves all been class teachers: not many class teachers have also been teacher educators or have the time available to acquire the relevant new skills. Many course tutors have spent considerable amounts of time in school and regularly work with practising teachers through continuing professional development and research activities. Having the combined perspectives of tutors, teachers and students themselves benefits everyone involved in the processes of teacher education, especially the children.

Having worked in schools with teachers, many students come back to the university desperate to know more about the theory behind classroom strategies or behaviour techniques or dealing with parents. Even when teachers have this knowledge (and many do), it is not always easy for them to articulate their effective practice as it is often 'second-nature'

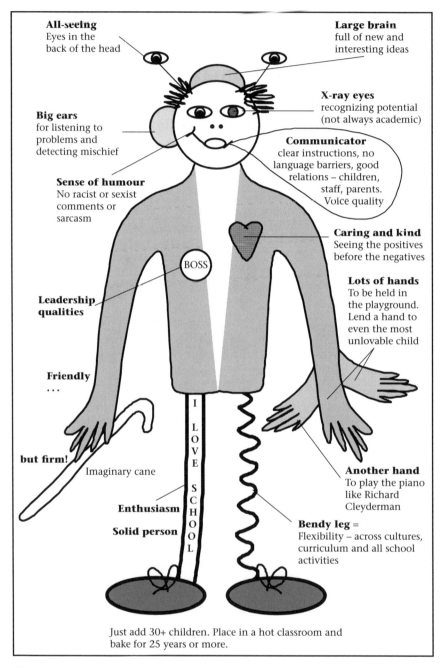

Figure 18.1   Recipe for the 'perfect' teacher

(see Moyles and Adams 2001). Opportunities for training will need to be given to classroom teachers for this to happen which, at the end of day, means more money (rather than less) being put into teacher education. In the meantime, education tutors frequently have this information to hand and the experience of dealing with adult groups to link the theory and practice effectively and efficiently.

The final statements in the book are left to those teachers just entering their first posts in primary schools all over the country and to those who are part of the teacher education system. Students just leaving ITE courses, and some who had left in the previous year, were asked to reflect (through the individual action planning processes mentioned in Chapter 4) on what advice they would wish to pass on to others in a similar situation. Teacher education tutors were also asked for their comments and reflections were also gathered from experienced teachers. The sample from all four groups constitutes much food-for-thought for beginner teachers and, undoubtedly, teachers at every stage in their careers.

We hope that, having read this book, you will be able to adopt (and adapt) some of this advice as you set out on the complex but rewarding professional journey that is primary teaching. Whereas some of the 'tips for teachers' might be familiar to you, there are others which, though unusual, are worth remembering. Many of these reiterate, albeit in a different way, the wealth of messages and insights that have comprised the chapters of this book.

Think twice! (teacher)

Know your own self-worth: value the skills you have and enjoy the children with their skills and understanding. (tutor)

Be up-front about our weaknesses with mentor teachers and tutors: share with them your own ideas and priorities. They will be grateful to you for the guidance of what they can help you with. (student teacher)

Avoid the perils of becoming a chocoholic – the pressure of the job leads to comfort eating on a massive scale. A 'Mars-a-day' is guaranteed to slow down your work, rest and play! Save the choc for the day you've been on playground duty! (tutor)

I think everyone has a good cry during their first year of teaching – but it doesn't mean you're useless! (NQT)

Learn the children's names as quickly as you can and use them as much as possible. You must *act* like a teacher – look as if you expect children to listen to you and they probably will! (tutor)

Don't be too proud or stubborn to learn from tutors and teachers: they have lots of experience and are there to help you to become a good teacher. (student teacher)

I've learned that all good teaching is based on relationships. Remember that children, like adults, tend to mirror the behaviour shown to them (especially if it's negative!) Always be patient, calm and courteous to the children whenever you can and don't 'lose your cool' (except as a deliberate strategy)! (teacher)

Treat children and others in school just as you would wish to be treated yourself. That way, you usually all find life as you like it. (tutor)

Try to ask yourself everyday – 'What did *I learn* in school/on the course today?' (student teacher)

Make one weekend day your own and cultivate friends who are not teachers – you will find that they offer a hearty laugh at some of the antics which go on in schools and thus offer you a sense of proportion. (tutor)

On my final teaching placement, I found that using practical activities with the children was less stressful than endless paper exercises. I found out more about what and how children were learning. When children did produce paper work, I wrote a comment on what they had shown they could do, or needed help to do, etc. and read this to the children. Even 5-year-olds appreciated this and it gave them motivation to try their best. (student teacher)

Good teachers have to be good learners. They have to learn *exactly* what it is the children (and they themselves) don't understand and then move heaven and earth to teach it so that they both *do* understand. (teacher)

Don't upset the caretaker and other support staff! (student teacher)

Try out new things on a Friday afternoon: that way you (and the other staff) can forget any disasters by Monday! (tutor)

Do your evaluating and assessing straight away after a lesson. When things are fresh, it helps you to think and helps you to work out progression for the children. (student teacher)

Having done written assignments on your teacher education course, you must use them as a tool for your work in school – if you have found out the theory and reflected on how you or others put that into practice (or not!), stop and then think about *how* this will affect your practice. Don't just rush on regardless! (NQT)

Getting the class 'with you' so that the child misbehaving becomes embarrassed without you having to shout! First give the child 'the withering look', then make them stand up (just for a little while), then ask them to settle down. It has usually worked for me. (student teacher)

Do remember that 'difficult' behaviour is usually the sign of an unhappy child – it is a challenge to you but it is not, at the end of the day, your *personal* problem. (course tutor)

Don't forget to speak clearly and *listen* hard to what the children are telling you. (student teacher)

Don't make promises you can't keep. If you say 'The next child who talks I'll get your parents in' and someone talks, get the parents! (Worst still, you might be tempted to suggest you'll throw them out of the window!) The corollary of this is *keep your promises*. (course tutor)

Especially with young children, don't be too shy to read stories in 'funny' voices. When I did, the children were 'knocked-out' by my Oscar-winning performance and I think I commanded much more respect afterwards. (student teacher)

Yes – you'll be tired, worn out, all-in, kn—ed (and every other exhaustion word you can think of!). *But* it's worth it at the end of day when even one child shows you he or she has actually *learned* something new. (teacher)

It would be unforgivable to leave a book about early years and primary education and children aged 3–11 years without giving some of them the final word. After all, it is because of children that most people enter the teaching profession in the first place.

Reference

Moyles, J. and Adams, S. (2001) *StEPs: A Playful Approach to Teaching*. Buckingham: Open University Press.

Index

ability, 256
  grouping by, 271–2
abstract art, 151–2
acceptance, 293–4
access to ICT, 198–9
accidents, 297, 300–1
accountability, 5, 28, 212
action plan, 88
active learning, 116, 122–3
activities, structuring, 116–20, 121
'advance organizers', 95–6
affective/emotional response, 239–41,
  244–5
affective objectives, 76
age groups, 34–7
Ager, R., 195
aims, 118
  art, 146
  Foundation Stage, 19–20
Alexander, R., 41, 45
analysing learning, 120–5
application of knowledge, 136
art, 9–10, 143–56
  artists' work in the classroom,
    150–2
  assessment, 152–3
  colour, 148–9

different ways to approach drawing,
  147–8
display, 153–4
making time for, 145–6
nurturing creativity, 149–50
three dimensional art, 150
time for art, 145–6
artist's work, 150–2
assault, 304–5
assessment, 10, 209–32
  art, 152–3
  equality and, 253
  formative, 53, 205, 215
  forms of, 214–16
  Foundation Stage, 22, 25, 216, 225
  ICT and, 195, 200, 205–7
  levels of, 215
  and planning for learning, 120–5
  priorities and issues, 211–13
  purpose, 213–14
  standards and, 79–80
  see also record keeping
attainment, 251–3, 265
attention, 91–7
  and distractions, 92–3
  and failure, 93
  levels of teacher attention, 117–18

span, 93–4
teacher's attentional skills, 94–5
attention grabbers, 94
attitudes, 253–5
audiences, 177–8, 188–9
audio recordings, 62

Ball, C., 23
'bananas to bed' cameo, 235, 236, 239–44
Barton, B., 163
baseline assessment, 216
baseline records, 216–17
battery, 304
Beacon Nurseries, 17
Bearne, E., 187
behaviour, 43–4, 265
beliefs, teachers', 32–3
Bennett, N., 110, 271
Berliner, D., 246
Bertram, A., 23
Bichard, M., 307
Bilton, H., 41
blame, 38
Bleach, K., 286
Boaler, J., 272
brain function, 23
brainstorming, 137
Bransford, J.D., 95
Bromley, H., 159, 166
Bruce, T., 26
Bruner, J., 99, 101

Cambourne, B., 175
care, duty of, 299–304
carers, 279–80
see also parents
carpet areas, 41
causal hypotheses, 135
'celebration' of children's work, 207
challenge, 293
Chambers, A., 183
checklists/grids, observation, 50, 51, 57, 58, 60–2
child-centred approach, 46
child development, 24, 37, 38–9
effect on learning, 81
see also cognitive development

children, *see* pupils
Children and Young Persons Act (1993), 309–10
citizenship, 24
class, social, 256
classifying data, 133–4
classroom assistants (CAs), 44, 45, 113–15, 203, 279
classroom management, 39–45, 79, 140–1
classroom organization, 39–45, 271–2
and management of ICT, 201–4
clay modelling, 150
Clement, R., 146
cognitive development, 98–100
children's developing strategies, 101–3
general trends, 100–1
cognitive objectives, 76
cognitive psychology, 23, 91–8
attention, perception and memory, 91–7
learning strategies, 97–8
collaborative learning, 187, 192, 200, 201
colour, 148–9
Commission on the Future of Multi-ethnic Britain, 256–7, 258, 264
communication, 44–5
mentor as 'good communicator', 287, 289–91
competences, 8–9, 73–89
changing perception of demands of standards, 85–8
characteristics of competences for teaching, 77–8
identification of, 82–3
meaning, 74–5
standards and, 78–85
within teaching and teacher education, 75–8
compositional writing skills, 186
computers, *see* information and communications technology
conductive hearing loss, 275–6
confidence, 37–8
conflict, 261, 273
confrontation, 238, 244, 247

consequence objectives, 76, 77
constructivism, 91
continuous records, 216–17, 224–7
control, 100
corporal punishment, 305
Costello, P., 37
creative development, 24
creativity, 129–30
  nurturing, 149–50
criterion-referenced assessment,
  214–15
critical friend, 82
critical thinking, 129–30
Croll, P., 64, 272
Crompton, R., 199
cross-curricular links, 111–12, 146
culture, 262
curriculum, 42, 108–9, 110, 264
  engaging with and equality, 250,
  262–3
  guidance for Foundation Stage,
  17–18, 54
  National Curriculum, *see* National
  Curriculum
  reflective practice and, 242
'Curriculum in Action' project, 210,
  211
curriculum planning, 24–6, 110

day-to-day records, 224, 224–7
De Boo, M., 37
Dean, C., 277
decisions, 240–1
decontextualized thinking, 100
demonstration, 201
Department for Education and
  Employment (DfEE), 6, 275
  Circular 4/98, 7, 197
  Circular 10/98, 305, 307, 307–9
  Code of Practice on SEN, 270, 274,
  277, 278, 279, 280
  Excellence for All Children, 274, 277
  Excellence in Schools, 251, 255
  National Curriculum Handbook, 257,
  258
desirable learning outcomes (DLOs),
  16
detailed planning, 116–20, 121

detention, 309–11
development
  child development, 24, 37, 38–9, 81
  cognitive, 98–103
Dewey, J., 237, 238
diagnostic assessment, 205, 213
diagnostic records, 224
difference, 255–6
Disability Discrimination Act (1995),
  256
discussion
  participation in, 64, 65
  pedagogical, 245–6
display, 153–4, 207
distractions, 92–3
Donaldson, M., 99, 100
Drummond, M.J., 19
Duffy, B., 147
Dunne, M., 271
duty of care, 299–304

Early, P., 88
Early Excellence Centres, 17
early learning goals (ELGs), 6, 18, 24
early years, *see* Foundation Stage
Education Act (1997), 305–6, 310
'education and training role' mentor,
  287, 291–4
elaborative strategies, 101–2
Elton Report, 305
email, 196
emotional/affective response, 239–41,
  244–5
employee, teacher as, 311
enactive representation, 101
English, 6
  National Curriculum, 162
  see also writing
English as an additional language
  (EAL), 215–16
entry phase, 82, 83–5
environment, 155
  organizing and managing learning/
  teaching environment, 39–45
  physical, 39–41, 265
equality, 10–11, 25, 249–66
  attitudes, 253–5
  difference, 255–6

legislation, 256–7
measuring success, 264–5
practice of, 257–60
principles, 250–1
procedures for, 260–4
social context, 251–3
teacher's role, 251
ethical issues, 242–3
ethnicity, 251–2, 256
ethnographic observation, 57
ethos, 272–3
evaluation, 214
children's learning experiences,
120–5
investigations, 135–6, 138, 140
evidence-informed teaching, 109
see also assessment; record keeping
exit phase, 83, 88
expectations of pupils, 81–2, 255,
273
experience, 112, 149–50
of listening to a story, 162–3
previous experience, 84–5
explanations, 135
exploratory objectives, 76
external agencies, 265

failure, learning, 93
fair tests, 135
false imprisonment, 310
family background, 34
see also parents
feedback
mentoring, 290–1
and writing, 180–1, 189
Fire of London storytelling activity,
168
First Steps *Oral Language: Resource
Book*, 161
Fisher, J., 37
Flanders' Interaction Analysis
Categories (FIAC), 65–6
force, use of, 304–7
foreseeable risk, 299, 300, 301, 301–2
formative assessment, 53, 205, 215
Foundation Stage (FS), 6, 8, 15–29
aims and values, 19–20
areas of learning, 17–18

assessment, 22, 25, 216, 225
children as learners, 23–4
collaborative teaching, 295
context of early years education,
5–7
curriculum guidance, 17–18, 24,
26–7, 54
curriculum planning, 24–6
getting to know the children,
20–1
links with parents, 21–2
managing learning with different
age groups, 35–7
teaching methods, 26–7
frames, writing, 188
Freire, P., 257

Galton, M., 57
gender, 252, 256
general and approved practice, 302–3
generalizations, 135, 139
genre, 188
Ghaye, T., 237
Gillborn, D., 251–2, 256
Gipps, C., 210, 252
glue ear, 275–6
governors, 265
Graves, D., 184, 185
Greenfield, S., 23
Gregory, E., 165
Gregory, S., 276
group work observation grid, 50, 51,
61–2
grouping, 44, 258, 264, 271–2
Grugeon, E., 160–1, 161
guided writing, 173–4, 179–82, 187

Hall, C., 293
Hall, E., 293
Hastings, N., 64
Headstart, 17
health and safety, 81, 201–2
duty of care, 299–304
hearing loss, 275–7
Heaslip, P., 246
hidden curriculum, 110
High/Scope, 17, 27
Hopkins, D., 64

House of Commons Education and
    Employment Committee, 6
Houston, W.R., 74
Howsam, R.B., 74
Hughes, M., 34
Human Rights Act (1998), 257
hypothesizing, 135

iconic representation, 101
ICT suite, 204
identity, 250, 259
images, 96
    stages in child development and,
    147
imagination, 10, 157–72
    role of, 163–4
immediate peer review, 180–1
impressions, 54–5
improvization, 170–1
in loco parentis, 34, 300
incident reports, 309
inclusion, 277–80
independence, children's, 37–9
independent writing, 174, 182–6, 187
individual (profile) level assessment,
    215
Individual Record Sheet, 58–60
individuals
    and art, 147–9
    children as, 38–9
induction tutor, 285
    see also mentoring
informal continuous assessment,
    225–7
information and communications
    technology (ICT), 10, 191–208
    access to, 198–9
    assessment, 195, 200, 205–7
    in the classroom, 202–3
    classroom organization and
    management of, 201–4
    health and safety, 201–2
    ICT suite, 204
    planning with, 197–200
    power and potential of, 194–6
    when to use, 196–7
    writing, 173–4, 179–82
information-giving talk, 65–9

initial teacher education, 6, 7, 8–9,
    75–89, 313–17
    and age groups, 34
    changing perception of demands of
    the standards, 85–8
    competences, 75–8
    use of standards, 82–5
insulator fabric investigation, 131–2,
    132–3
Integrated Learning packages, 205
intensive (case-study) level
    assessment, 215
interactivity, 195
interdependence, 259–60
intermediary phase, 82–3, 85–7
internal influences, 255
Internet, 196
investigative thinking/skills, 9, 100,
    127–42
    classroom management and ethos,
    140–1
    developing science investigating
    skills, 132–6
    mathematical investigations,
    138–40
    reasons to develop, 129–30
    science investigations, 130–2
    technological investigations, 136–8
isaptive assessment, 215
ITT partnerships, 7

Jacobsen, L., 273
Johnson, M.K., 95

Klein, G., 254
Knight, P., 275
knowledge
    application of, 136
    standards and, 78–9
Kress, G., 188

language, 256, 261–2
law, 11, 80, 297–312
    duty of care, 299–304
    and equality, 256–7
    physical contact with pupils, 304–9
    punishment, 309–11
    teacher as employee, 311

Lawrence, D., 277
Lawrence, J., 27
layout, classroom, 40–1
learned helplessness, 93
learner: engaging with, 250, 260–2
  see also pupils
learning, 9, 90–104
  analysing and evaluating children's
    learning, 120–5
  attention, perception and memory,
    91–7
  child development effect on, 81
  children's developing strategies,
    101–3
  cognitive development, 98–100
  engaging with and equality, 250,
    263–4
  Foundation Stage, 20, 23–4
  general trends in development,
    100–1
  objectives, 76–7, 118
  planning for, 111–16
  processes, 6–7, 17
  strategies, 97–8
  understanding and remembering, 97
learning context/environment, 8,
    30–47
  children 3–11 years, 33–9
  organizing and managing learning
    environment, 39–45
  teachers' beliefs, 32–3
learning support assistants, 44, 45,
    113–15, 203, 279
Lee, B., 116
legislation, *see* law
lesson planning, 200
  see also planning
level descriptions, 215
Lewis, M., 188
links
  cross-curricular, 111–12, 146
  story, 163
listening to an oral story, 162–3
literacy hour, 42, 160–1
Local Government Act (1988) Section
    28, 257
longhand notes, 58, 58–60
look, cover, write, check, 97

Mackey, M., 179
managerial talk, 65–9
Manchester Early Literacy Project,
    222, 223
Mann, P., 199
maps, 63–5
mark books, 227
matching technique, 134–5
mathematics, 6, 114
  investigations, 138–40
Maude, T., 38, 41
McAlpine, A., 290
McConnell, C., 275
McDonald, J., 77
McIntyre, D., 238
McNair, Justice, 300
McNamara, D., 77, 78
measuring, 134–5
Meek, M., 184
media, 253
Meltzoff, A., 23
memory, 91–7
mentoring, 11, 44, 284–96
  'good communicator', 287, 289–91
  'perceptive observer', 287, 288–9
  structures and strategies, 287–94
  teacher who appreciates education
    and training role, 287, 291–4
  working relationships with other
    adults, 294–5
Mercer, N., 179
Merry, R., 37
metacognition, 102–3
Mirza, S., 251–2, 256
mistakes, learning from, 140
mixed ability groups, 272
modality preferences, 96–7
monitoring, 10, 79–80
  see also assessment; record keeping
moral issues, 242–3
Morgan, M., 154
Moyles, J., 31, 57, 116, 242, 279, 295

NASEN, 278–9, 280
National Curriculum, 5, 6, 24, 35, 262
  assessment, 215
  ICT, 192, 194, 199
  oral storytelling, 162

standards, 78–9
writing, 188
National Literacy Strategy (NLS),
    160–1, 161, 187
National Writing Project, 188
negligence, 299–304
networks, computer, 204
newcomers, 260–1
Newly Qualified Teachers (NQTs), 5,
    7, 25, 83
non-forceful contact, 307–9
norm-referenced assessment, 214
numeracy hour, 42
nursery nurses, 295
nursery vouchers, 16

objectives
    learning objectives, 76–7, 118
    realization in art, 146
observation, 8, 48–72
    difference between looking and,
        54–5
    hints and stumbling blocks, 69–70
    maps and plans, 63–5
    mentor as 'perceptive observer',
        287, 288–9
    observing teachers, 65–9
    open-ended vs structured, 57–62
    purpose, 56–7
    in science investigations, 132–3
    systematic, 57
    types of, 57
    video, 62–3
observation records, 225
obvious folly, doctrine of, 302
Office for Standards in Education
    (Ofsted), 4, 6, 27, 53, 280
    *Raising the Attainment of Minority
    Ethnic Pupils*, 251
oracy, 10, 122, 157–72
    experience of listening to an oral
        story, 162–3
    power of oral stories, 159–60
Osborne, J., 130
outcomes
    valuing a range of in investigations,
        140
    writing, 186–7

outdoor activities, 41
Owen, R., 303
ownership of writing, 182
Oxford Reading Tree Scheme, 225

Papert, S., 192
parents
    attitudes and equality, 253–4
    children with SEN, 279–80
    links with, 21–2, 34, 265
    reports to, 224
participant observation, 57
participation in discussion, 64, 65
Pascal, C., 23
pattern recognition, 139
pedagogical understanding, 238–9,
    246–7, 247
peer review, 180–1
perception, 91–7
    different perceptions, 95
    'perceptive observer', 287, 288–9
Perera, K., 185
'perfect' teacher, 313, 314
performance, teaching as, 77
performance objectives, 76
performance-related pay, 5
personal skills, 2–4
personal, social and emotional
    development, 24
philosophy of learning, 241–2
physical contact with pupils, 304–9
physical development, 24
physical environment, 39–41, 265
Piaget, J., 98–9
planning, 9, 79, 107–26
    curriculum, 24–6, 110
    detailed planning and
        implementation, 116–20, 121
    'golden rules' for, 112–13
    with ICT, 197–200
    interpreting and evaluating
        children's experiences, 120–5
    for learning, 111–16
    specialist teaching, 115–16
    support staff, 113–15
planning charts, 117–18
planning diaries, 115
plans, classroom, 41, 51, 52, 63–5

play, 23–4, 28
policies, whole-school, 265, 278–9
political context, 5–7
political issues, 242–3
portfolios, 217
pragmatic response, 241, 245–6
prediction, 135
prescription, 4–5
previous experience, 84–5
prewriting, 186
problem solving, 100
   see also investigative skills
processes
   art and, 146
   learning processes, 6–7, 17
   writing process, 186–7
product-led art, 146
products, testing, 136–8
professional development, 235, 236,
   244–6
professional discussion, 245–6
professional role, 80
professional skills, 2–4
protection, mentoring and, 292
prudent teacher, 303–4
psychometric approach to assessment,
   214–15
punishment, 309–11
pupils, 33–9
   engaging with the learner, 250,
     260–2
   expectations of, 81–2, 255, 273
   family background, 34
   getting to know, 20–1, 273–7
   grouping, 44, 258, 264, 271–2
   independence, 37–9
   involvement, 112, 140, 212, 225, 229
   managing learning with different
     age groups, 34–7
   physical contact with, 304–9
purpose
   of assessment, 213–14
   writing and, 188–9

Qualifications and Curriculum
   Authority (QCA), 4, 17
   Curriculum Guidance for Foundation
     Stage, 17–18, 24, 26–7

ICT, 198
   records, 216
   Teaching Speaking and Listening,
     162
Qualified Teacher Status (QTS), 7, 53,
   289
quality, 250, 258–9

Race Relations Act (1976 and 2000),
   256
Raison, G., 161
reading, 185
Reading 2000 Storytime Individual
   Assessment Record, 227, 228
reasonable force, 305–7
recipe for the 'perfect' teacher, 313,
   314
recognized authority, 305
record keeping, 10, 206–7, 216–29
   day-to-day records, 224, 224–7
   framework, 222–4
   learning about children with SEN
     from records, 273
   portfolios and RoA, 217–22
   summary records, 216–17, 224,
     227–9
recording, data, 134–5
Records of Achievement (RoA), 212,
   217–22
reflective practice, 10, 77, 235–48
   affective response, 239–41, 244–5
   curriculum response, 242
   levels of reflection, 243–4
   philosophical response, 241–2
   political/ethical/moral issues,
     242–3
   pragmatic response, 241, 245–6
   processes of, 237–8
   purposes of, 238–44
religion, 256, 262
remembering, 97
reporting methods, 135–6
reports to parents, 224
representation, 147
   stages of development, 101
Resnick, L.B., 100
resources, 265
   investigations, 140

responding to children's writing,
   189–90
responsibilities, 42–3
rewriting, 186
Reynolds, D., 271
Richardson, J.T.E., 103
rights, 43
Robinson, G., 146, 149, 154
Rosen, B., 164–5
Rosenthal, R., 273
rote strategies, 101
routines, 41–3
rules, 43
Runnymede Trust, 256–7, 258, 264

scaffolding, 99
schemes of work, 108
science investigations, 130–6
   applying knowledge acquired, 136
   data classification and organization,
      133–4
   evaluating and drawing conclusions,
      135–6
   fair tests, 135
   observation, 132–3
   prediction and hypothesizing, 135
   recording and measuring, 134–5
   science concepts, 130
screening (survey) level of assessment,
   215
seating arrangements, 40–1
Section 28 of Local Government Act
   (1988), 257
self-efficacy, 236
self-esteem, 277
SEN and Disability Rights in
   Education Bill, 277
Sex Discrimination Act (1975 and
   1999), 256
sexuality, 256, 257
shared writing, 173, 175–9, 187
Sharples, M., 181
Shephard, T., 141
simulation, 196
sketchbooks, 147–8, 149
skills, 75
   see also competences
small group discussion, 140

snowman storytelling activity, 166–7
social class, 256
social context, 99
society, 250, 259–60
sorting, 133–4
sources, story, 163
span of attention, 93–4
special educational needs (SEN), 11,
   25, 267–83
   classroom organization and
      grouping, 271–2
   creating, 270–1
   creating a positive ethos, 272–3
   defining, 274
   inclusion, 277–80
   knowing the children and building
      on their success, 273–7
   spectrum of need, 274–5
'special friend', 261
specialist teaching, 115–16
spelling, 181–2
spiral curriculum, 99
staff
   attitudes, 254–5
   training, 265
   see also classroom assistants;
      teachers
standard assessment tasks/tests, 215
standards, 212
Standards for QTS, 5, 7, 9, 25, 53,
   78–85
   changing perception of demands of
      standards, 85–8
   expectations, 81–2
   health and safety, 81
   learning and development, 81
   liaising with parents and carers,
      20–1
   student responses, 83–5
   use by students, 82–5
'Stepping Stones', 24
stimulus/starting point, 154
storytelling, 10, 157–72
   in the classroom, 165–6
   experience of listening to oral
      stories, 162–3
   impact of literacy hour, 160–1
   improvization, 170–1

power of oral stories, 159–60
role of imagination, 163–4
story sources and story links, 163
storytelling activities, 166–70
teacher as model, 164–5
story game, 167, 168–9
storybox, 166
strategies
children's developing strategies,
101–3
learning, 97–8
mentoring, 287–94
structured observation, 57–8, 60–2
structures, 41–3
subject curriculum, 6–7, 110
Sukhnandon, L., 116
summary records, 216–17, 224, 227–9
summative assessment, 205, 215
'super skills', 23
support, 292
support staff, 113–15, 294–5
see also classroom assistants
Sure Start programme, 17
Suschitzky, W., 279, 295
Swanwick, R., 275
Sylva, K., 27
symbolic representation, 101

take-home tasks, 225–6
Task Forces on Literacy/Numeracy,
4
Task Group on Assessment and
Testing (TGAT) Report, 212
teacher assessments, 215
teacher-centred approach, 46
teacher education, see initial teacher
education
Teacher Interaction with Child (TIC)
Record format, 226–7
teacher observation sheets, 66–8
Teacher Training Agency (TTA), 4, 54,
257
teachers
assessing teacher's role in learning,
124–5
attentional skills, 94–5
attitudes, 254–5
beliefs, 32–3

as employees, 311
levels of teacher attention, 117–18
observing, 65–9
professional and personal mix, 2–4
recipe for the 'perfect' teacher, 313,
314
role, 2, 124–5, 251
teacher as model in storytelling,
159, 164–5
working relationships, 294–5
teacher's log, 224–7
teaching
competences within, 75–8
environment, see learning context/
environment
mentor's role and, 291–2
specialist, 113–16
teaching methods, 26–7
teaching talk, 66–9
technology, 199
ICT, see information and
communications technology
investigations, 136–8
themes, 111–12, 146
thinking
children's independence, 37
developing in art, 9–10, 143–56
investigative, 9, 100, 127–42
tracking children's movements, 51,
52
traditional tales, 163, 165
Trainee's Career Entry Profile, 83
transcriptional writing skills, 186
trespass to the person, 304–6, 310

unanswerable questions, 141
understanding
and remembering, 97
standards and, 78–9

values, 19–20, 27
vicarious liability, doctrine of, 311
video recordings, 62–3
voice, 166
Vygotsky, L.S., 99–100, 277

Webster, A., 275
Weir, L., 157

welfare records, 224
'What if . . . ?' storytelling activity, 169–70
whole-class teaching, 271
whole-school policies, 265, 278–9
willow pattern plate story, 167–8
Wilson, A., 175
wireless local area networks (LANs), 204
Wolfendale, S., 280
working relationships, 294–5
Wragg, E.C., 68
Wray, D., 188

writing, 10, 166, 173–90
    evaluating children's learning, 122
    guided writing, 173–4, 179–82, 187
    independent writing, 174, 182–6, 187
    process and outcomes, 186–7
    purposes and audiences, 188–9
    responding to children's writing, 189–90
    shared writing, 173, 175–9, 187
writing frames, 188

zone of proximal development (ZPD), 99–100

LITERACY AND LEARNING THROUGH TALK
STRATEGIES FOR THE PRIMARY CLASSROOM

Roy Corden

This book focuses on the inter-relationship between reading, writing, speaking and listening. Psychologists and educationalists, influenced by the work of Vygotsky, have emphasized the importance of social interaction in learning, and the National Writing, Oracy and LINC Projects highlighted the need for quality interactive pupil discourse and effective teacher–pupil interaction. However, although the DfEE claims that the successful teaching of literacy is characterized by good quality oral work, speaking and listening is not included in the National Literacy Strategy Framework and the Literacy Training Pack does not address the issue.

Literacy and Learning through Talk blends theory, research and practice to show how an integrated programme of work can be developed to ensure that literacy is taught in a vibrant and stimulating way. Strategies for developing successful group work and whole class, interactive discourse are examined, and effective teaching roles and questioning techniques are explored. Transcripts of group discussions and examples of children's work illustrate various points and work plans and practical classroom activities are described.

Contents
Introduction – Talking, learning and literacy – The discourse of literacy – Planning for talk – Group work – The role of the teacher – Exploratory talk – Speaking and listening to reading and writing: story making, storytelling – Children's literature – References – Index.

204pp   0 335 20450 3 (Paperback)   0 335 20451 1 (Hardback)

STEPS: STATEMENTS OF ENTITLEMENT TO PLAY
A FRAMEWORK FOR PLAYFUL TEACHING

Janet Moyles and Siân Adams

The basis of this video and book Pack – StEPs – is a belief in the rights of the young child to appropriate opportunities to *be* children and to learn in playful and meaningful ways. It is also predicated upon a view that practitioners working with young children have equal rights to teach using playful strategies.

Children and adults are responsible for making the most of the playful learning and teaching opportunities provided in quality early childhood settings and to ensure that the curriculum – statutory or recommended – is implemented efficiently and effectively. The view taken throughout is that there is no conflict between being accountable to parents, politicians or providers for children's learning and offering play experiences as the basis for that learning.

Playful teaching and learning are discussed and exemplified throughout the two elements of the Pack. The video offers viewers a chance to see some of the practitioners who contributed to the Pack, in their own settings using aspects of StEPs to support their everyday teaching and learning. One of the major intentions of the Pack is that it should be used by practitioners and settings – or those undertaking training sessions with them – to both evaluate and extend play practices. The video, child development charts, planning sheets and other documentation, explained in various sections, support a variety of uses across a range of settings reflecting different backgrounds and ethos. Once the framework is understood, the StEPs themselves offer endless opportunities for development of quality learning experiences for children and for articulation, explanation and advocacy of quality practice by practitioners to parents, inspectors and those who evaluate settings.

Contents
Section 1 Introduction: a framework for playful teaching – Section 2 The practitioner-researchers: who are we and what do we do? – Section 3 Using the materials within the Pack: let the children – and practitioners – play! – Section 4 Using the video: what we can learn by observing children and practitioners playing – Section 5 The statements of entitlement to play: explanation and charts – Section 6 StEPs and curricular links – Section 7 Using the six entitlements: interpreting StEPs in action in the setting – Section 8 Child development charts – References – Annotated bibliography – Topic index – Author index.

112pp   0 335 20717 0 Paperback and Video Pack